Courtesy of the Thomas Keene Collection, Mansfield, Ohio.

A TREASURY OF BOOKS
FOR BIBLE STUDY

A TREASURY OF BOOKS
FOR BIBLE STUDY

By

WILBUR M. SMITH

W. A. WILDE COMPANY

Natick, Massachusetts

INTRODUCTION

The Christian Church is witnessing the greatest era of the publication of significant books relating to Biblical interpretation since that period of 1870 to 1895, when major Bible dictionaries were being compiled, and we were introduced to the exegetical works of Godet, Westcott, Lightfoot, Bishop Moule, and the commentaries edited by Lange, Schaff, Bishop Ellicott, etc. The literature today, however, is far more extensive than it was sixty or ninety years ago, and the average clergyman is bound to be somewhat bewildered as he sees announcements of such a multitude of new and important works in the field of Biblical interpretation in every religious journal he opens.

There are a few men who have the ability to master everything, in three or four languages, relative to some large area of Biblical revelation. The late Professor James Moffatt—however we may disagree with his conclusions—was one of these men; Professor H. H. Rowley is another, along with Dr. F. F. Bruce, and Professor Bruce Metzger of Princeton Seminary. I am not one of these phenomenal men—polymaths, we would call them—but I, with many others, do have a longing to become acquainted with some of the principal literature in certain areas of Biblical investigation. For over forty years I have been reviewing books; I have a love for Biblical literature and a desire to pass on good things to others who are looking for help. It is my good fortune to have a large library from which to work.

This past summer when in London I picked up a brochure listing 825 titles of religious books that had been published, in Great Britain alone, between January 1957 and June 1,

1958. Now, even if one had nothing else to do but read, and even if he had the ability to read with unusual rapidity, he could not read this literature as fast as it was being produced. And what of the thousands of books in the areas of the Christian religion, church history, Biblical interpretation, etc., worth reading and acquiring, published long before this mass of current literature appeared? In other words, no Christian in the world today can keep up with all that is being published relating to the Christian religion and the Word of God. The busy pastor, the equally busy professor in a theological seminary, and the unusually busy missionary will not be able to carry a phenomenal reading schedule—if they read one hundred serious books a year, they are doing well, I think. Each person will have to choose what he is going to read, and much will depend upon that choice: his own mental life, his knowledge of the Word of God, his desire to stimulate others, his recognized authority in his own field of investigation, and, for a minister, his eagerness to meet the questions and problems which will arise in the minds of members of his church who are enrolled in our secular colleges and universities.

In 1952 I began editing a department known as "In the Study" for *Moody Monthly,* and into these columns I have endeavored to pour some of the results of these years of reading. Sometimes all of the allotted space for a given month is devoted to a single subject, and at other times five or six subjects might be considered. At the request of my publishers, the W. A. Wilde Company, I have here attempted to bring together articles from "In the Study" of more or less permanent value. These chapters are not to be considered exhaustive in their treatment of any one subject. The opinions are my own, and carry no spirit of finality in their expression.

From communications regularly coming to my desk, from

ministers and laymen on both sides of the water, I am led
to believe that many look to these columns for guidance in
their choice of books. Through the years men and women
have told me that they have built their libraries around my
bibliographical suggestions, particularly those appearing in
Profitable Bible Study. No one should conclude from this
work that there are not other important books, which a
minister should purchase and seriously study, not mentioned
in these pages. Thus, e.g., one of the finest helps for Bible
study issued in the twentieth century is the Lexicon of the
Greek New Testament by Gingrich and Arnt—perhaps more
helpful than any one work referred to here—but I am not
the person to write a long article on Gingrich, and that is
the reason there is no examination of the volume in this
book.

The factors which will determine the choice of books—
and I shall be confining myself to the areas of Church history,
theology and Biblical interpretation—are basically important, and can reveal great extremes. First of all, this choice
of books will be determined by one's own immediate needs.
A man who has given his life to missionary activity in some
Islamic territory along the North Africa coast will find that
he *needs* most to read books that would be in no way essential for the pastor of a rural church in Idaho. If a minister
is about to begin a series of expository sermons from the
Epistle to the Romans, he must read some of the major commentaries on this Epistle, and some works on Pauline theology. A professor in a theological seminary who is planning
to write a volume on Old Testament Theology will be re-
quired to investigate works different from the two previously
mentioned. If a Christian is a farmer and has time and
strength for only six or eight hours of reading in Christian
literature each week, his needs will be still different.

A second factor in ascertaining what one should acquire and read is his capacity. I receive many letters from both younger and older men asking what they should read for an understanding of the Scriptures—a much weightier problem than they are aware of, I think. In replying to such an inquiry, one must have some knowledge of the person's education. A man who left school in the eighth grade and went to work in a machine shop will want a volume altogether different from one recommended to a university graduate majoring in classical languages. This would apply, e.g., to a man who desires to know something, e.g., about the Epistle to the Romans. There is no point in suggesting to a minister who has never been in a seminary, or had any Greek, a commentary on the Greek text of Romans (it will only irritate him), unless he is going to acquire some knowledge of Greek by his own efforts, and many have done this. Some books will be found difficult even for men who have spent their lives in theological study. One of my own colleagues, with two doctorate degrees, told me recently of a scholarly treatise on Mark's Gospel that he himself had to read twice before he understood what the author meant.

A third factor involved in this choice of books is a simple one: what does one possess, or what has he already read? It is difficult to give reading suggestions to an active pastor, let us say, until one knows what this man has already absorbed.

A fourth factor—which ought not to dominate one's thinking but which cannot be wholly overlooked, and should not be—is our own personal interests. I personally am intensely interested in Biblical archaeology, and any page on this subject written with authority I read with eagerness. If Biblical archaeology is a bore to someone, let him forget the subject. I do not think people should torture themselves by thinking they must read certain things which will weary them. Of course there are exceptions. Whether or not we like theology, we should occasionally read some great theological treatise. Whatever he may think of Calvin, Luther or Augustine, a well-educated minister will train himself to read frequently in the glorious, inexhaustive pages of these mighty Christian thinkers. We are born with certain instincts, likes and dislikes, but as the years come and go we surely should experience an enrichment of interests: we should be more vitally interested in many more subjects at fifty years of age than we were at twenty.

There is another factor, the reality of which cannot be denied, and that is, one's own theological viewpoint, conservative or liberal. I am a conservative. I have read thousands of pages by liberal scholars, but must say that I have today no intention of trying to read through ten or fifteen volumes on the person of Christ, published within the last five years, which deny His virgin birth, His deity, and His bodily resurrection. After one gets to know the flimsy arguments advanced in repudiating these sacred themes, one becomes weary of this type of literature—and right here I must say that, in my opinion, conservative scholars today are far better acquainted with the literature of liberalism than are the liberal scholars with the works of conservative theologians.

Other factors need not be entered into with any detail here. Each individual will have to reckon with some things according to his own circumstances, e.g., the amount of money available for books, his access to large theological libraries, time available for reading, the number of messages to be prepared each week—how different are the demands upon a man who addresses his congregation twice every Sunday, and once on Wednesday night, from those upon a pastor who has no evening service and no prayer meeting.

Many wonderful volumes now being published are not

mentioned in these pages; in fact, there are scores of worthwhile books coming from religious publishing houses just now which, I regret to say, I will never get time to read, though many of them are here in my library waiting to be read. I do hope that the publication of this volume will at least quicken the interest of many Christian people in our land in reading serious literature, which is able to enlarge our comprehension of divine truth, and help us to grow in grace, and in the wisdom and knowledge of God.

Finally, I trust that some of my readers will begin to specialize in some one area of Biblical literature. Though it is a rather expensive project, a collection of books on the Bible in Art would be most fascinating. Never before have so many notable books on this subject been issued as in the last ten years. Or, one might begin to gather different reference Bibles in the English language. Often these can be purchased for a very small sum, in second-hand bookstores; actually, that is where most of them will have to be found, for many reference Bibles are now out-of-print. Undoubtedly the greatest subject in all the world for consideration, study, and meditation, is the Person and Work of the Lord Jesus Christ. I would estimate that there are at least 65,000 different volumes on the life of Christ in the languages of western Europe! If one should wish to confine oneself to a single area in this inexhaustible theme, I would earnestly commend those volumes which relate to our Lord's holy death, including literature on the Atonement, the Cross, the Seven Last Words, and related subjects.

Through the years, I have often been asked, at conferences and at other gatherings, "How do you get so much reading done?" May I say here, again, that there is only one way to get any reading done, and that is to read. Whatever reading

I may do, I do not deprive myself of needed sleep, and am always in bed for at least eight hours every night; I do not withdraw myself from society; and I am not a man free from obligations, that is, I have been a minister or professor all my adult life, and thus many hours of the day are not my own. There is only one way to get any reading done, and that is to read. If one does not wish to read, he will not read—but if he does not, his ministry will be impoverished indeed. We must acknowledge, however, that some men whose lives have been a channel of true blessing to others have not been known to read five books a year. Reading is not a synonym for a life of obedience to God, nor for holiness, nor even for fruitfulness. Preaching and evangelizing are of pre-eminent importance.

I trust that the bringing together of these studies, chiefly relating to Biblical subjects, will arouse in many ministers a desire for a more serious, constant study of the Word of God, and of the great books that have been written to help us understand these Divine oracles. And I can also hope that some things set forth here will save many from wasting money and time in the purchase and reading of those superficial works which, however glowing might be their blurbs and advertising, will fade into oblivion before a given year is past. Some of the chapters are not primarily guides to literature, but, occasionally, outlines of some Biblical subject.

In these pages I am only attempting to give some guidance to those who want to read, and who know they should read, but who are bewildered by the large number of books they observe in the bookstores or see advertised in religious journals. Even the Apostle Paul, author of the most profound treatises the Church will ever know, after all those wonderful years of evangelism, in the last days of his life on earth, knowing that at any time he might be called out of the

Mamertine Prison to lay down his life for Christ, asked Timothy to bring "the books and the parchments." He never lost his love for reading, and no doubt he never had the time for reading all that he longed to read.

Both the publishers and I wish to thank the Moody Bible Institute for granting permission to reprint this material from the columns of *Moody Monthly*.

Wilbur M. Smith

Fuller Theological Seminary,
Pasadena, California

TABLE OF CONTENTS

A TREASURY OF BOOKS
FOR BIBLE STUDY

I

COLLECTIONS OF TRIBUTES
TO THE LORD JESUS CHRIST

In the *Reader's Digest* for January, 1954, there appears a glowing tribute to the greatness of Jesus (nothing is said here about His deity, His atoning death, or His resurrection), which, I would judge, was uttered by a Unitarian. The editors say that though this statement was made years ago and has been reprinted in many anthologies, and often quoted, no one has been able to definitely identify its author. They add, "To try to determine its origin, the editors have consulted libraries and prominent ministers. All agree that it is a piece of great distinction, but none can name the author."

The moment I saw this, my mind went to a folder of notes which I have been gathering on what might be called "The Anthologies of Christ," or, "A Collection of the Great Tributes Offered to Christ Through the Centuries." Possibly nothing could be quite as interesting, and perhaps profitable, to the readers of *Moody Monthly,* as a discussion of such volumes, some of which are easily obtainable, and all of which make a genuine contribution to the subject.

There is no theme in all the world so exalted, so cleansing, so satisfying as that of the Lord Jesus Christ. At the very beginning of John's Gospel, we read, "And the Word became flesh, and dwelt among us (and we beheld his glory, glory as of the only begotten from the Father), full of grace and truth." (1:14).

It has been the joy, the indefinable experience of the disciples of Christ, in all centuries since, to behold His glory, to look into His face, and to look forward to that day when we shall be like Him, when we shall see Him as He is.

Actually, almost every book about Christ that discusses Him according to the revelation of Holy Scripture is a confession of His pre-eminence. The very title of a work such as *The Deity of Jesus Christ*—and there are scores of volumes bearing that title—places Him above every other man or woman who ever lived, for no book has ever been written on the deity of Mohammed, or Joseph Smith, or Mary Baker Eddy. The term *incarnation* is never used in reference to such people. One cannot use the word *sinlessness* in the title of any biography or discussion of anyone who ever lived on this earth, except the Lord Jesus Christ. In his index to the principal works in every department of religious literature, published over eighty years ago, Howard Malcolm lists more than 150 volumes under the single subject of the deity of Christ!

All creeds contain tributes to Jesus Christ; all the early councils of the Church record marvelous confessions of the greatness and glory of the Lord Jesus Christ; and hundreds of hymns written through the ages are in reality tributes to the saving power, to the greatness, to the loveliness of Christ. Some of these areas have never been touched, in the anthologies we are about to consider.

Indeed, one might well begin this study by making a careful classification of the confessions of men in the New Testament concerning Christ, which, as far as I know, has not been adequately done. It would make a fascinating series of Sunday evening sermons, of a strong evangelistic nature. If any of my readers should undertake this, may I recommend a volume which seems to be known to very few, a series of studies devoted only to the Gospels, *Jesus As Judged by His*

Enemies, written by Dr. James H. Snowden (1922), for many years professor of Systematic Theology at Western Theological Seminary.

I shall begin this list with an older work, now seldom come upon, which enjoyed great fame for some years after its publication, and I will then proceed to what might be called strict anthologies concerning our Lord. The volumes are arranged in order of publication dates. As far as I know, this is the first attempt that has been made to construct such a list as this. Strange to say, there is no section on tributes to Christ in the notable bibliographical work, *Jesus Christ our Lord,* by S. G. Ayres, done a half-century ago, though it lists over five thousand books relating to Christ.

Testimonies of the Ante-Nicene Fathers to the Divinity of Christ, by Edward Burton. 2nd ed., Oxford, 1829. pp. xvii, 489 (5). This work is still of greatest value. It was done by the Regius Professor of Divinity at Oxford, one of the great scholars of his day, and contains an excellent index both to texts and subjects.

The Person of Christ, the Perfection of His Humanity Viewed as a Proof of His Divinity; with a Collection of Impartial Testimonies to the Character of Jesus, by Philip Schaff. 12th ed., enl. and rev., New York, 1882. pp. viii, 298. First published in 1865, this volume received acclaim everywhere, and was translated into six or seven European languages. The collection of tributes, pp. 183-298, is one of the best ever published. The French material is especially good. Here in both French and English, is the marvelous testimony of Napoleon to the greatness of Christ, given during his last days on St. Helena.

In the life of Dr. Schaff by his son (p. 244) is an incident regarding this volume which is so good that I cannot refrain from quoting it here: "Attending a lecture by a well-known personage, Dr. Schaff was surprised to hear him borrow, without acknowledgment, whole paragraphs from its pages. The lecturer, being introduced to him, showed embarrassment and said, 'I have quoted you a great deal tonight and in my manuscript here I have given you credit,' He replied, 'Books are written to be used, and I think you have turned mine to account for the public good.' " We shall again come upon the name of Schaff in a later section of this list.

God-Man: Search and Manifestations, by Luther T. Townsend. Boston, 1872. pp. 446. Under "Divinity of Jesus" are the following divisions: "Apostolic Opinions," "Contemporaneous Public Opinion," "His Personal Testimony," "Early Christian Opinion," "Modern Opinions and Estimates." For the most part, sources are not given for the last section. There are some tributes here, as in subsequent books, from men who were actually disbelievers in the Christian faith, as Goethe, Hegel, Thomas Paine, and Lord Byron. The author was one of our leading apologetic writers at the close of the nineteenth and beginning of the twentieth centuries. The *Dictionary of American Biography* says, "Few teachers of practical theology have made a more marked impression than he upon his students; his class lectures were rich in content, admirably organized and unusually stimulating."

Christ in Literature, or the Words and Acts of Jesus with Choice Illustrative Readings from the Great Writers of All Ages, and Embracing Their Best Thoughts, by Edward Eggleston. Chicago 1876. pp. 421. This volume contains an excellent index of authors, and subjects, embracing 50 pages. Arranged in 42 sections, the work follows the chronological order of events in the life of our Lord. Many commentators are quoted without specific references to books and pages. Some of the statements are from Eggleston's own pen, most are in prose, and are generally brief—on an average of 250 words. The work begins with Edmund Spenser's "Hymn of Heavenly Love," and includes such famous pieces as that on the raising of Lazarus, by Dodd-ridge. Eggleston was one of the most popular writers of his generation, author of *Hoosier School-Master* and, a work that had a vast circulation, *A History of the United States and Its People,* etc. He gradually drifted into a position of extreme Unitarianism, almost agnosticism. Sometime before 1881, a volume which I have been unable to locate was published entitled, *Christ in Literature: Treasury of Readings in Prose and Verse Illustrative of Acts and Words of Jesus.* Whether this is a variation of the Eggleston title, or an entirely different work, I do not know.

Testimony of Nineteen Centuries of Jesus of Nazareth, by James Herman Whitmore. 1889. pp. 722. The subtitle reads: "An unrivalled and unique collection of rare and remarkable tributes from many countries and centuries; which the research and genius, the learning and devotion, of more than three hundred eminent scholars, statesmen, orators, philosophers, and divines have paid to the fault-less character, peerless life, and spiritual influence of the Founder of Christianity." This is the *largest* single volume of tributes of Christ I have come upon. A very full general index of 35 pages is included, and references are given for nearly all the quotations, one of them as late as the year in which this work was published. There are many statements here from the works of Ullmann, Rudolf Stier, J. P. Lang, F. W. Farrar, and from Albert Barnes' famous *Evidences of Christianity.* The section on the testimony of the writers of the New Testament is not complete. The book was sold only by subscription.

A Cloud of Witnesses. The Greatest Men in the World for Christ and the Book, by Stephen Abbott Northrop. Chicago, 1894. pp. xlii, 524. Some words from the Preface to this book will give us an idea of its contents: "These testimonies have been obtained during years of painstaking research in city, national, and university libraries, and by an extensive correspondence with distinguished men of two continents up to the present hour. The references . . . are of indisputable authority, so that those who wish to quote or investigate may feel perfectly assured of their accuracy. Testimonies with *facsimile* signatures are trustworthy in every case. The original letters are in possession of the undersigned—deposited under lock and key for safekeeping or any possible appeal."

No attempt has been made to indicate the volumes from which the selections have been taken. The material is arranged alphabetically, by profession, e.g., artists, authors, educators, financiers, governors of states, historians, kings and nobility, lawyers, philosophers, physicians, poets, presidents of the United States, scientists, soldiers, statesmen, etc. A fourth edition of this work was published some years later, with 26 additional pages. Some months ago I was told that there were only three copies of this book in the United States, of which my copy was one. Unable to believe this, I looked up the title in the Printed Catalog of the Library of Congress, and it was not there. I wrote to ask if it was not on their shelves, and they graciously replied that it was, in three different editions. The section on religion in the Library of Congress is the most miserably catalogued section in the entire library, and thousands of its religious volumes have never been recorded on printed cards, and therefore are not to be found in their otherwise indispensable Printed Catalog.

Greatest Thoughts About Jesus Christ, by J. Gilchrist Lawson. New York, 1918. pp. viii, 322. Though the book is well done, the author should not have said that it is a collection of "all the greatest thoughts and sayings about our Lord and Saviour Jesus Christ." A part of this book is classified according to profession, and part according to subject, e.g., "The Deity of Christ," "The Supremacy of Christ," "Second Coming of Christ," etc. Quite a number of these quotations were lifted from Whitmore and Northrop, without credit. Some of the authors are quite unknown, and a portion of the material is from periodicals, generally without references. Included here is an excellent statement from Gladstone, though it differs from a similar quotation in the next volume we are to consider. The chapter on "Sceptics' Opinions concerning Christ" is good reading.

Tributes of Great Men to Jesus Christ, by Arthur H. DeLong and Allen P. DeLong. New York, 1918. pp. 126. This is an excellent work for its size, the index naming 260 authors. The first fifteen pages contain only Biblical statements, so that with ten pages of Preface, there are actually less than one hundred pages of testimonies. In view of this, the authors must have been grossly ignorant of similar books previously published, or they would not have declared that these pages "contain the largest and best collections of the sayings of great men concerning the Christ ever published."

Anthology of Jesus, arranged and edited by Sir James Marchant. New York, 1926. pp. vii, 419. In my mind, this is the finest work of its kind that has yet been done, especially in the fullness and accuracy of references. The reference material alone, locating each item quoted, occupies 20 pages; the index of authors, seven pages. Here is the story of Charles Lamb discussing with Leigh Hunt and others, the great people they would like to have met, concluding with the verdict that if Christ came into the room where they were sitting, "We should all fall and try to kiss the hem of His garment." Brought together by one of the best Christian anthologists of the twentieth century, the work contains 422 items. Beautifully printed.

Whom Do Men Say That I Am? A Collection of the Views of the Most Notable Christian and Non-Christian Modern Authors about Jesus of Nazareth, chosen and edited by H. Osborne. London, 1932. pp. xv, 410. Going back to writers of the earlier part of the nineteenth century—Emerson, Darwin, Strauss, etc.—the work contains more quotations from modern intellectuals than anything issued up to that time. Forty pages are devoted to Jewish opinions of Christ, 35 to Mohammedan verdicts, 100 pages to "Philosophy and Science," and 120 to "Literature." I find 22 pages of material from such a blasphemer as Nietzsche, 20 from H. G. Wells, who, while recognizing the greatness of Jesus, spoke shamelessly of His virgin birth, etc. There are, however, some fine things from Archbishop Temple, Bishop Gore, and others. This is the only volume, thus far listed, which contains biographical notices of the authors quoted.

Behold the Man; An Anthology of Jesus Christ, edited by Ralph L. Woods. New York: Macmillan, 1944. pp. xx, 565. The collection here is divided into eight sections: Christ as Man, Christ as God, Teacher, Redeemer, Leader, Messiah, Reformer, and Prophet. I notice that under the subject, "Christ as God," some of the quotations are a denial of His diety.

* * * * *

There is a number of volumes which, while not strictly anthologies of tributes to Christ, do contain a number of such statements. The following are but examples:

Christ and the Fine Arts. An Anthology of Pictures, Poetry, Music and Stories Centering in the Life of Christ, by Cynthia Pearl Maus. New York: Harper, 1938. pp. viii, 764.

The Story of Jesus in the World's Literature, by Edward C. Wagenknecht. New York: Creative Age Press, 1946. pp. 11, 473. This large quarto volume arranges its excellent collection of material under the following headings: His Coming, The Hidden Years, Legends, His Work on Earth, The Social Gospel, The Passion Drama, Christ as Redeemer and Saviour, Afterwards, Christ Universal.

The great poems about Christ of course represent another source of material for this particular study. I believe the following works are the more important in this area:

Christ in Song. Hymns of Immanuel, by Philip Schaff. New York, 1870. pp. xxiv. 711.

The Vision of Christ in the Poets, by Charles M. Stuart. Selected studies of the Christian faith as interpreted by Milton, Wordsworth, the Brownings, Tennyson, Whittier, Longfellow, Lowell. Rev. ed., New York, 1906. pp. 320.

Christ in the Poetry of Today. An Anthology from American Poets, by Martha Foote Crow. New York: Woman's Press, 1918. pp. (16) 227. This work was revised by Elvira Slack, and republished as *Christ in the Poetry of Today. An Anthology of American Verse.* New York, 1928. pp. 287.

The Poets' Life of Christ, by Norman Ault. London: Oxford

University Press, 1922; 2d impression, 1923. pp. xxviii, 276.
The Master of Men. Quotable Poems about Jesus, by
Thomas Curtis Clark. New York: Richard R. Smith, 1930.
pp. 243.

In Schaff's *Library of Religious Poetry* (1881) is a section of
200 double-column pages entitled, "The Poet Contem-
plates the Saviour," a superb collection.

*   *   *   *   *

Jewish testimonies to Jesus form a separate subject, and
more properly should be included in a discussion of the
history of the doctrine of Christ than in this bibliography of
tributes to Christ. For this material, one might first consult
the article, "Christ in Jewish Literature," by R. T. Herford,
in Hastings' *Dictionary of Christ and the Gospels,* Vol. II,
pp. 876 ff. Quite an exhaustive study is that in Rabbi Morris
Goldstein's *Jesus in the Jewish Tradition,* New York: Macmillan, 1950, pp. 319; with elaborate notes. Of a somewhat
different nature is the more recent work, *Walls are Crumbling,* by John M. Oesterreicher, a Jew converted to the
Catholic faith by the writings of Cardinal Newman. This
volume, published by the Devin-Adair Company, New York,
1953, has never received the attention it deserves. Here is a
scholarly discussion of the attitude of seven modern Jewish
philosophers to Christ, including Henri Bergson. A monu-
ment of learning, the work is supported by nearly one
thousand footnotes. There are also a number of important
statements concerning Jesus in that epochal work by Professor
Joseph Klausner, *Jesus of Nazareth* (Eng. tr.).

A number of volumes carries titles that would *seem* to indicate that they are anthologies of tributes to Christ, but the
titles are misleading. For example, in 1858 a volume was
published entitled *Opinions Concerning Jesus Christ,* by

Peter Davidson, a Presbyterian clergyman of Edinburgh. This is actually a series of seven addresses on Jewish opinions of Christ, chiefly from the New Testament, then infidel opinions, followed by a long discussion of Arianism and Roman Catholicism. Several months ago the William Sloane Associates of New York issued a large volume of over 600 pages, *Jesus Through the Centuries, His Figure and Teachings as Reflected in the Minds of Many Men,* by Manuel Komroff. Containing neither Table of Contents nor Index, the work is really quite a piece of confusion. We have here extended quotations from the New Testament, chapters from Sholem Asch, H. G. Wells, Thomas Jefferson, Daniel Defoe, sections on "The Invention of the Holy Cross," the far-fetched story, however beautiful, of "Robin Redbreast," and a fantastic chapter, "Did Our Lord Visit Great Britain," by C. C. Dobson—22 pages of myth, etc., etc.

There is still room for a definitive anthology of Christ, beyond anything that has appeared in our language, embracing poetry and prose. Some of the most beautiful tributes to Christ are to be found in the biographies of His servants through the ages, a glorious body of material that has hardly been touched.

2

THE SIGNIFICANCE OF CELESTIAL PHENOMENA
IN BIBLICAL PROPHECY

Although since our mastery of the air and the development of the airplane, our attention has been directed to aerial activity, and we speak of this as an aerial age, it was not until the launching of the first Sputnik that the thoughts of all civilized people were turned to the subject of unusual celestial phenomena—pertaining to the moon, the planets, the sun and the stars. The Bible says a great deal about disturbances in the celestial sphere that are to occur at the end of the age, and with the advent of Sputnik a number of articles was written on this subject, some of them containing some very foolish statements. I have attempted to present here but an outline arrangement, without any elaborate interpretation, of practically all references in the Old and New Testaments to celestial disturbances.

I. The First Basic Statement

A. It is generally thought that Joel was the first of the writing prophets. In his comparatively brief but important book we have an announcement regarding celestial phenomena that is repeated in later prophecies, both in the Old and New Testaments (2:10, 30, 31; 3:15). These prophecies, as the text clearly indicates, refer to the time known as "the day of the Lord" (see 1:15 and 2:1, 11). Joel 2:28-32a is quoted by St. Peter in his great Pentecostal sermon (Acts 2:16-21). While there was an outpouring of the Holy Spirit on that day, the celestial disturbances here spoken of did *not* occur. This means, of course, that the prophecy must have its complete fulfillment in the future.

B. The reiteration of these predictions by Isaiah.

1. "For the stars of heaven and the constellations thereof shall not give their light; the sun shall be darkened in its going forth, and the moon shall not cause its light to shine" (Isa. 13:10). Note that the time when these things shall occur is said to be, as in Joel, in "the day of the Lord" (13:6, 9). Though this prediction is placed in a chapter concerning judgment upon Babylon, it embraces a much larger sphere, for the Lord here declares, "I will punish the world."

2. The most interesting of all prophecies of this nature is found at the conclusion of Chapter 24: "And it shall come to pass in that day, that Jehovah will punish the host of the high ones on high, and the kings of the earth upon the earth. And they shall be gathered together, as prisoners are gathered in the pit, and shall be shut up in the prison; and after many days shall they be visited. Then the moon shall be confounded, and the sun ashamed; for Jehovah of hosts will reign in Mount Zion and in Jerusalem; and before his elders shall be glory" (v.v. 21-23).

The forceful comment of the Biblical scholar Delitzsch on these lines is so profound that I would like to quote it: " 'The host on high' refers to personal powers, namely, the angelic army. Both the context and the parallelism show that the reference must be to a penal visitation in the spiritual world, which stands in the closest connection with the history of man, and in fact with the history of the nations. Consequently the host on high will refer to the angels of the nations and kingdoms; and the prophecy here presupposes what is affirmed in Deut. 32:8 (LXX), 'When the most High divided the nations, when he separated the sons of Adam, he set the bounds of the nations according to the number of the angels of God,' and sustained in the book of Daniel, when it speaks of a prince of Persia, Javan, and even the people of Israel.

Delitzsch goes on to say: "Just as, according to the scriptural view, both good and evil angels attach themselves to particular men, and an elevated state of mind may sometimes afford a glimpse of this encircling company and this conflict of spirits, so do angels contend for the rule over nations and kingdoms, either to guide them in the way of God or to lead them astray from God; and therefore the judgment upon the nations which the prophet here foretells will be a judgment upon angels also. The kingdom of spirits has its own history running parallel to the destinies of Men."

C. There is one group of prophecies in which the shaking of the heavens and the shaking of the earth are placed together; Isaiah 13:13; 34:4; Joel 3:16; Haggai 2:6, 7, the last of which is quoted in Hebrews 12:26.

II. References to Celestial Phenomena in Our Lord's Olivet Discourse

A. In Luke's account, one phenomenon of this type is located before the tribulation: "And there shall be great earthquakes, and in diverse places famines and pestilences; and there shall be terrors and great signs from heaven" (21:11). What these "great signs" will be is not indicated.

B. In Matthew's record of this great prophetic utterance, the word *heaven* occurs, significantly, five times in three successive verses (Matt. 24:29, 31) .

1. "Immediately after the tribulation of those days shall the sun be darkened and the moon shall not give her light, and the stars shall fall from heaven" (also Mark 13:24; Luke 21:25).

2. "And the powers of the heavens shall be shaken" (also

Mark 13:25b; Luke 21:26b). There is no unity of interpretation among commentators on this verse. My own view is that this corresponds to "the hosts of the high ones" referred to above.

3. "And then shall appear the sign of the Son of man in heaven." This phrase is in Matthew only. Here again the interpretations down through the ages have been many, some holding that this refers to an appearance of Christ, others, that it is a prediction of a great illuminated cross to appear in the sky, etc.

4. "Then shall all the tribes of the earth mourn, and they shall see the Son of man coming on the clouds of heaven with power and great glory" (also Mark 13:26; 21:27). On Christ's coming in the clouds of glory, see also Matthew 26:64, and with great glory, 25:31; 13:26.

5. "And he shall send forth his angels with a great sound of a trumpet, and they shall gather together his elect from the four winds, from one end of heaven to the other" (also Mark 13:27).

Note that all (with the single exception of Luke 21:11) these celestial phenomena refer to the period "after the tribulation," and therefore fulfillment cannot be looked for in this hour in which we are living. One here recalls the phrase, "we would see a sign from heaven," in Matthew 12:38; 16:1, and Mark 8:11. Here also perhaps should be included the words of our Lord, "I beheld Satan fallen as lightning from heaven" (Luke 10:18; compare Isa. 14:12).

III. In the Epistles of the New Testament

A. St. Paul tells us, in his familiar statement on the second advent, that when the Lord descends from heaven, the Church will be caught up to meet Him "in the air" (I Thess. 4:17).

B. One of the most pregnant utterances of St. Paul is that in which he refers to Satan as "the prince of the power of the air" (Eph. 2:2). May I direct attention to a chapter on this phrase in my volume, *This Atomic Age and the Word of God*, pp. 222-248.

C. St. Peter, in a famous but difficult passage (II Peter 3:7, 10, 11), speaks of the elements melting with fervent heat, etc. See an extended discussion of this, also in my *This Atomic Age*, pp. 126-163.

IV. In the Book of Revelation

A. During the seven-seal judgment, at the time of the opening of the sixth seal: "And the sun became black as sackcloth of hair, and the whole moon became as blood; and the stars of the heaven fell unto the earth, as a fig tree casteth her unripe figs when she is shaken of a great wind. And the heaven was removed as a scroll when it is rolled up" (6:12b-14).

B. During the trumpet judgments
1. At the first trumpet (8:8)
2. At the third trumpet (8:10, 11)
3. At the fourth trumpet (8:12)
4. At the fifth trumpet (9:1, 2)

C. At the time of the war in heaven. Immediately preceding this conflict there was "great hail" (11:9). There it is said of Satan, "And his tail draweth the third part of the stars of heaven, and did cast them to the earth" (12:4). Finally, Satan himself is cast down to earth (12:9). Of the dark period of the reign of the beast we read, "And he doeth great signs, that he should even make fire to come down out of heaven upon the earth in the sight of men" (13:13).

D. During the vial judgments.

1. The fourth vial: "And the fourth poured out his bowl upon the sun; and it was given unto it to scorch men with fire" (16:8).

2. The fifth vial: "And the fifth poured out his bowl upon the throne of the beast; and his kingdom was darkened; and they gnawed their tongues for pain" (16:10).

3. The seventh vial: "And the seventh poured out his bowl upon the air; and there came forth a great voice out of the temple, from the throne, saying, It is done: and there were lightnings and voices, and thunders; and there was a great earthquake . . . and great hail, every stone about the weight of a talent, cometh down out of heaven upon men" (16:17, 18, 21). I cannot but believe there is some connection between "upon the air" and Ephesians 2:2.

E. The new heavens and the new earth (Rev. 20:11 and 21:1; with his compare Isa. 65:17).

The above arrangement of all the passages in the Old and New Testaments relating to celestial disturbances would seem to indicate that we are not to consider any unusual celestial aberrations before the tribulation period as having prophetic significance—and certainly these devices known as the Sputnik, the Explorer, the Pioneer, etc., important as they are, and others may become, in the armaments race, have no bearing upon these prophecies. It should be remembered that while all these are man-made and man-directed the celestial phenomena referred to in the prophetic Scriptures are controlled by God himself, and involve judgments sent by God.

In reading these passages concerning the darkness to come upon the world in the day of the Lord, a time of judgment, we recall two *historical occasions* of divine judgment in which *darkness was experienced,* though in a local and brief extent: in the ninth plague upon Egypt (Ex. 10:21-23), and at the time of our Lord's crucifixion (Matt. 27:45; Mark 15:33; Luke 23:45).

Our Lord himself came down *from heaven,* as the New Testament frequently reminds us (John 6:42; I Cor. 15:47; I Thess. 1:10, 4:16; II Thess. 1:7).

God is spoken of as being *in the heavens* (see e.g., in Matthew alone, 5:16, 34, 45, 48; 6:1, 9; 7:11; 10:32; 11:25; 12:50; 16:17; 18:10, 14, 19).

A truth of great comfort is that uttered by our Lord just before He went into glory: "All power is given unto me in heaven and earth." (Matt. 28:18).

3

SOME OF THE MORE IMPORTANT LITERATURE RELATING TO THE HISTORY OF PREACHING

Six great areas of *historical* study are open for investigation to every serious student of the Bible and the Christian Church—more than present themselves to the followers of any other profession in the world.

First of all there is the inexhaustible subject, now richer and more satisfying than ever, *Biblical* history, extending from the days of the patriarchs to the close of the first century. This is followed by the numerous subjects of *Church* history, on which thousands of books have been written, and its corollary, the history of *doctrine,* called by some, historical theology. Parallel with these two themes is the history of *missions,* to which e.g., Professor Latourette has made such an outstanding contribution during the last quarter of a century. A field which has not been adequately developed is the history of the *influence of the Bible* in the literature and civilization of the world.

Finally, an area in which few ministers, I fear, have done much reading, but one of the most interesting and profitable lines of investigation for anyone holding a high view of this holy task, is the history of *preaching*. As John Kelman said many years ago, "No study could be more interesting, and few perhaps more profitable, than a historical review of the great preachers of the past."

The reissuing of the most comprehensive history of preaching as a whole in our language, that by Dargan, and the appearance of the first volume of what will ultimately be the most exhaustive history of preaching in Great Britain and America ever published—to both of which works we shall refer later in this discussion—makes this the opportune occasion for briefly surveying some of the major works on the history of preaching that have appeared in the last sixty years. It is only in the last three generations that anything of importance, in our language, has been done in this area. We might begin by being reminded of what Dargan says, in the opening chapter of his monumental work:

"The Graeco-Roman oratory at its best state was lacking in one great essential, to the highest eloquence. It had no religious content and but incidentally a moral one. The accepted division of oratory into its kinds was three-fold, deliberative, or political; forensic, or judicial; and epideictic or declamatory. The last at first was meant to embrace funeral or memorial orations, or panegyrical discourses upon living persons, or patriotic speeches, or, as Aristotle defines it, was concerned chiefly with praise and blame. But in this classification of orations there is notable omission of the didactic element. *There was nothing in ancient oratory corresponding to our lecture platform or pulpit.* Lectures by teachers were hardly considered as belonging to oratory at all, and their declamations, given as models to their pupils, would probably have been classed under the third division if anywhere."

It is interesting to observe that while Great Britain, though embracing less than one-half the population of the United States, produced far more great preachers in the nineteenth century than could be found within the borders of this country, yet the best books on homiletics and the history of preaching appearing during the last three-quarters of a century have been written by American authors. In fact, what might be called the pioneer volume in this field was that done in 1876 by Dr. John A. Broadus, of the Southern Baptist Theological Seminary, author of the most notable work on preparation of sermons of modern times. The title of Broadus' work was simply, *The History of Preaching* (241 pages), to which all subsequent writers down to the time of Dargan were deeply indebted, as they acknowledged. This volume resulted from a series of lectures which Dr. Broadus delivered at Newton Theological Seminary in the early part of that year.

As far as I can discover, the first work by a British scholar surveying the history of preaching was also in the form of a series of lectures, given by John Ker, *Lectures on the History of Preaching,* first issued in 1889. The volume begins with a chapter on "Preaching in the Old Testament," a subject rarely considered by any writer. Ker is entitled to a further word here.

Of the Greek Orthodox Church, Ker rightly said, "A great torpor has benumbed the preaching of this church for centuries. No great name stirring the hearts of the masses and shining out to lands beyond has appeared for more than a thousand years." The larger part of the work is devoted to the history of German preaching (pp. 145-388), and constituted the best survey of preaching in that country available in our language until the appearance of Dargan's second volume in 1912. Ker calls attention to the fact that Luther himself was at first unwilling to preach, though he moved Western Europe with his preaching in subsequent years.

Two German preachers to whom Ker gives considerable space are practically unknown to this generation of American ministers. One is Ludwig Hofacker (1798-1828), who died at the age of thirty, but whose sermons sold over 100,000 copies, most of them after his death; indeed, twenty-two editions were called for up to 1839. Ker says that though Hofacker "had no arts of eloquence or sensational novelties, with his soul he preached Christ and Him crucified." I would like to know more of Klaus Harms (1778-1855), of Kiel, whose sermons attacking contemporary rationalism were so powerful that as a result of them, and his famous "Ninety-Five Theses" in defense of the evangelical faith, over two hundred pamphlets by rationalists were written against him and his conservative views!

John Brown delivered the Lyman Beecher Lectures on Preaching at Yale in 1899, and published them a year later under the title, *Puritan Preaching in England.* To the early friars of the thirteenth century, he devoted twenty-eight pages, but apparently had no knowledge of the earlier preaching in England such as is now set forth so fully in Webber's work.

There are some good things here on the value of expository preaching (pp. 40-45), and an interesting chapter on the Cambridge Puritans, of whom you and I know so little today. There was Lawrence Chaderton, for fifty years the afternoon lecturer at St. Clement's Church, Cambridge; Henry Smith (1500-1591), called "the prime preacher of the nation," whose collected sermons went through one large edition after another, but about whom I could not write two accurate sentences; and Thomas Adams, of the same period, called "the Shakespeare of the Puritans."

We could well go back for edification to the volumes of some of these men. Here is an excellent chapter on "John Bunyan as a Life Study for Preachers," and another on Richard Baxter, who, Brown reminds us, hardly knew an hour free from pain for over fourteen years. One section is devoted to what Professor Brown calls "the modern Puritans" —Spurgeon, Dale and Maclaren.

In 1903 appeared what was, up to that time, the most complete work in this field, *The History of Christian Preaching,* by T. Harwood Pattison (1838-1904). Pattison was the professor of Homiletics and Pastoral Theology at Rochester

Theological Seminary. At the end of the work is an interesting "Chronology of Preachers." Here are chapters on "Prophet and Synagogue," "The Preaching of Jesus," "Apostolic Preaching," etc. The brief chapter on the preaching of the period extending from the fifth to the tenth centuries is entitled, "Darkness and Light"; the section on the seventeenth century, to which the author gives extensive treatment (pp. 163-213), is called "The Golden Age of English Preaching."

Of Thomas Hooker (1553-1600) Pattison says, "In the annals of the pulpit one illustrious name belongs entirely to the reign of Elizabeth." What mighty servants of God could be heard in the pulpits of England from 1575-1675: Henry Smith, Lancelot Andrewes, John Donne, Joseph Hall, Thomas Fuller, Samuel Rutherford, Robert Leighton, Thomas Goodwin, John Owen, and Jeremy Taylor!

In a worthwhile chapter on "French Preachers of the Seventeenth Century," the author refers to Bourdaloue (1632-1704) as "the greatest preacher of his age." There are later sections on British preaching in the nineteenth century, and two concluding chapters on American preaching, emphasizing especially the work of Beecher and Phillips Brooks. Pattison reminds us that Gladstone considered Henry Melvill the greatest Anglican preacher of his generation —today scarcely read at all.

The year following the publication of Pattison's work saw an altogether different type of the study of preaching in the volume *Representative Modern Preachers,* by the then professor of Practical Theology at Yale University, Louis Brastow. These nine chapters are really studies of nine of the great preachers of the nineteenth century: Schleiermacher, F. W. Robertson, Henry Ward Beecher, Horace Bushnell, Phillips Brooks, John Henry Newman, J. B. Mozley, Thomas

Guthrie, and Charles Haddon Spurgeon. Since in this volume of over four hundred pages Brastow attempts to cover the preaching of only nine men, he is able to more carefully and exhaustively analyze the fundamental factors that made their preaching outstanding, beyond anything that had yet been done by writers in this area of Christian literature. In 1906, when over seventy years of age, Brastow issued his second volume, *The Modern Pulpit, A Study of Homiletic Sources and Characteristics,* in which is revealed a good deal of sympathy with the more liberal thinkers of his day.

In 1905 appeared the first volume of the most thorough survey of the history of preaching in the Christian Church down to the end of the nineteenth century that had ever been attempted in our language, simply called *A History of Preaching,* by Edwin Charles Dargan (1852-1930), for many years the professor of Homiletics at the Southern Baptist Theological Seminary at Louisville, Ky., successor to Dr. John A. Broadus, and his close friend for decades. Thus, both the *initial* attempt to survey the history of preaching in modern times, and the later more comprehensive work on the subject to be published, came from professors in the same theological seminary.

The work of Dargan appeared in two volumes (1905 and 1912), totaling 1,168 pages, including 33 columns of index. Professor Dargan planned to issue a third volume, covering the entire history of preaching in the United States, a subject he had not dwelt upon in these first two volumes, but he was not able to complete the work. I remember as a young minister, perhaps about 1920, writing to this beloved teacher of the South, to ask when we might expect this third volume, and receiving from him a most gracious letter, which I have treasured through the years, telling me that because of his new responsibility with the Board of Publication of the

Southern Baptist Church, he was sure the task would never be finished.

I would estimate that Dargan's work extends to 440,000 words. The first volume carries us down to 1572; the second opens with preaching in Europe at the end of the sixteenth century.

This superb survey had become very scarce, so much so that I know of at least one theological seminary that tried in vain for ten years to purchase a copy for its own library. All must be grateful indeed to the Baker Book House of Grand Rapids for recently bringing out a reprint of the work, now bound in one volume, and making it available again to a new generation.

It is not possible here to go into detail regarding Dargan's work, but I would simply say that it is without rival, to the present time, in the area it covers. I read it with great interest many years ago, and have recently been turning the pages to reread some of the passages then underlined, and some of the notes I made in the margin. From these pages, any minister, whatever his handicaps and limitations, will be encouraged to go on striving to be a more effective and worthy minister of the Word of God. Thus, of Gregory Nazianzen, the author says that though he held a high, firm place among the world's great preachers, "he was small of stature and unprepossessing in appearance, and had no majestic presence to help out the flash and force of his oratorical genius. He was sensitive, vain, ambitious, yet struggling with these and other infirmities ever toward the better things in character and usefulness." Over and over again the author emphasizes the truth that at all times the character of the preacher either enforces or enfeebles his preaching. The work is a gold mine of illustrations on the tremendous influence of the Word of God upon the lives of many, when proclaimed with the power that the New Testament always identifies with true preaching.

The virtues of the work are many, the shortcomings few indeed. One is surprised to note that there is no mention of that truly great preacher, to whom I shall refer later, John Flavel, or of Matthew Henry, who was an able preacher of the Word as well as the peer of commentators. A perusal of these pages will pull any sensitive minister out of the doldrums.

For that invaluable series, the International Theological Library, Professor Alfred Ernest Garvie did the volume, *The Preachers of the Church* (London, 1926), which was too brief a work (245 pages) to allow this gifted scholar to do justice to his subject. In 1942 appeared a work covering a more limited period than those we have thus far considered here, by a noted Presbyterian American clergyman, Dr. Hugh Thompson Kerr, *Preaching in the Early Church*. This includes chapters on "Apostolic Preaching"; "The Preaching of the Greek Apologists," mostly apologetic preaching; "The Preaching of the Latin Apologists," principally Tertullian and Cyprian, and concludes with a discussion of the great Greek and Latin preachers. Dr. Kerr did a good piece of work here, but there is not much in his pages that cannot be found in the more comprehensive study by Dargan.

Before turning to the monumental work of Webber the first volume of which has just been published, I think we might mention here some volumes on the history of preaching which limit themselves to certain periods of Church history. The two better known surveys of medieval preaching in England are by G. W. Owst, *Preaching in Medieval England*, and, *Literature and Pulpit in Medieval England*, published in Cambridge in 1926 and 1939 respectively. On the seventeenth century, there are two fine, scholarly volumes, *English*

Preachers and Preaching (1604-1670) by Caroline Frances Richardson (New York, 1928), and *English Pulpit Oratory, from Andrewes to Tillotson* (1932). Professor W. G. Blaikie did a notable work some years ago, still worth reading, *The Preachers of Scotland from the Sixth to the Nineteenth Centuries* (Edinburgh, 1888). There is a fascinating work on *New England Clergy in the American Revolution* by Alexander Baldwin (1928), and a later scholarly piece of genuine research, *Preaching in the First Half Century of New England History,* by Babette May Levy (Hartford, 1945, American Society of Church History).

For some reason, the most important work on the history of preaching published in our country in nearly a half century has escaped notice in our leading religious periodicals. I have never seen an extended review of the book, and came upon the title almost by accident. It is the first volume of *A History of Preaching in Britain and America* by F. R. Webber, a Lutheran, an authority on Church architecture, and a native of southern England (Milwaukee: Northwestern Publishing House, 1952). This first volume of 758 pages takes us through the nineteenth century in England alone; the second will survey the history of preaching in Ireland, Scotland, and Wales; and the third will be devoted to America. (Since this review was written the two concluding volumes of this great work have appeared).

Two outstanding virtues presented themselves to me in the reading of this initial volume. Fundamentally we have here, for the first time in our language, a true account of the earliest preaching in Great Britain, in what would be called the Celtic Church, and secondly, we have an approach to the great preachers of England by a conservative who passes judgment on many of the men he discusses in their relationship to the Word of God and the basic Christian truths, which is invaluable.

Here, for the first time in a history of preaching, is set forth the amazing power of evangelical preaching in the early Celtic Church in England. The author has been able to do this so satisfactorily for two reasons. First of all, he lived in this part of England for years, and thus knows its history and literature intimately; and then, it has been only since 1916 that we have had books written as the result of extensive research in this formerly almost unknown period of Christian activity. Many of the great preachers of the Celtic Church listed here cannot be found in the *Dictionary of National Biography*.

For years the Roman Catholic Church has attempted to prove that British Christianity derived from Rome, but Webber proves with overwhelming evidence that the earliest Christianity, which had nothing to do with the superstitions and beclouding traditions of Roman Catholicism, originated in Gaul.

There are excellent discussions here of Liddon, Parker, Farrar, Spurgeon, Meyer, and even, to my astonishment, A. C. Dixon, who, though an American preacher, and one of the finest, was for a few years in the First World War, pastor of Spurgeon's Tabernacle, London. Among the notable preachers whom for some reason the author missed are Samuel Chadwick, Robert Haldane, Marcus Rainsford, Adolph Saphir, and C. J. Vaughan. I only wish there was space for quoting some of the excellent passages in this monumental work. I commend it to every minister in America as a "must" for his library, for his reading, and for his education.

The literature on preachers is vast, and I am not here attempting a complete bibliography. Among the more significant is the delightful volume by Sir Robertson Nicoll, gifted editor of *The British Weekly*, entitled *Princes of the Church*, brilliant biographical sketches of many of the outstanding preachers of the nineteenth century known intimately to Nicoll, and others. An earlier volume that included some of the names found in the Nicoll volume is *Nine Great Preachers* by Albert H. Currier (400 pages), which begins with Chrysostom and includes chapters on Richard Baxter and John Bunyan. Dr. Clarence Edward Macartney, one of the prominent preachers of our generation a quarter of a century ago, wrote a volume now almost forgotten, *Sons of Thunder*, ten chapters on preachers, including Samuel Davies, James Waddel, and Eliphalet Nott. In 1921, Professor Arthur S. Hoyt issued his *The Pulpit and American Life* and some years ago Sir James Marchant edited a work entitled, *British Preachers*.

A rich piece of ecclesiastical scholarship is that huge volume, found in the libraries of many ministers today but I am afraid seldom read, *History and Repository of Pulpit Eloquence* by H. C. Fish. There are invaluable biographies of most of the notable American preachers of a century ago in that epochal work by William Buell Sprague (1795-1876), *Annals of the American Pulpit*, issued in nine volumes between 1857 and 1869, containing material not found in any other work in our language. A title which looks most attractive, but which I have never seen, is *Classic Preachers of the English Church* by J. E. Kempe (2 vols., 1877-1878) .

A brilliant work of nearly five hundred pages by E. Paxton Hood (1888) will abide as a volume of true inspiration—*The Throne of Eloquence: Great Preachers, Ancient and Modern*. Of less significance, but still interesting, is *Princes of the Christian Pulpit and Pastorate* by Dr. Harry C. Howard of Emory University (1927) , fifteen biographical chapters, beginning with Francis of Assisi and ending with that peer of preachers, John Henry Jowett.

If there is an adequate history of preaching as set forth in the New Testament, it is not known to me. Here perhaps is an opportunity for the writing of a volume which could open up new veins of Biblical truth. Some years ago Albert Richmond Bond published a work which has not been given much attention, *The Master Preacher, A Study of the Homiletics of Jesus.* We have many books on Christ as teacher, but practically none of real value on Christ as preacher.

In the preaching of the Apostle Paul, we are more adequately provided for. A century ago John Eadie wrote a volume that is still important, *St. Paul the Preacher;* and, more recently, Maurice Jones did an excellent piece of work in his volume, *St. Paul the Orator,* published in London in 1910. I know of nothing worthy of note on the preaching of the Apostle Peter, though the data for such a subject fills almost one-half of the Book of Acts.

The most neglected sermons of a great preacher of modern times, in all the volumes relating to this subject, are those of Charles John Vaughan (1816-1897), dean of Llandaff, and for some years headmaster of Harrow. Of his work at Harrow, the sketch in the *Dictionary of National Biography* says, "During the last dozen years of his life, it is probable that no school stood higher than Harrow. . . . No headmaster, Arnold excepted, gathered around him a more gifted band of scholars or colleagues." Vaughan published over sixty volumes, and those of sermons contain some of the greatest preached in England in a day marked by good preaching. Among these are *Epiphany, Lent and Easter* (1865) ; *Lessons of Life and Godliness* (1862); *Words from the Gospels* (1863) ; *Foes of Faith* (1873) ; *Life's Work and God's Discipline* (1873); *The Two Great Temptations* (1875) ;

Temple Sermons (1881). Many of these volumes went through many editions. His works also include the helpful *Lectures on St. Paul's Epistle to the Philippians; Lectures on the Revelation of St. John; The Church of the First Days* (Acts), etc. Somewhere I have seen the statement that Bishop Westcott read one of Vaughan's sermons every Sunday afternoon for nearly thirty years. Here is an area of investigation for someone doing a master's thesis in the field of homiletics.

Let me close this study of literature on the history of preaching with the following paragraph of encouragement from Professor Ker: "Each true Christian minister has had his place and circle, and he may have still. He may be a man of genius—there is room for him—or of the plainest, most realistic understanding. He may be as learned as the library of Alexandria, or a man of one book, provided it be the true Book. He may be a philosopher of the schools, or a scholar of common life. He may be original to the verge of eccentricity, or a traveler in well-worn paths. Let him only be resolved to make his gifts the property of his fellow men in loyal obedience to His Master."

4

HISTORICAL SURVEYS IN THE OLD
AND NEW TESTAMENTS

Historical themes are set forth in the Holy Scriptures in three basic types of composition. There are first of all, of course, what might be called straight historical narratives, some with considerable detail and some with brevity. Such periods, for example, as the wanderings of the patriarchs in Palestine, the wanderings of the children of Israel in the wilderness, the life of David, the building of the temple, the reigns of Ahab and Hezekiah, the Perean ministry of our Lord, and the events of Friday of Holy Week are recorded with great detail. On the other hand, sometimes the events of scores of years are compressed into a short summary, as the sufferings of the children of Israel under the Pharaoh of the oppression in the early chapters of Exodus, some of the conquests of Joshua, and some of the reigns of the kings of Israel and Judah. By way of illustration, the reign of Joash extending for thirty-seven years is assigned only twenty-one verses in the book of Kings.

A second form of composition, setting forth major historical events, is the prophetic. Thus, in Leviticus 26, and Deuteronomy 29 and 30, we have a prophetic outline of the entire *history* of Israel; in Jeremiah 25, one of the most important prophetic chapters in all of the Bible, a panoramic view is given of the three great judgments of nations in God's redemptive program: upon Israel, then upon Babylon, and finally God's future judgment upon all the nations of the earth. In Daniel 2 and 7 we have prophetic outlines of the age of the Gentiles, from the reign of Nebuchadnezzar to the return of Christ. In Matthew 24 (and in the Synoptic parallels) we have our Lord's prophetic foreview of the course of this age, while in I Corinthians 15:20-28 we are given a remarkably condensed survey of basic events in Christ's conflict with antagonistic authorities and powers.

It is, however, the third type of composition found in the Bible, in relation to setting forth great historic events with which we shall be primarily concerned in this study. I refer to those remarkable and numerous passages of the Old and New Testament scriptures in which we have set before us what might be called *panoramic synopses* of past historic events.

Though there are some sixteen different compressed surveys of Biblical history in the Bible, the subject, as far as I know, has never been given any consideration in the many works that we have at our disposal on the subject of Biblical History.

Here I want only to attempt a brief survey of the relevant material, hoping that this study will stimulate a number of Bible students to pursue the matter further—and perhaps someone will be led to write an entire book on this one theme.

GEOGRAPHY OF THE FORTY YEARS OF WANDERING

The first historical *survey* of past events, I believe, found in the Scriptures is in the thirty-third chapter of the book of Numbers, one of the most remarkable geographical passages in all the Bible. It enumerates forty different places which the Israelites visited or passed through during their forty years of wilderness wandering, from the time they left Egypt to the time they came down to the Jordan River opposite Jericho. Of these forty-eight places, twenty-four are designated in the *Westminster Historical Atlas* as either "uncertain" or "unknown." Thus, for example, the places mentioned in verse 13 and nearly all of the places in verses 19 to 29 are spoken of nowhere else in the Old Testament. Verses 30 to 34 are practically a duplication of Deuteronomy 10:6, 7. Verse 36 refers to one of the most interesting sites in all of the Old Testament outside of Palestine, Ezion-geber. This is where, many years later, Solomon would build smelting furnaces (I Kings 9:26), abundant remains of which have been explored by Dr. Nelson Glueck.

MOSES' REVIEW OF ISRAEL'S FAILURES

The first three chapters of the book of Deuteronomy record one of the great addresses of Moses, delivered when Israel was encamped on the plains of Moab, somewhere near 1400 B.C. To me, for years the passage seemed exceedingly difficult to outline, but I believe at last I have discovered a genuine sequence here, and I would like to place it before my readers in outline form.

I. The first approach to Palestine 1:6-46
  1. The command to leave Mount Horeb vv. 6-8 (Num. 20:11)
  2. The appointment of judges to assist Moses vv. 9-18 (Ex. 18:13-26)
  3. From Horeb to Kadesh-barnea v. 19 (Num. 10:12)
  4. The report of the spies vv. 20-25 (Num. 13:1—14:39)
  5. The numbering of the people vv. 26-40
  6. Israel defeated by the Amorites vv. 40-46 (Num. 14:40-45)

II. The second approach to Palestine 2:1—3:7
  1. The departure from Kadesh-barnea and the circuit of Mount Seir 2:1-8a (Num. 20:1-13)
  2. The arrival at the border of Moab vv. 8b-15 (Num. 21:11-20). In verses 10 to 12 we have a very interest-

ing archaeological note regarding the pre-Canaanite inhabitants of Palestine. Between Numbers 20:13 and 20:14 a period of thirty-seven years must be inserted.

3. The defeat of Sihon, King of Heshbon 2:16-36 (Num. 21:21-32)
4. The defeat of Og, King of Bashan 3:13 (Num. 21:33-35)

III. The Allotment of territory east of Jordan 3:8-17 (Num. 32)

We discover in this passage one of the most interesting and important factors to be found in nearly all of these historical surveys, namely, that some data appears which is not found in the original historical narrative. Here, e.g., follows a prayer of Moses (3:23-29) which is not to be found in the earlier narratives covering this period of Israel's history. While normally one would not assign any great importance to the original narrative in Numbers 21, the Old Testament writers made much of these two victories over Sihon and Gog. Not only are they repeated here, but we also have references to them later in this book, 29:7 and 31:4; four times in the book of Joshua 2:10; 9:10; 12:4; 13:12, 30, 31; also in Nehemiah 9:22; and twice in the Psalms, 135:11; 136:20.

Moses' Second, Briefer Survey

This same book of Deuteronomy (9:7—10:11) contains a second, more condensed survey of Israel's history during the Mosaic period, with a greater emphasis upon the ethical, or we might say the unethical, aspects of Israel's attitude toward God. The long stay at Mount Sinai is summarized, verses 8 to 21; then we have a short account of the report of the spies, verses 23 to 29 (Num. 11, 12), followed by a notice of the command to Moses to make a second table of the ten commandments, 10:1-5 (Ex. 34). There is a reference in 10:6, 7 to Numbers 33:31-33, and in 10:8, 9 to Numbers 3:6 and 8:14, while in verse 16 we have a reference to Exodus 34:28. From this, one immediately becomes aware that these historical surveys must be given most careful consideration before one comes to a final conclusion as to the specific events to which they refer.

Joshua's Last Message

When Joshua came to the end of his life he, like many other great leaders of the Old Testament, delivered an exhortatory message, looking backward in recalling God's wonderful and many mercies, and also looking forward, seeing, far down the corridor of time, the coming of a period of apostasy and rebellion.

Joshua (24:1-13) begins his survey with the call of Abraham, passes on to the evil work of Balaam, and then gives a short summary of the conquest of Palestine, which had been accomplished, by the grace of God, under his leadership. Here again we have a detail concerning the life of the first patriarch not found in the book of Genesis: "They served other gods," that is in their native home in Ur.

The Brief Survey in the Book of Judges

In Judges 2:1-15, we have a brief survey going back to the Exodus, verses 1 and 2, and then proceeding to the work of Joshua, verses 6 to 9, and the tragic events that followed soon after Joshua's death, verses 10 to 15. Here again, is a reference to an event taking place sometime before this, not found in the preceding Biblical record, namely, the weeping of the children of Israel at Bochim.

THE ONE HISTORICAL SURVEY IN THE BOOK OF KINGS

One would have thought that in the books of Kings and Chronicles we would find a number of surveys of past history, but strange to say we do not. In II Kings 17:7-23 we have a very simple résumé of those sins which brought Israel to her doom and captivity in 721 B.C. This review begins with the deliverance from Egypt (v. 7), and then proceeds to an enumeration of Israel's great sins after she was brought into the land (vv. 8-17), including idolatry, divination, the disregard of the messages of the prophets, and the worship of the hosts of heaven. The end of this catalogue includes a reference (vv. 21, 22) to the division of Israel and Judah following the death of Solomon.

THE GREAT GENEALOGICAL TABLE

In the first nine chapters of the First Book of Chronicles we have the most extended and important collection of genealogical data to be found anywhere in the Scriptures. For our purpose it is not necessary to go into detail here. An indication of the major sections will be sufficient.

The first chapter repeats most of the genealogy of the book of Genesis. Chapter 2 covers the period from the exodus to David. Chapter 3 enumerates the descendants of David. The genealogies of all the other tribes are given in the following five chapters, and the entire section closes with a genealogy of the priests and Levites in Chapter 9.

Here again a number of names are found which appear nowhere else in the Bible, e.g., Azarias in 2:8, Jerahmeel in 2:9, and Zeruiah, a sister of David, in 2:16. The genealogical records bring us down to the middle of the sixth century B.C., the time of Zerubbabel. As many have indicated, these genealogical tables all point to one great theme, the life and work of King David. *The Catholic Bible Commentary* significantly reminds us, "it is remarkable that the Chronicler with his interest in the Temple and public worship nowhere gives us a list of the high priests as such." The best general discussion of Biblical genealogies known to me is the article by P. W. Crannell, in the *International Standard Bible Encyclopaedia* (Vol. III, pp. 1183-1196).

The Prayer of the Levites

Somewhere near the middle of the fifth century B.C. the priests and Levites in a great prayer of confession, review the amazing mercies and kindnesses of God as a background for setting forth in all their darkness the sins of rebellion in Israel's successive centuries. Their prayer (Neh. 9) is an enumeration of these events in their exact order: Creation, verse 6; Abraham, verses 7 and 8, the Exodus, verses 9 to 11; the Wilderness experience, verses 12 to 21; Israel in the land, verses 20-30a; the Captivity, verses 30b to 35; and the Return, in which Nehemiah was participating, verses 36-38.

The Rebellion of Israel in Ezekiel's Prophecy

As far as I have been able to discover, there seems to be only one extended historical survey of Israel's history in all of the prophetic books of the Old Testament, strange as it may seem. It is found in Ezekiel 20, in a message given to those who came to inquire of the prophet concerning the will of God in a matter not specifically mentioned. The words were uttered, probably, about 591 B.C. The sequence is not difficult. He begins with the deliverance from Egypt, verses 5 to 9; he recounts the mercies of God to Israel in the wilderness, verses 10 to 26; he acknowledges Israel's constant rebellion against God in the land, verses 27 to 32; and concludes with a prophecy of Israel's dispersion, verses 33 to 39 and Israel's return, verses 40 to 44.

Incidentally, in this chapter we have quotations, in this order, from Leviticus 18:24; 18:5, 21; and 20:8. Three times in this chapter it is stated that Israel *rebelled*, verses 8, 13, 21; there is also the famous characterizing title for Palestine, "the glory of all lands," verses 6 and 15; and the significant phrase in the warning that God would bring Israel "into the wilderness of the people," verse 35. (There is a rich discussion of this chapter in Patrick Fairbairn's *Ezekiel and the Book of His Prophecy,* 3rd. ed., 1863. pp. 209-230.)

The Historical Surveys in the Psalms

There are five *different* surveys of Israel's history in the Psalter. The first, in Psalm 81, begins with Jacob and Joseph, verses 4 to 6, proceeds to the wanderings, verses 7 to 10, closing with the statement of Israel's disobedience.

In Psalm 135:1-11 we have an expression of gratitude to God for His glorious work in creation, verses 6 and 7; His deliverance of Israel from Egypt, verses 8 and 9; and Israel's conquest in the land, verses 10 to 12. Kirkpatrick says that this Psalm is "little more than a mosaic of fragments and remains from Law, Prophets and other Psalms."

Psalm 136 is a great hymn of thanksgiving, going back to creation, verses 5 to 9, leaping over the intervening periods to the Exodus, verses 10 to 15, and then giving thanks to God for His overruling providence in Israel's wanderings and conquest, verses 16 to 22.

The most remarkable survey of history in the Psalter, and perhaps in the whole of the Old Testament, almost a cosmorama, is found in a series of four Psalms, 104 to 107. Psalm 104 is a poetic expression of the story of creation, Genesis 1:3 to 2:3. Psalm 105 begins with God's covenant with the patriarchs and brings one down to the settlement in Canaan verses 42 to 45. This same incident is also mentioned in I Chronicles 16:7-36.

The Psalmist in the next Psalm repeats God's goodness to Israel in Egypt, verses 7 to 12, and in the wilderness, verses 13 to 33 and in the land, verses 34 to 36. But throughout the Psalm (something which is very rare in the Psalter,) we have a constant reference to that tragic theme of Israel's stubborn resistance to God. The two concluding verses are prophetic. Although Psalm 107 begins a new book in the Psalter, it belongs to the preceding Psalms, for here, surely, is a prophecy of Israel's final return and restoration.

Stephen's Review of the Unbelief of Israel

In some ways, the most amazing single survey of redemptive history in all the Scriptures is that given by Stephen, when he stood before the Sanhedrin on trial for his life, an address that terminated with his martyrdom.

He begins with God's covenant with Abraham, and Abraham's unswerving obedience (Acts 7:2-8). From this he enters into the general theme of the address, the unbelief of the later patriarchs, beginning with the sons of Jacob who sold their brother Joseph into slavery (vv. 9-16).

The central portion of the defense, an account of Israel's rejection of Moses and her manifestations of unbelief in the wilderness journey (vv. 17-44), is followed by a brief discussion of the periods of Joshua, David and Solomon (vv. 45-50). The survey concludes, as the others did not, with a summarizing indictment, "Ye stiffnecked and uncircumcised in heart and ears, ye do always resist the Holy Spirit: as your fathers did, so do ye."

A number of things in Stephen's address are not set forth

elsewhere in Scripture. Here alone we read that Moses was "instructed in all the wisdom of the Egyptians" (v. 22), and that he was forced to flee Egypt when forty years of age. Here only is the revelation at Sinai designated as the "living oracles," and here alone are we told that this revelation was given through an angel.

The entire discourse bristles with difficulties. Rackham, in his great commentary on Acts (pp. 99-102) points out fifteen variations from the Old Testament records in this one address. (For a helpful discussion of these, see the volume on the Book of Acts by Stokes, pp. 309-318 and, best of all, the work by T. Walker on Acts, in the *Indian Commentary Series*.)

In one way, Stephen's discourse is but an echo of the surveys previously considered, given by the leaders of Israel in the Old Testament—one more presentation of the undeniable fact that down through her history Israel failed to appreciate and act upon the goodness and mercy of God, but stubbornly went her own way.

A careful study of this chapter will reveal how Stephen, in a masterly way, places the unbelief of Israel against a background of what should have been sufficient evidence to persuade Israel to walk in the will of God. Of their leader, Moses, against whom they constantly murmured, it is said that he was "instructed in all the wisdom of the Egyptians, and was mighty in words and works" (v. 22); he had a revelation from God (vv. 30-33); he had a commission from God (vv. 34, 35); he "wrought wonders and signs" (v. 36); and he was spoken to by an angel (v. 38). In addition to this, the Israelites had "the tent of testimony in the wilderness" (v. 44).

With this in mind, let us look at the words and phrases which emphasize Israel's tragic failure to believe: "they understood not" (v. 25); they "thrust him away" (vv. 27, 39);

"they refused" (v. 35); they "would not be obedient" (v. 39); and in relation to the Lord, they persecuted and killed (v. 32).

Paul's Address in Antioch of Pisidia

In Luke's record of the first missionary journey is one of the few detailed accounts of a sermon from the apostle Paul, one that he preached in Antioch of Pisidia (Acts 13:14-41).

Without mentioning any of the names of the patriarchs, Paul begins, as do most of the other surveys, with the call of the "fathers" of Israel, and proceeds to the Exodus from Egypt and the wanderings in the wilderness. In reviewing the conquests of Palestine, he—and only he—uses the phrase, "the seven nations in the land of Canaan," which are enumerated in Deuteronomy 7:1.

A name new in these surveys is here mentioned, that of Samuel the prophet, which leads to a reference to the choosing of Saul and to the founding of the Davidic line (vv. 21, 22). Passing over the intervening centuries of Israel's history, the apostle moves from David the king to David's seed, the Saviour, Jesus, whom John the Baptist introduced.

Omitting any reference to the ministry of Christ, he dwells in detail upon the supreme act of rejection in Israel's history —the slaying of her own Messiah "because they knew him not, nor the voices of the prophets." It is frequently said that Paul knows nothing about the tomb of Christ; but it is too often forgotten that he speaks of the *empty* tomb, as in v. 29. In its treatment of the death and resurrection of Christ, Paul's speech here is almost parallel to that of the apostle Peter on the day of Pentecost.

The Epistle to the Hebrews

The final survey of redemptive history is the famous eleventh chapter of Hebrews, which has been called the Westminster Abbey of Faith. The résumé is unique in that it does not refer to the unbelief of Israel, but rather, to the deep faith and consequent acts of many of her great leaders. It is the only survey of Biblical history (apart from those of the Psalter) which does not emphasize disobedience, rebellion, and unbelief.

Here again, as in the Psalms, we are taken back to creation. Verses 4 to 31 comprise a roll call, as it were, of certain men and one woman, of faith, from Abel to Rahab: six names taken from the Book of Genesis, followed by an account of the faith of Moses and his parents (vv. 23-29), and a reference to an episode involving Rahab, found in the opening chapters of Joshua.

The chapter gives a number of facts regarding familiar events in the Old Testament which are not contained in the original narratives nor in any subsequent commentary upon them. For example, only here are we told that Abel's sacrifice was "by faith," which implies faith in a revelation from God—a fact that one would almost necessarily assume in reading Genesis; and here alone we are informed in relation to Abraham's offering up of Isaac that he knew, should Isaac be slain, that God would raise him from the dead (v. 19).

The extended discussion of Moses includes the remarkable statement that he would "rather to share ill treatment with the people of God, than to enjoy the pleasures of sin for a season: accounting the reproach of Christ greater riches than the treasures of Egypt: for he looked unto the recompense of reward" (vv. 25, 26, A.S.V.).

Following these illustrations of faith from the lives of specific individuals, the writer proceeds to recount, without names, what might be called some exploits of faith. Many references here are to Old Testament passages: e.g., stopping the mouths of lions (Dan. 6:16, I Sam. 17:34), etc., while perhaps others are from post-Biblical history as recorded in the Book of Maccabees. As in so many other surveys, the conclusion looks to the future, and thus ends with a prophecy.

There are a number of *brief* summaries of Israel's history which I have not attempted to analyze, among which are Isaiah 41:8; 51:2; Jer. 33:26; Amos 2:9-12; Hosea 11:1-4; 12-13; Micah 6:4, 5; Matt. 23:35; Jude 5.

Summary

Of these sixteen surveys, five began with creation, five with the patriarchs, and five with the exodus. A review of the writers of the Old Testament, the composers of the Psalms, the prophets, Stephen, Paul, and the writer of the Hebrews, all of whom spoke and wrote under the guidance of the Holy Spirit, reveals that they primarily emphasized five great acts of God: the creation, the call of Abraham, the Exodus from Egypt, the giving of the Law, and the initial victories over the kings in Transjordania. How strange it is that no major event in the history of Israel from the days of the judges to the return from Babylon is similarly repeated in these surveys!

The one tragic undertone running through all these surveys (except that of Hebrews 11) when the author is discussing not what God has done but what man has done, is that of failure, unbelief and rebellion. Is not this likewise the underlying note of Paul's last epistle (II Timothy), of II Peter and Jude, that the Church of Christ in the last days will manifest the same unbelief which marked the history of God's chosen people of an earlier dispensation?

I would like to repeat what I said at the beginning of this study, this entire subject of historical *surveys* in the Scriptures has not been worthily brought to the attention of Bible students.

5

"AT THE FEET OF JESUS"—
A NEGLECTED SERMON SUBJECT

Through the kindness of my friend Dr. David J. Laurie, formerly of Edinburgh and now of Mount Hermon, Calif., I have come into the possession of a book previously unknown to me, a volume of sermons, entitled *The Feet of Jesus in Life, Death, Resurrection and Glory,* by Philip Bennett Power, M. A., once a clergyman of Christ Church, Worthing, England. The book of more than 300 pages, was published in London in 1872.

Power was a voluminous writer, though he is little remembered today. He was the author of *The "I Will's" of the Psalms* and *The "I Will's of Christ;* also *Behold,* a series of meditations of passages of Scripture in which, as he says, "God arrests the attention of man by the use of the word *Behold."* The printed catalogs of the Library of Congress do not list any volume of Power as being in that vast collection.

In view of the many references to the feet of our Lord in the Gospels, and occasionally in the Epistles and the Book of Revelation, it is surprising to note the scarcity of sermons relating to men and women found at the feet of Christ.

The subject of the feet of Jesus is not listed in the indexes of *The Expositor's Bible,* Joseph Parker's *The People's Bible,* Maclaren's *Expositions of Holy Scripture,* or Hastings' *Great Texts of the Bible.* Furthermore, there is no reference to such in the 180 columns of the index to the first eighteen volumes of *The Speaker's Bible,* in the *Imperial Bible Dictionary,* or in the *International Standard Bible Encyclopedia.*

There is, however, an interesting *summary* of references to the feet of Jesus in the article *"Feet"* by John Reid, in James Hastings' *Dictionary of Christ and the Gospels,* Vol. I, pp. 586-587, and a short article of H. Wheeler Robinson, in Hastings' *Dictionary of the Apostolic Church,* Vol. I, p. 404. In neither of these discussions is there any reference to sermonic material.

However, I do find a characteristically helpful sermon on Luke 7:38 by Charles H. Spurgeon, "Our Place: At Jesus' Feet," in the *Metropolitan Tabernacle Pulpit* for 1889, Vol. XXXV, No. 2066. Inasmuch as many of my readers may not be fortunate enough to own this set, I would like to give here the outline of this sermon of Spurgeon's.

 I. At His Feet is a Becoming Posture
    1. because of the Majesty of His Person
    2. because of the Unworthiness of Ourselves
    3. because of His Well-Beloved Claims Upon Us
    4. because He is All in All.
II. It is a Very Helpful Posture
    1. for a weeping penitent
    2. for a new convert
    3. for a pleading intercessor
    4. for a willing learner
    5. for an ever-grateful worshiper.

Spurgeon gives Gospel references for most of these points, and concludes by quoting a stanza of the hymn, "Lo, at His Feet."

> Lo, at his feet with awful joy,
>   The adoring armies fall!
> With joy they shrink to nothing there,
>   Before the eternal All.

Spurgeon has another sermon on Luke 1:39, "Mary also sat at Jesus' feet and heard His Word," which he entitles, "Love At Leisure." Much is said about the feet of Jesus as Spurgeon develops the theme, "Let us sit at Jesus' feet because our salvation is complete," and sets forth the idea of our unworthiness, concluding, "Sink; go on sinking; be little; be less; be less still; be still less; be least of all; be nothing." (*Metropolitan Tabernacle Pulpit,* 1905, Vol. LI, pp. 133-142). Undoubtedly there are many other sermons on this subject, but after a careful search, I have failed to find such.

Returning to this remarkable work by Power, I think the best thing would be for me to give simply the titles for the sermons with the relevant texts.

   I. The Feet of Jesus, the Place for Helpless Misery, Matthew 15:30

  II. The Feet of Jesus, the Place for Personal Ministration. Luke 7:37, 38. (The author does not refer to the other familiar verse in this paragraph in which the feet of our Lord are mentioned, v. 44.)

 III. The Feet of Jesus, the Place for Personal Necessity (Jairus at the Feet), Luke 8:41. (To which should be added the parallel, Mark 5:22.)

  IV. The Feet of Jesus, the Place for Personal Necessity (The Syrophoenician Woman at the Feet), Mark 7:25, 26

   V. The Feet of Jesus, the Place for Personal Necessity (Mary at the Feet), John 11:32

  VI. The Feet of Jesus, the Place for Personal Necessity (Mary at Jesus' Feet), Luke 10:39

 VII. How the Demoniac Came to be at the Feet of Jesus, Luke 8:35

VIII. The Demoniac Sitting at the Feet of Jesus, Luke 8:35

   IX. The Man as Seen at the Feet of Jesus, Luke 8:35
    X. The Man as Sent Away from the Feet of Jesus, Luke
        8:37
   XI. The Feet of Jesus, the Place of Personal Suffering,
        Psalm 22:16
  XII. The Angels Sitting at the Head and Feet of the Place
        where the Body of Jesus had Lain, John 22:12.
        (The author devotes fifty pages to this verse, though
        strictly speaking the feet of Jesus are not in the
        text.)
 XIII. The Feet of Jesus, the Place of Worship, Matthew
        28:9, 10
  XIV. The Feet of Jesus, the Place of Comfort, Luke 24:40.
        (With this compare John 20:20, a verse upon which
        Power does not comment.)
   XV. The Feet of Jesus, the Place of Manifested Glory,
        Revelation 1:15
  XVI. The Feet of Jesus, the Place of Manifested Power,
        Revelation 1:15
 XVII. The Feet of Jesus, the Place of Strength, Revelation
        1:17

It is significant that of the first six references all but the
first relate either to women at the feet of Jesus or, as in the
case of Jairus, a man pleading for a woman who was ill.
There are some rather notable omissions here; e.g., the
record of the grateful leper falling at the feet of Jesus (Luke
17:16), and the beautiful story of Mary anointing Jesus' feet
at the home in Bethany (John 12:3).

The writers of the New Testament, in referring to that
day when Christ shall put all enemies under His feet, often
quote Psalm 8:6: "Thou madest him to have dominion over
the works of thy hands; thou hast put all things under his
feet" (See I Cor. 15:25; Eph. 1:22; Heb. 2:8).

Some of the more familiar references to the feet of Jesus in literature and hymnology may appropriately conclude our discussion. Some years ago P. P. Bliss penned the words and music to a hymn once frequently sung but now seldom heard, "At the Feet of Jesus" (*Gospel Hymns* Nos. 1-6, No. 75):

> At the feet of Jesus, listening to His word:
> Learning wisdom's lesson from her loving Lord:
> Mary, led by heav-nly grace,
> Chose the meek disciple's place.
>
> At the feet of Jesus is the place for me;
> There a humble learner would I choose to be.
> At the feet of Jesus, pouring perfume rare,
> Mary did her Saviour for the grave prepare:
> And, from love the 'good work' done,
> She her Lord's approval won.
>
> At the feet of Jesus is the place for me,
> There in sweetest service would I be.
> At the feet of Jesus, in that morning hour,
> Loving hearts receiving Resurrection power:
> Haste with joy to preach the Word:
> 'Christ is risen, Praise the Lord!'
> At the feet of Jesus, risen now for me,
> I shall sing His praises through eternity."

A hymn bearing the same title, "At the Feet of Jesus," written by J. H. (otherwise not identified), appears in *Christ in Song* (Review and Herald Publishing Assn., Washington, D.C., 1908):

> Sitting at the feet of Jesus, O what words
>   I hear him say!
> Happy place! so near, so precious! May
>   it find me there each day;
> Sitting at the feet of Jesus, I would
>   look upon the past,
> For his love has been so gracious, it has
>   won my heart at last.

> Sitting at the feet of Jesus, where
>   can mortal be more blest?
> There I lay my sins and sorrows, and,
>   when weary find sweet rest;
> Sitting at the feet of Jesus, there I love
>   to weep and pray,
> While I from his fulness gather grace
>   and comfort every day.
>
> Bless me, O my Saviour, bless me as
>   I'm waiting at thy feet,
> O look down in love upon me, let me
>   see thy face so sweet;
> Give me, Lord, the mind of Jesus, make
>   me holy as he is,
> May I prove I've been with Jesus, who is
>   all my righteousness.

The autobiographical poem by J. N. Darby on this theme is also worth quoting:

> Low at Thy feet, Lord Jesus,
> This is the place for me,
> Here I have learned deep lessons,
> Truth that has set me free.
>
> Free from myself, Lord Jesus;
> Free from the ways of men;
> Chains of thought that have bound me,
> Never can view again.
>
> Only Thyself, Lord Jesus,
> Conquered my wayward will;
> But for Thy love constraining,
> I had been wayward still.

In *Evangeline* (pt. II, Sec. V line 35,) Longfellow speaks of the feet of our Lord in these simple words:

> Other hope had she none, nor wish in
>   life, but to follow

> Meekly, with reverent steps, the sacred
> feet of her Saviour.

In his helpful volume, *Studies of the Man Christ Jesus,*
Robert E. Speer quotes the following lines:

> As once toward heaven my face was set,
> I came up to a place where two ways met.
> One led to Paradise and one away;
> And fearful of myself lest I should stray,
>   I paused that I might know
> Which was the way wherein I ought to go.
> The first was one my weary eyes to please,
> Winding along thro' pleasant fields of ease,
> Beneath the shadows of fair branching trees.
> 'This path of calm and solitude
> Surely must lead to heaven,' I cried,
>   In joyous mood.
> 'Yon rugged one, so rough for weary feet
> The footpath of the world's too busy street,
> Can never be the narrow way of life.'
> But at that moment I thereon espied
> A footprint bearing trace of having bled,
> And knew it for the Christ's, so bowed
>   my head,
> And followed where He led.

Perhaps the most famous reference in all of literature to
the feet of Jesus are the words of Shakespeare in *Henry IV,*
(Pt. I, Act I, Scene I, line 24 ff.):

> In those holy fields.
> Over whose acres walk'd those blessed
>   feet
> Which, fourteen hundred years ago,
>   were nail'd
> For our advantage on the bitter cross.

A poem by George MacDonald entitled "Mary" begins
with the words, "She sitteth at the Master's feet . . ." The

entire poem may be found in the book edited by W. Garrett Horder, *The Poet's Bible: New Testament* (London, 1883), pp. 260-262.

Somewhere William Cowper has the following lines:

> 'Tis joy enough, my All in All
>   At Thy dear feet to lie;
> Thou wilt not let me lower fall
>   And none can higher fly.

6

THE LITERATURE OF THE FLORA OF THE BIBLE

The occasion for writing at length on this subject at this time (1953) is the appearance of the most notable work on biblical flora that has been published in our language to the present time, a work that will no doubt remain as the definitive volume on this subject for many years to come. I refer to the book published by Chronica Botanica Company of Waltham, Mass., late in 1952, *Plants of the Bible,* by Dr. Harold N. Moldenke, assisted by Alma L. Moldenke.

The subject of trees and plants play a far greater part in biblical revelation than Bible students generally realize. Not only are plants given considerable space in the account of creation, and Adam assigned the task of gardening, but the very temptation itself revolves around those two mysterious trees, the tree of the knowledge of good and evil, and the tree of life.

After the fall, our first parents are said to have made aprons of the leaves of the fig tree, and among the judgments upon mankind for disobedience was the pronouncement that the ground should bring forth thorns and thistles. As the fall of man came through disobedience regarding a command pertaining to the fruit of a tree in Eden, so our redemption was purchased by Christ's dying on a tree (Acts 5:30; 10:39; 13:29; Gal. 3:13), though the Bible nowhere gives a hint as to what species of tree this might have been.

Again and again, righteous men are likened to palm trees and cedar trees. Indeed, in a passage which I must confess I had not noticed until recently, we read that "as the days of a tree shall be the days of my people" (Isa. 65:22). Atonement and cleansing are repeatedly connected with the word *hyssop*, which we shall consider later in our study.

Wheat, generally translated "corn" in most of our versions, was the dominant problem in Joseph's administration in Egypt, and brought the family of Jacob into that land of bondage. The frailty of man is often likened to grass (Isa. 40:6-8; I Pet. 1:24), or to the fading of leaves (Isa. 1:30; 64:6), and the promise is given that those who serve the Lord shall be like the leaf that does not fade (Ps. 1:3).

When the historian of Solomon's reign speaks of the king's great wisdom, he says, in part, that Solomon "spoke of trees, from the cedar that is in Lebanon even unto the hyssop that springeth out of the wall" (I Kings 4:33).

Many of our Lord's parables referred to the laws of plant life, as the parables of the sower, of the wheat and tares, and of the vine. Even in the description of the New Jerusalem, whether the passage be taken symbolically or literally, we read that on either side of the river of the water of life was "the tree of life, bearing twelve manner of fruits, yielding its fruit every month: and the leaves of the tree were for the healing of the nations" (Rev. 22:2).

Dr. Moldenke well says:

"There is no other branch of botany in which so many persons have spoken, argued and written without ever bothering to investigate the controversial matters by direct observation. It seemed entirely unnecessary—and even irrelevant—to these older writers, chiefly theologians, divines, and classical scholars, to inquire as to what plants actually were growing in biblical lands in their day. Kitto aptly summed up the situation in the following words: 'The natural histories of the Bible form a class by themselves, having less connection than any other with the science of nature. They are rather works of criticism than of natural history —rather the product of philologists than of natural historians.'"

EARLY WORKS ON BIBLICAL FLORA

The first work ever published that dealt entirely with biblical flora was that of Levinus Lemmens, issued in 1566, with a long title, beginning, *Herbarum atque Arborum quae in Bibliis*. . . . This work, often reprinted, was translated into English by Thomas Newton and published at Oxford, in 1577, a volume of some 287 pages. A number of volumes were issued at the end of the sixteenth century, and the beginning of the seventeenth, the outstanding one being the work by J. H. Ursinus, a 638-page volume (1663), *Arboretum Biblicum*, etc. Ursinus added to this a *Continuatio historiae plantarum biblicae*, the two works appearing as one, in two volumes, in 1699.

About a century later, the founder of modern botany, Carolus Linnaeus, edited a work originally written by his student, F. Hasselquist, who was aroused to visit Syria and Palestine to explore their botanical treasures upon hearing Linnaeus state in a lecture in 1747 that among those countries of which men were generally ignorant regarding the natural history was Palestine. Hasselquist died in Smyrna at the age of thirty-one and Linnaeus published his notes, with elaborate additions, in 1757, *Inter Palaestinum*.

The work was immediately translated into German, English, and French, the English edition being entitled, *Voyages and Travels in the Levant in the Years 1749, 50, 51, 52, etc.*, which, says Dr. Moldenke, "imperfect as it is, because of the short time that Hasselquist lived in Palestine before he succumbed, is still one of the most valuable books ever written on the subject, and marks the beginning of a new era. For the first time in history a writer on natural history of the Bible had actually visited biblical lands and had there studied firsthand the natural features of the region."

Almost one hundred years went by before any further advance was made in the study of biblical botany. In fact, we are told that as late as 1863, a writer visiting the great British Museum of Natural History in South Kensington, found there specimens of plants and animals from all the world in great abundance, but hardly anything from Palestine.

In the middle of the nineteenth century, one of the outstanding botanists of Great Britain was John Hutton Balfour (1809-1884). For many years he was professor of Botany at Glasgow University (succeeding the famous Sir W. J. Hooker), and then professor of Botany at the University of Edinburgh, as well as keeper of the Royal Botanical Garden. His lectures and botanical tours met with enthusiastic support, as did his botanical textbooks, which went into numerous editions. Balfour published *Lessons From Bible Plants,* and in the same year, 1851, a volume entitled *Phyto-Theology; or Botanical Sketches Intended to Illustrate the Works of God in the Structure, Functions, and General Distribution of Plants.* (For most of the above I am indebted to Dr. Moldenke's preliminary "Historical Sketch.")

The two men who did more to advance our knowledge of the flora of the Bible, in the last half of the nineteenth century, were clergymen, both deeply interested in Christian missions. The first was Canon H. B. Tristram (1822-1906), who between 1861 and 1897 made five trips to Palestine, with two primary objectives: to extend the work of the Church Missionary Society, and to investigate the natural history of the Holy Land.

Out of this came his many invaluable articles on various subjects relating to biblical natural history which he wrote for William Smith's epochal *Dictionary of the Bible*; and then his own classic work, *Natural History of the Bible,* published in 1867, which went through ten editions (the botanical portion of the last edition, pp. 330-493). Tristram is especially good on the palm tree (pp. 378-386), the vine (pp. 402-413), and thorns (pp. 423-432). In 1884, he issued his *Fauna and Flora of Palestine,* a volume in the famous *Survey of Western Palestine* series, seldom come upon today.

The other outstanding contributor to this subject was an American, Dr. George Edward Post (1838-1909), one of the most brilliant missionaries ever to leave the American shores. He received a degree in medicine in New York City in 1860, a degree in theology at Union Theological Seminary the following year, and a degree from the Baltimore College of Dentistry in 1863. Almost his entire missionary life was spent in Syria, where he obtained a reputation throughout the Near East for surgical skill, a mastery of Arabic, unusual ability in preaching, and as a writer of great fluency.

In 1883, Post published a work of over nine hundred pages that immediately took its place as the outstanding authority on the subject in the Western world, *The Flora of Syria, Palestine, and Sinai.* A second edition of this work, in two volumes, was published by Oxford University Press in 1932. Dr. Post wrote many of the articles on botanical subjects for Hastings' *Dictionary of the Bible,* and contributed extensively over many years to the *Sunday School Times.*

An important work for illuminating the particular field to which it is devoted is *From Cedar to Hyssop, a Study of the Folklore of Plants in Palestine,* by Louise Baldensperger and Grace M. Crowfoot (London: The Shelton Press, pp. 196, including 56 pages of drawings). I met Miss Baldensperger some years ago in Palestine, and when I (foolishly) asked her if she spoke Arabic, she replied indignantly, and with well-deserved pride, "I speak it like a native." The folk-lore of the book is for the most part from Arabic sources, and is well done.

In 1941 an American student of botany—with a great amount of help from Dr. Moldenke, which she fully acknowl-edges—Eleanor Anthony King, issued through Macmillan's a most interesting volume, *Bible Plants for American Gardens,* which went out of print almost immediately, and is now difficult to secure. The chapters on perfumes and precious woods, and thorns and thistles are especially fascinating. More recently, another American, Allstair J. MacKay, has issued a most informative volume, *Farming and Gardening in the Bible* (Rodale Press, Emmaus, Pa., 1950).

A Monumental Work

We now turn to this definitive work by Dr. Moldenke, which must have been at least twenty years in writing. While I do not have any information on this, it is clear from his bibliography that his father, or some other member of the family of the preceding generation, C. E. Moldenke, was interested in the subject of Egyptian botany, having pub-lished as early as 1887 a work on the trees of ancient Egypt. Dr. Moldenke himself was for a quarter-century—just re-cently retired—the curator and administrator of the Her-barium in the New York Botanical Garden, where his garden of biblical plants, the best in America, drew thousands of visitors annually. In 1940 he published a volume bearing the same title though much smaller in scope. This new work brings the knowledge of biblical botany down to the latest investigation.

It is estimated, though I think Dr. Moldenke does not himself say this, that there are some 3,500 species of plants to be found from northern Syria to Sinai, grouped in 850 genera, representing 124 orders. It is generally stated that there are 280 different plants mentioned in the Bible, though not all of them can as yet be identified. This work (I would judge that the text devoted to the description of species embraces about 155,000 words) describes 230 species. The material is arranged alphabetically, according to the Latin name of the species, beginning with *Acacia nilotica,* the scientific term for a form of acacia which some believe was the species of the bush which Moses saw aflame, as recorded in Exodus 3:2-4.

Before discussing any one species, he quotes in full all the verses, both of the Old and New Testaments, in which a particular species is referred to—a truly valuable feature. Some descriptions receive only a half-page, others are given four or five pages. Especially interesting is his discussion of the species represented by the words incense (pp. 56-59), mustard seed (pp. 59-62), cedar (pp. 66-70), barley (111-113), the lily of the valley of the Song of Solomon (114-116), linen or flax (pp. 129-133), the olive tree (pp. 157-160), the palm tree (pp. 169-172), the oak (pp. 193-199; a very difficult subject), corn (pp. 228-233; by which of course is meant wheat), and the grape vine (pp. 240-244).

One of the most important words in biblical botanical nomenclature is *hyssop.* Hyssop was designated to be used at the time of the Passover (Exod. 12:22), in the cleansing of lepers, and the cleansing of a house (Lex. 14:6, 49). It was used in the sin offering for sprinkling the ashes and water (Num. 19:6, 18); and the writer of the Epistle of the Hebrews tells us that Moses "sprinkled both the book, and all the people," using hyssop (9:19). All Bible readers know of the cry of David, "Purify me with hyssop, and I shall be clean: wash me, and I shall be whiter than snow" (Ps. 51:7).

Exactly what this plant was has been a matter of wide

disagreement. Moldenke says that the Hebrew word thus translated "is unquestionably the most puzzling and controversial of all the words in the Bible, applying or believed to apply to plants and plant products." Celsius, in his botanical work of two centuries ago, devotes forty-two pages to this subject and enumerates eighteen different species that had thus far been suggested as the one meant by the biblical writers.

Some scholars still insist that the plant is what is now known as *Hyssopus officinalis;* but Moldenke makes out a good case for the small plant belonging to the mint family, giving forth an aromatic substance, the hairy stems of which "if assembled in a bunch with their leaves and flowers, would hold water very well and would make an excellent sprinkler." This plant was designated by Linneaus as *Origanum maru.* There are some good things on this in the work by Miss Baldensperger (pp. 71-78). In their annual celebration of the Passover, the Samaritans still use this plant.

Another biblical term that has given rise to many theories and legends is *apple.* The idea that the tree from which Eve plucked the fruit that brought about the fall of our first parents was an apple tree is widespread, but probably does not go back farther than Milton's *Paradise Lost.* We shall probably never be able to identify the nature of the "tree of the knowledge of good and evil." However, frequently in the Song of Solomon, and in Joel 1:12, our English text reads *apple,* and no doubt the writers meant a specific tree. Some have contended that this was the orange tree, especially because of Proverbs 25:11, but the idea is generally repudiated by botanical scholars. Moldenke argues strongly—and in this he follows Tristram—for identifying the apple with the *apricot, Prunus armeniaca.*

Our Lord's famous statement regarding "the lilies of the field" has long been understood as not referring to what we call lilies today, but to a member of the anemone family, *coronaria*, also called the wind flower. (Our author devotes 3,300 words to an interesting discussion of this subject.)

There have been many different views held regarding the wood of the cross on which our Lord was crucified, some legends insisting that it was made up of four pieces, but all this is based on late tradition and need not arrest our attention here.

There are approximately 300 species of passion flowers, we are told, but none of them is found in Palestine. The plant used in making a crown of thorns for our Lord was no doubt *Paliurus spina christi*, though there are twenty-two Hebrew and Greek words used in the Bible to refer to spiny, thorny and prickly plants. The very complicated subject of what is called *mandrake* in our version, in Genesis 30, is elaborately entered into here (pp. 137-139).

The bibliography in Dr. Moldenke's book is without doubt the most exhaustive list of works on the subject of biblical flora that has appeared in our language. It numbers 605 items, many of which, of course, are simply later editions of an earlier named work; e.g., Tristram's *Natural History of the Bible* is given four different designations in the bibliography, Nos. 322-325. In spite of the great care with which this has been constructed, there are some important works that should have been included. The earliest of these would be a work by Wilhelm Sarcerii, *Herbaium Spirituale*, published at Frankfort in 1573. In 1592, a work was published by Prosper Alpenus, *The Historia Naturalis Aegypt*, which Canon Farrar once referred to as among the five most important works in print on biblical botany.

An Englishman, John Denne, published a volume in 1733, *The Wisdom and Goodness of God in the Vegetable Creation,* which, while not a work on biblical botany as such, does discuss the deeper significance of plant life in relation to natural theology. Certainly the famous work by the French botanist Alphonse L. P. DeCandolle, *The Origin of Cultivated Plants,* translated into English years ago, should have a place in such a bibliography as this; also, the excellent notes, however brief, on biblical botany in A. P. Stanley's classic volume, *Sinai and Palestine.* There are some very excellent pages on biblical botany in the well-known edition of Calmet's *Dictionary of the Bible* by Taylor.

The work of Harris, *The Natural History of the Bible,* to which Moldenke refers, also had a German edition (Leipzig, 1825). The writings of Canon Hanauer are worthy of consideration when studying the subject of biblical plants. There is a monumental work, still in process of publication I believe, by Vivi and Gunnar Täckholm, *The Flora of Egypt,* the first volume of which was published by the Fouad I University, Cairo, in 1941, a work of 570 pages.

Such a bibliography as Dr. Moldenke has here constructed could have been made even more useful by the addition of a section on the principal articles on plants in the various biblical encyclopedias, such as that by E. W. G. Masterman in the *International Standard Bible Encyclopedia,* Vol. I, pp. 505-509, and by Charles L. Souvai in the *Catholic Encyclopedia,* Vol. XII, pp. 149-157. Incidentally, Souvai mentions a number of works not to be found in Dr. Moldenke's bibliography, especially a volume published at Westminster in 1894 by Bonavia, *The Flora of the Assyrian Monuments and Its Outcomes,* and the beautifully printed work by Fillion published in Paris in 1884, *Atlas d' Histoire Naturelle de la Bible.*

Biblical Flora and Israel

In spite of these years of labor which one of our outstanding botanists has given to the subject of biblical flora, there is no doubt much more yet to be learned, and he is the first to acknowledge this. He frequently declares that he is confident much valuable light is still to be shed on this subject by Dr. Ha-Reubeni, of the National Hebrew University of Jerusalem, who is probably the greatest authority on biblical botany in the Holy Land today. I shall never forget my surprise, when, in 1937, it was my privilege to visit his beautiful museum of biblical botany, to find huge cases labeled, "The Botany of the Gospels," and actually seeing here in the National Hebrew University the plant identified as that used for making the crown of thorns for our Lord.

This whole matter of biblical flora is taking on a new and deeper significance because of the events in the State of Israel. On the one hand, Israel is planting millions of trees, for forests and fruit, and developing the Balfour Forest in the Plain of Jezreel, and the great Herzl Forest. Dr. Gindel of Israel's Forest Research Station says, "More trees mean more shade, more oxygen, more moisture in the soil, more organic matter on its surface, more raw materials for our farms and factories.

Also in preparation, they say, for the third temple, there is a great deal of interest apparent in the matter of Herbs. An article in *The Jewish Observer and Middle East Review* for June 16, 1952, states that a Mr. Mordehai Klein, who came to Israel two years ago from Czechoslovakia, claims that there are 25,000 herbs growing in Israel, of which at least 1,000 are of medicinal value.

BIBLICAL FLORA IN SERMONIC LITERATURE

In writing this review of Dr. Moldenke's book I cannot refrain from saying something about the sermonic literature which derives from passages in the Bible containing botanical terms. The one who has produced more of this than any other minister of modern times is Dr. Hugh Macmillan (1833-1903), one of the most gifted ministers of Scotland, at the end of the last century; from 1869 to 1878, minister of Free St. Peter's Church, Glasgow, and from 1878 to 1901, of the Free West Church of Greenock.

Dr. Macmillan began publishing botanical material before he was thirty years of age, with a small book, *Footprints from the Pages of Nature, or First Forms of Vegetables.* In 1866, he published his famous work, *Bible Teachings in Nature,* which had reached a fifteenth edition by 1899, and by 1903 in England alone had sold 30,000 copies! It was translated into French, German, Norwegian, Danish and Italian. I have gone through my volumes of Macmillan, a practically complete set, and think perhaps it would be of interest to many to have a list of his principal sermons on botanical subjects. This list is in textual order followed by title of sermon, and the volume and pages in which it may be found.

Genesis 1:11, "Visible Music," *Daisies of Nazareth,* 162-169.
2:4, 5, "The Leaf," *Bible Teachings in Nature,* 130-151.
2:16, "Every Tree of the Garden," *The Clock of Nature,* 228-239.
3:17, 18, "Weeds," *Two Worlds Are Ours,* 62-79.
"The Thistle," *The Gate Beautiful,* 60-69.
"Thorns: The Curse of Adam and the Crown of Christ," *The Ministry of Nature,* 97-120.
8:11, "The Olive Leaf," *The Olive Leaf,* 1-14.

Deuteronomy 32:32, "Apples of Sodom," *The Olive Leaf,* 280-300.

Joshua 5:12, "Manna and Corn," *Two Worlds are Ours,* 177-189.

Proverbs 25:11, "Apples of Gold in Pictures of Silver," *Daisies of Nazareth,* 179-190.

Psalm 1:3, 4, "The Fruit Tree and the Chaff," *Two Worlds are Ours,* 203-212.

   65:9, "Corn," *Bible Teachings in Nature,* 90-107.

   78:24, "The Corn of Heaven," *The Corn of Heaven,* 1-13.

   104:14, "Food for Cattle and for Man," *The Isles and the Gospels,* 55-66.

   104:16, "The Trees of the Lord," *Bible Teachings in Nature,* 65-89.

   104:17, "The Hospitalities of Nature," *The Olive Leaf,* 39-59.

Song of Solomon 2:5, "An Apple," *Two Worlds are Ours,* 213-229.

   6:3, "Feeding Among the Lilies," *The Sabbath of the Fields,* 28-51.

Isaiah 40:7, "Summer Blossoms," *Two Worlds Are Ours,* 97-116.

   53:2, "The Root Out of Dry Ground," *Bible Teachings in Nature,* 210-231.

   64:6, "Faded and Wind-Driven Leaves," *The Gate Beautiful,* 265-273.

   "Fading Leaves," *Bible Teachings in Nature,* 191-209.

   65:22, "As the Days of a Tree," *Two Worlds Are Ours,* 301-327.

Amos 8:9, "A Basket of Summer Fruit," *The Clock of Nature,* 212-227.

Matthew 6:28, "Lessons From the Lilies," *The Sabbath of the Fields,* 340-358.

"The Daisies of Nazareth," *The Daisies of Nazareth,* 9-24.

21:19, Luke 19:4, 5, "The Two Fig-Trees," *The Spring of the Day,* 207-218.

Mark 4:28, "First the Blade," *Daisies of Nazareth,* 25-36.

John 12:20-25, "A Corn of Wheat," *Two Worlds Are Ours,* 230-252.

15:5, "The Vine and Its Branches," *Bible Teachings in Nature,* 174-190.

Dr. Macmillan did an entire volume on the vine, a work of 320 pages, entitled *The True Vine,* published in 1872. A general sermon on "Grass" will be found in *Bible Teachings in Nature,* pp. 45-64; and a number of interesting subjects without texts in the work published the year he died, *The Deeper Teaching of Plant Life.* Dr. Henry C. McCook, an American clergyman of the latter part of the nineteenth century, in his *The Gospel in Nature* (1887), has three sermons on the Song of Solomon 2:11-13 (pp. 244-290).

Though it does not relate directly to biblical flora, there is a verse in our New Testament that refers to an imperishable plant, the *amaranth,* in St. Peter's phrase, "that fadeth not away" (I Pet. 1:4). This is no doubt the plant technically known as *Gomphrena globosa.* Among the Greeks this plant was a symbol of long life, or even of things imperishable.

Dr. Macmillan has some remarkable words on this text in his book, *The Olive Leaf.* The word *amaranth* does not refer to "a distinction between the species but is the type of a peculiar class of plants, comprehending many species and even genera, which, on account of their dry, juiceless texture, retain their color and form indefinitely, and are therefore called immortelles, or everlasting flowers." Dr. Macmillan concludes with this penetrating remark: "The changeless asphodel and amaranth may form the adorning of the pagan heaven; but they have no place in the Christian's fields of living green beyond the river."

There are a number of volumes of sermons based on statements in the Gospels in which Jesus used various phenomena in nature for presenting spiritual truth. I am sure that there are far more volumes in this area than are known to me. One of the best in this group was published years ago by the late gifted Bishop William A. Quayle, *Out of Doors with Jesus.* Another volume of carefully prepared messages by one of the outstanding Methodist preachers of his day is *Nature Sermons* by Charles E. Jefferson; and, of later date, 1937, the book published by the Cokesbury Press, *Christ of the Countryside,* by Malcolm Dana.

There is also some relevant material in a volume of sermons by some of the outstanding British preachers at the beginning of our century, *Jesus in the Cornfield,* published in Manchester in 1903 by James Robinson. There is, of course, a large literature on the olive tree. One of the finest discussions of the significance of olive culture in the Mediterranean area one will unexpectedly find in Adolf Deissmann's great work, *St. Paul, a Study in Social and Religious History,* pp. 39-41.

A Final Word

While the subject of the flora of the Bible is a more serious and important matter than floral traditions and floral lore developed through the ages, the religious significance attached to flowers has its interest, even though the data does not come by divine inspiration. In closing this discussion, therefore, may I call attention to a volume in my library (not mentioned by Dr. Moldenke) *The Flora of the Sacred*

Nativity, by Alfred E. P. Raymund Dowling, at one time of St. John's College, Oxford, a very attractively printed book published in London in 1900.

The author here attempts to collect the principal legends and ancient dedications of plants connected in popular tradition with the life of our Lord from His nativity to the flight into Egypt. The work is prefaced by a most interesting essay, "Flora Sacra," a theme rarely come upon today, and I would like to include here his opening lines:

"Flowers seem to have retained more of the fragrance of a world which dwelt around the gates of the terrestrial Paradise than anything else in creation. To be in contact with them is purifying, refining, ennobling; their simple, gentle life soothes and softens the mind fretful and feverish with the restlessness of the milling crowd and the traffic of life's stage; and in their companionship we apprise at its value the artificial existence of modern life, as our better nature realizes that man was originally created to live in a garden, and not in a town, and that in wandering from the memory even of his old home he is working against the color, and a law of his being. If we agree with Bacon, that God Almighty planted a garden, we may be very sure that He intended us to follow His example."

It is a very dangerous thing to speak of a book in any article about which one knows absolutely nothing, but I am yielding to that temptation here. In my card files I have the following title—where I got it and what it means, I do not know: *The Botany of Three Historical Records: Pharaoh's Dream, The Sower, and the King's Measure,* by A. Stephen Wilson, otherwise unknown to me (Edinburgh, 1878). It is not found in the printed catalogs of the Library of Congress.

Inevitably the whole study of biblical natural history leads to the vast, complicated, yet important, subject of natural theology, about which we hear so little today—certainly a study that needs to be revived in our theological seminaries.

For a very scholarly treatment of the Christian concept of nature, see an article by T. Rees in Volume IX of the monumental Hastings' *Dictionary of Religion and Ethics,* pp. 201-207. Paley in his century, and Thomas Chalmers in the middle of the nineteenth century, wrote works of everlasting value in this field.

And we would recall the old but still interesting work by the former president of Princeton University, James McCosh, *Typical Forms and Special Ends in Creation,* published in 1855, a work of over 500 pages. Finally, just to stir up interest in a great subject, may I mention here a two-volume work, translated from the German by the then professor of Catholic Theology in the University of Bonn, Dr. F. H. Reusch, *Nature and the Bible* (Edinburgh, 1886). This work, as well as a number of others mentioned previously, does not seem to be in our Library of Congress. As this volume was being prepared for the press, I acquired a more recently published work, previously unknown to me—*Plants of the Bible,* by A. W. Anderson, of the Royal Institute of Horticulture, New Zealand (London, 1956, pp. 72), which discusses twenty-four biblical plants, with twelve beautiful colored plates accompanying the text.

7

LETTER TO AN ADULT FRIEND WHO IS BEGINNING SERIOUS BIBLE STUDY

Recently I received a letter from one who has been very close to me through the years, a devout churchman now in his mid-fifties, in which he said that his daughter, a freshman at a well-known university in the Midwest—a young lady of great charm, with a high IQ, and athletic ability as well—had been quite deeply moved by an address given by a visiting clergyman at the school, and wanted to begin the serious study of the Bible.

The father said that he might like to begin such a study himself, and perhaps both of them could carry on a systematic search of the Scriptures. He asked what I would suggest for foundational reading, and just how they might begin such a program. While I have answered hundreds of letters through the years about different aspects of Bible study, and have published various bibliographies, to the answer of no other similar communication have I given quite so much care.

Perhaps there are others who would like to undertake a similar program, or who have been approached by someone who had such an idea in mind, and would appreciate some help in the line of basic reading. My reply to this man's, inquiry, with the omission of all personal references, is quoted in the following paragraphs.

To my great joy, his prompt acknowledgment of the communication told of his keen interest and delight in the possibilities now unfolding before him. He went on to say that an older son had just been visiting from another state, the father of three children himself, and had spontaneously re-marked without having any knowledge of what the father was planning, that he too had a longing to begin a study of the Scriptures. No one can estimate the results which may accrue from such a program undertaken in one family. Similar activity in ten thousand families across our land could revitalize many areas of the Christian Church. A portion of the letter follows:

Dear Friend:

You have certainly handed me a very important but at the same time a very difficult problem, as to what one should read as he begins a systematic study of the Holy Scriptures, especially when this study is to be carried on by father and daughter, separated by thirty years in age, one attending college about the time of the First World War, and the other now, in the midst of this strange twentieth century. I am not going to consider for one moment anything superficial or trivial, for I think you and I both agree that people do have leisure today and can, if they wish, give some six to ten good hours a week to the serious study of the Word of God. Though I have been recommending books and constructing bibliographies in various fields of Biblical investigation for over a quarter-century, this is the first time I have ever drawn up suggestions for this particular type of program for Bible study.

It seems to me that first of all one ought to have in his hands a sort of introduction to the Bible, which will give him a background of its growth, its history, and the primary contents of its greatly varying books. I need not tell you that your own denomination has issued such a volume, *The Holy Scriptures,* by Dr. Robert C. Dentan (The National Council of the Protestant Episcopal Church, 1951; pp. 221), though in parts the work seems to me unsatisfactory. While it is true to the person of our Lord, as one would expect in a creedal church, there are things here regarding the Scriptures which seem to arise from an imperfect conception of the inspiration of the Bible, and which would weaken the faith of some in the authority of the Book.

For example, the author says that Daniel is not a book of prophecy, and was written in the second century B.C., rather than in the sixth century B.C., that the latter part of Isaiah was not written by Isaiah; that the great fish in the Book of Jonah "is merely a bit of picturesque detail" which the author introduces in order to make his story more colorful and interesting—in other words, the book is a piece of fiction. The volume is especially weak in its interpretation of Biblical prophecy, and its extensive bibliography carefully avoids the more conservative literature. I think, then, that the best introductory volume is still the one published in 1947 by the Inter-Varsity Fellowship entitled *The New Bible Handbook,* by G. T. Manley. You will find this an exceedingly helpful work.

A good Bible dictionary is almost indispensable. The standard one-volume conservative Bible dictionary is the one edited by the late Dr. John D. Davis, the fourth edition of which appeared in 1924. The book was given a thorough revision by Dr. Henry S. Gehman of Princeton and reissued in 1944. Since this veered to the left in some of its articles, the original 1924 edition has been reprinted by another publishing house.

The finest Bible dictionary for archaeology, geography and history, beautifully illustrated, is *Harper's Bible Dictionary* (1952). If you wholly ignore its theology—and we ought not to take our theology from a Bible dictionary—this is the book.

Along with these, one should have the indispensable *Westminster Historical Atlas to the Bible,* edited by Dr. Wright and Dr. Filson (Westminster Press, 1945). The maps here are simply superb.

While you need not read the book at once, before getting into a study of the Scriptures proper, it is very important to have some idea of how the Bible grew, some information regarding its languages, how the canon was formed, and the various versions which have been used around the world through these centuries. The finest book for this type of study appeared in 1950—*The Books and the Parchments,* by F. F. Bruce. The appendix contains an excellent list of books for further study along this line.

Nothing, however, can substitute for the actual study of the text, and for this one will want the very best helps. The most dependable, scholarly, stimulating and comprehensive one-volume commentary on the Bible in our language appeared recently, *The New Bible Commentary,* edited by Professor F. Davidson, and published by the Inter-Varsity Fellowship, simultaneously in London and in this country. It is a beautifully printed work of 1,200 double-column pages, with excellent introductory articles on the authority of Scripture, the poetry of the Old Testament, the four-fold Gospel, etc., with good maps and chronological tables. This is a must for every Bible student today.

Anyone beginning such a study as this will be asking himself the question, Where shall I *begin* to read and study in this vast literature called the Bible? Well, I think there is only one answer to this—begin with the Book of Genesis. By this I do not mean that Exodus should follow automatically, and then the other books of the Old Testament in their canonical order; rather, take first the Book of Genesis, then the Gospels, then the remaining books of the Pentateuch, then Acts, the Pauline epistles, etc. Of course it would be impossible and unnecessary, in a letter like this, to give a list of commentaries on each of the books of the Bible, but let me attempt it for what we might call the fundamental portions.

For Genesis, one of the most interesting, spiritually help-ful works in our language is the three-volume commentary by Dr. W. H. Griffith Thomas, appearing in the *Devotional Commentary* series (London, 1909), which has brought great blessing to many throughout the Western world.

Should you become interested in an advanced study of the book, let me recommend a volume too-little known today, outside of Lutheran circles, *Exposition of Genesis,* by Profes-sor H. C. Leupold (Wartburg Press, Columbus, Ohio, 1942), a work (of something over 1,200 pages) that never disap-points.

There has lately come from the press a volume that both you and your daughter must read, a work that is already taking its place as one of the outstanding publications of our generation and, on the subjects dealt with, by far the best. It is *The Christian View of Science and Scripture,* by Dr. Bernard Ramm (Eerdmans Publishing Co., 1954). How the author covered all this literature and thought through all these problems is somewhat of a mystery to me. In our own seminary here, I have not heard any recent book so highly and rigorously praised as this volume.

Then, because so many of its chapters deal with matters discussed in Genesis, you will want to secure another recently issued work which will at once take a high place in this field, *Archaeology of the Old Testament,* by Dr. Merrill F. Unger (Zondervan Publishing House). Here you will find chapters on the Biblical and Babylonian accounts of creation, the flood in Sumerian and Babylonian tradition, the Bible and the flood, the table of nations, Abraham and his age, etc.

Inasmuch as I will not be giving additional titles for the other books of the Pentateuch, let me suggest an invaluable work for the study of Exodus and Leviticus, long out of print but recently reprinted, *Studies in the Mosaic Institutions,* by William G. Moorehead. This will give you a clear conception of the sacrifices of the Old Testament, the meaning of the tabernacle, the priesthood, and other related subjects.

Of course, the greatest theme of the Word of God, and of all ages, is the person and work of Jesus Christ. The Gospels are the most beautiful, and the most important documents in all the history of literature. First of all then, one should have a good harmony of the Gospels, and I believe that the one published by Dr. Albert C. Wieand (first ed., 1947; third ed., 1953) is the best. This is now issued by Eerdmans of Grand Rapids, Mich. The marginal notes, the outlines and charts make it the most satisfactory work of its kind in our language. The finest *small* one-volume life of Christ is that classic work published some years ago, *The Life of Christ,* by James Stalker. For something more detailed, Edersheim's famous, widely used work *The Life and Times of Jesus the Messiah,* is still the best.

One might continue his study of the life of our Lord with two works by Dr. G. Campbell Morgan, *The Crises of the Christ* (1903), and, *The Teachings of Christ* (1913), the former being probably the greatest single volume Morgan ever did. For an examination of any one Gospel, Morgan on Matthew, and on Luke, will be found most revealing.

Then, of course, one should become thoroughly familiar with all the events that center in the death of Christ. For this, a good introduction is James Stalker's *The Trial and Death of Jesus Christ;* then Krummacher's epochal volume, *The Suffering Saviour,* which I had the privilege of editing as the first volume in the now well-known Wycliffe Series of Christian Classics, published by Moody Press.

Turning back to the Old Testament, the best one-volume introduction to the prophetic writings, from a conservative viewpoint, is the recently published work by H. L. Ellison, *Men Spake From God; Studies in the Hebrew Prophets* (Paternoster Press, London, 1952). We still await a volume that comprehensively and adequately covers all the great prophecies of the Word of God.

To one undertaking a study of the Book of Acts, I would highly commend two books: Stifler's *Introduction to the Book of Acts,* and *The Acts of the Apostles* by G. Campbell Morgan. It is not necessary to list here commentaries on any of the other books of the Bible, but may I refer to the new edition of my own *Profitable Bible Study,* the last half of which is devoted exclusively to an annotated, classified list of nearly two hundred books for Bible students, where you will find additional titles.

In addition to these study books, covering certain portions of the text itself, you will want to read from time to time books that discuss the influence, the beauty, the unity, the power and structure of the Word of God. Some years ago, Adolph Saphir did two classic works which every Christian should read and ponder—*Christ and the Scriptures* and *The Divine Unity of Scripture.* Saphir had a beautiful style, saw deeply into the Word of God, and his writings will confirm the faith of any who read them.

My friend Dr. Frank Gaebelein has a very fine small book entitled *Exploring the Bible: A Study of Background and Principles,* which ought to be read early in one's pursuit of this study. Some years ago Dr. Arthur T. Pierson wrote two volumes which have had wide influence and which are still worthy of careful consideration—*Many Infallible Proofs: The Written and Living Word of God* and *God's Living Oracles*. These works by Saphir and Pierson may be out of print, but you should try to secure them.

The one-time president of McCormick Theological Seminary, Dr. James G. K. McClure, was the author of a classic work, *The Supreme Book of Mankind,* which Scribners published in 1930. A most interesting volume, full of unique information, is *Our Roving Bible: Tracking Its Influence Through English and American Life,* by Lawrence E. Nelson (Abingdon-Cokesbury Press, 1945).

Perchance you might be interested, either now or later, in the influence of the Bible on English literature and the fine arts, I am sending you with this letter my own bibliography of this subject which appeared some time ago in the Bulletin of the Fuller Seminary Library, together with four remarkable booklets published by the American Bible Society, including one on the English Bible in British and American life.

For the study of Bible biographies, you should secure— volume by volume if you do not wish to get the entire set at once—a marvelous series by Alexander Whyte, one of the greatest preachers in the world of a generation ago, simply called *Bible Characters.* No one has analyzed these characters so vividly and penetratingly as Whyte. Every page is edifying and suggestive.

The William Wise Company of New York two years ago put out a magnificent work in four volumes called *The Story of the Bible.* The text in some places is liberally slanted, but I recommend it for the illustrations, of which there are *twelve hundred,* in color and monotone, the most elaborate collection of pictures and photographs relating to the

Scriptures that we now have in the English language. Try to pick up a second-hand copy. It is beautifully bound, and will provide delightful reading and study for many days in any family.

Well, you are about to enter upon a thrilling experience. You will find the study of the Scriptures the most exhilarating, fascinating and satisfying work you have ever undertaken. The Bible is inexhaustible, and has had more written about it, of course, than has been written about the twenty greatest classics of world literature combined—and we have still not exhausted its wealth. Its truths are forever settled in heaven; its prophecies mold the destinies of nations; as the water of life, it cleanses our souls; as a seed, it imparts life; as bread, it nourishes us; and the entrance of the Word into our hearts delivers us from darkness and fear. May the Spirit of God Himself take the things of Christ and reveal them unto you both day by day, and page by page.

There is one more thing that I ought to speak of, though you may not wish to act upon it at once. It is something that deserves thought, however. I have always found for myself that one of the greatest incentives to thorough study is an opportunity for passing on what I have learned to others. Many years ago in Baltimore I initiated a Saturday night Bible class in my own home for some young people in the church, meeting for just one hour, from seven to eight o'clock. We met for a study of the Book of Genesis. The notes I made for those two years of study are more valuable than any other notes now in my possession. There were only about ten of us, but these young people never missed an evening. Though they sometimes came in full dress for some evening occasion to follow, they still came to class. There was no pressure, no organization, no dues, no attendance record.

I do not know what you might ultimately want to do along this line, whether it would be to take a class in your own church, or have a group in your home; but after you have felt your way through some of this material, and it begins to organize itself in your mind, and you have some good notes, it would be a double joy to pass on to others some of the things you have gleaned.

8

SOME GREAT DICTIONARIES OF THE BIBLE

Some twenty years ago, while a pastor in Coatesville, Pa., sitting down one Saturday evening to read the *Philadelphia Evening Bulletin,* I was directed to a text, the meaning of which had somehow escaped me. Every Saturday for many years the *Bulletin* printed a sermon by Dr. George P. Purves —at that time reprints, of course, since Dr. Purves was then deceased. As I recall, the title of the sermon was "Treasures in Books," and this was his text: "Search was made in the house of the books, where the treasures were laid up" (Ezra 6:1).

As the Biblical narrative goes, Tattenai was attempting to prevent the building of the second temple in Jerusalem, and had sent an official letter to Darius the Mede, asking for an investigation into the matter of permission to rebuild this temple, which permission the Jews claimed they had been given. The entire verse reads: "Then Darius the king made a decree, and search was made in the house of the archives, where the treasures were laid up in Babylon." The margin of the American Standard Version translates "archives" as "books," and this is how Dr. Purves got the title for his sermon.

I am sure that all ministers of the gospel, and many lay Bible students have volumes in their libraries containing, as yet, undiscovered treasures. Here I have in mind especially our Bible dictionaries. The matter has been newly impressed upon me as I have been looking through my own Bible dictionaries and encyclopedias for principal articles relating to the subject of Eschatology. During my search I have come upon many articles which I did not know were in these volumes, and which would have proved of great help to me through the years in preaching, writing, and teaching various subjects, had I been aware of them.

There is, by the way, a most comprehensive article on dictionaries by the gifted bibliographer and librarian of Princeton University, Dr. E. C. Richardson, in the *International Standard Bible Encyclopedia*, Vol. II, pp. 843-48.

The greatest editor of dictionaries in Great Britain (or America), from 1840 to 1890 was William Smith (1813-1893), a brilliant classical scholar, who probably did more for the revival of interest in classical studies in Great Britain than any other one man of his day. Before he was thirty years of age, Smith edited the *Dictionary of Greek and Roman Antiquities* (1842), and in 1844 he brought out a large, three-volume work *Dictionary of Greek and Roman Biography and Mythology* (1,100 pages to a volume). Here Bible students who are also students of history will find material still of the greatest value. For example, there is the article on Cicero, extending to about 45,000 words, containing the most exhaustive discussion of Cicero's writings that I have come upon in any English dictionary or encyclopaedia. The section on Aristotle embraces 50 columns. It is surprising to see a number of Christian characters included here, such as Barnabas and Chrysostom, and an interesting article on Altius, the famous atheist of Antioch, who flourished in the middle of the fourth century.

In turning these pages, I could not help but note how many hundreds of names once appearing in dictionaries are practically unknown to us today, and are really, it would seem, of no particular importance in this swiftly changing time of world crisis. Here are 50 different men, thought worthy of being mentioned in this work, by the name of Demetrius, and 68 by the name of Dionysius. Most of us could name five or six different men called Antiochus, but there are 35 of them here, and 58 known in history as Apollonius.

Passing over for a moment the most noteworthy dictionary that William Smith issued, I should mention the two-volume *Dictionary of Christian Antiquities* (1875-1880), each volume extending to more than one thousand pages. Here (and remember, I am speaking only of the first volumne of any series) are many articles of importance to all students of the Bible, and of the history of Christianity. In this time of carelessness in matters of sex, one comes upon the *48-column* article on "Adultery" with a degree of surprise. "Apostolical Canons" receive 20 columns, and "Apostolical Constitutions" 14 columns. I wonder how many realize the true significance of that which takes in less than a minute at the close of our services, on the Lord's Day—the benediction. This is here given a rich treatment in 13 columns.

In our day, when among so many conservatives there appears such a regrettable indifference to the Church as a divine institution, to its officers and sacraments, it is refreshing to be reminded that a century ago this was not true. "Bishop" here receives 65 columns of comment; the "Consecration of Churches," 16 columns; "Lectionary," 27 columns; "Liturgy," 50 columns, and the "Liturgical Books and Literature," 15 additional columns, embracing something over 30,000 words. In view of the recent coronation of the Queen of England, the articles "Coronation," in 12 columns, and "Prayer for Kings," 5 columns, are timely. There are good pages here on "Christmas," especially its history; the "Crucifixion," is given 18 columns; and "Gems," 10,000 words (with many illustrations).

The article that pulled me up with the greatest start was

that on "Exomologesis." And what might that be? It is the Greek verb in Matthew 11:25, translated *thank:* "At that season Jesus answered and said, I thank thee, O Father, Lord of heaven and earth, that thou didst hide these things from the wise and understanding, and didst reveal them unto babes." The early Church Fathers used this word to indicate the whole course of penitential discipline, and subsequently it came to mean the public acknowledgment of sin, which formed so important a part of penitence. How the meaning of a word can change through the centuries!

We are now ready to consider the greatest work that Dr. Smith did, through the pages of which he brought treasures of Biblical scholarship to thousands of clergymen on both sides of the Atlantic. His *Dictionary of the Bible,* in four volumes of approximately 900 pages each, is eminently worth consulting, though the articles on archaeological and some historical subjects need rewriting, of course, or rather, new articles.

The first English edition appeared in 1863, for the writing of which Dr. Smith had the help of sixty of the outstanding Biblical scholars of his day—such a group I am sure could not be gathered together today, and possibly never will be found again in any one generation. Here are great names indeed: Dean Alford, Bishop Ellicott, F. W. Farrar, Lord Hervey, the famous botanist Joseph D. Hooker, Principal Howson (of the Conybeare and Howson *Life of St. Paul*), J. B. Lightfoot, the Perownes, Reginald S. Poole of the British Museum, George Rawlinson—the distinguished professor of English History at Oxford, Dean Stanley, Samuel Tregelles, Henry Tristram (the best authority on Palestine in his day), Canon Wordsworth, the inimitable Bishop Westcott, etc.

Four years later an American edition appeared, edited and

revised by Professor H. B. Hackett of the Theological In-
stitution of Newton, Mass., and Ezra Abbot of Harvard
College, assisted by Professor Park, Professor Peabody, Dr.
Schaff, President Woolsey of Yale College, and many others.

In the first volume of this work, extending to the word
"Gennesaret," are excellent articles on many subjects that
do not receive the consideration they deserve from Christian
students today; e.g., "Aceldama," "Air," "Behemoth,"
"Cherub" (7 columns), "Chronology" (a magnificent study
in 40 columns), "David" (30 columns), and, very interesting,
"Day's Journey." Of course there is material here on the
"Tower of Babel," "Arabia," "Bethel," "Cain," "Daniel,"
etc.

But in the middle of this volume is something which I
myself did not know was there until recently. After some 16
columns of text on the "Church," one comes upon five
columns of bibliography on this one subject, in its various
aspects: "Church in General," "Church and the State,"
"History of the Eastern Churches," "History of the Reformation," "History of the Church of England," and "Other
Branches of the Church in England and America." This is
the most important bibliography of the Christian Church I
have seen in any dictionary in the English language.

Before the work of Smith, a general advance in Biblical encyclopedias was made when John Kitto (1804-1884) published
his *Encyclopedia of Biblical Literature* in 1845, in two large
volumes. A second edition was soon called for, and a third, in
1862, in three volumes. Here, e.g., we have, I think, the longest
article on "Adam" to appear in any Bible dictionary to that
time (pp. 56-65), an unusually long discussion of "Arima-
thaea" (pp. 209-212), and a well-illustrated section on "Burial
in Tombs" (pp. 369-403). I do not know any Biblical encyclopedia that has a more comprehensive article on "Con-

cordances" (pp. 550-553). All that was known at that time of the First Book of Esdras, and of the Book of Enoch is here set before Bible students (pp. 819-24, 791-96).

Some of the titles will not be recognized by the ordinary reader, and that is one reason why anyone possessing this set should go through it with some care and index it. Thus, e.g., the article "Agrielaia" (pp. 87-88) is a thorough discussion of the wild olive, referred to in Romans 11:17, 24; "Bassan" (pp. 311-312) has to do with the balsam tree. Here is an article of three thousand words on "Becher," the second son of Benjamin and, also, the second son of Ephraim, and a most learned discussion of "the apparent discrepancies of the genealogical list," with which I am acquainted. Incidentally, this third edition of Kitto's work incorporates a good deal of material from an earlier edition of Smith's *Dictionary of the Bible.*

In 1887, William Smith, in co-operation with Dean Henry Wace, gave to the world the last of his famous dictionaries, *A Dictionary of Christian Biography, Literature, Sects and Doctrines,* a four-volume work covering every important name in the history of the Christian Church down to the eighth century; superior, I would say, to any other dictionary of this period in any language. Many of the longer articles were written by the greatest Biblical scholars of the latter part of the nineteenth century—Hort, Westcott, Lightfoot, etc. In some of our more popular magazines today we occasionally see sensational announcements of some work entitled, "The Lost Books of the Bible," or "The Book of Adam and Eve," etc., but eighty years ago the famous classical scholar F. J. Hort wrote an article of ten columns for this work entitled, "The Book of Adam."

In the first volume are magnificent discussions of "Angels," "Antichrist," the apologist "Athanasius" (25,000 words), and a ten-column article on "Attila the Hun." The section on "Basilides," the founder of Gnosticism in the second century extends to 13 pages, and that on "Basil," bishop of Caesarea, to 15 pages. The 28,000 words on "Judah and Judaism" could well constitute a separate book on the subjects. Here we find exhaustive discussions of "Chrysostom," "Clement of Alexandria," "Constantine" (50 columns), the "Coptic Church," "Cyril of Jerusalem" (14 pages), "Donatism" (32 columns), "Demonology," the *"Chronicon Paschal,"* etc. There has been no great addition to our knowledge of most of these subjects since these volumes were published. They offer an education in Church history to anyone who will shut the door and soberly study these pages.

One can still profit from the work, now almost ninety years old, found on the shelves of most serious Bible students of a former generation, *The Cyclopedia of Biblical, Theological and Ecclesiastical Literature,* appearing in ten massive volumes from 1867 to 1881, edited by John M'Clintock and James Strong, with two supplementary volumes to appear in 1890. John M'Clintock (1814-70), first president of Drew Theological Seminary, who lived to see only the first three volumes published, has been called "the most universally accomplished man American Methodism had produced." James Strong (1822-94) devoted many years of his life to the epochal *Exhaustive Concordance of the Bible* (1890).

Here are articles not only on the principal Biblical and theological subjects, some of which are quite detailed (e.g., three and one-half columns on the word "Ant"), but many biographical sketches, in some instances of men whose names are now almost wholly forgotten. I came upon such a one, "Nathan Bangs," a bishop of the Methodist Church, who is here given about 3,500 words, but about whom I knew nothing. He does appear in the *Dictionary of American*

Biography, but nearly one hundred years ago M'Clintock and Strong gave more details of his life than the now standard American biographical dictionary.

The greatest contribution of this encyclopedia, however, is its bibliographies, I do not know who was responsible for putting so much emphasis on bibliographical details. (This, incidentally, is the weakest point in nearly all the Hastings' dictionaries.) Let us take, e.g., the article on "Antichrist," embracing approximately 25,000 words—a small book. Here is not only a detailed discussion of the various aspects of Antichrist, but the most exhaustive treatment of the different views held on Antichrist from the earliest Church period down to the middle of the nineteenth century that I have seen anywhere in our language. All the literature on the various identifications of Antichrist is given, in addition to over a thousand words of bibliography exclusively at the conclusion of the article.

In the 1880's one of the outstanding Biblical scholars of Great Britain, a true conservative, Dr. Patrick Fairbairn, who had already become famous by his writings on the typology of Scripture and his commentary on Ezekiel, edited *The Imperial Bible Dictionary,* in six beautifully illustrated volumes (including about seven hundred engravings). The last issue of this work, after Dr. Fairbairn's death, was that of 1886, with new introduction, etc. The volumes are especially helpful in the areas of Biblical biography, geography and botany. Here is a masterly discussion of "Adam" extending to over 12 columns, and a superb article on "Mount Ararat," with a full account of the various explorers who have ascended this mountain.

A truly epochal work, the *New Schaff-Herzog Encyclopedia* of *Religious Knowledge,* appearing in 1908 in twelve volumes, is a condensed and modified form of the third edition of the famous *Realencyklopädie,* founded by J. J. Herzog, and edited by Albert Hauck. Dr. Philip Schaff, the Church historian, was responsible for bringing out the first edition of this work in our country; the third and last edition was edited by Dr. Samuel Macauley Jackson, with the assistance of more than six hundred scholars and specialists.

This work contains biographical, historical, ecclesiastical, biblical, and theological articles. The Biblical material here is generally considered the least important, though the bibliographies are still unsurpassed; e.g., the six columns on "Adam" are followed by the most extensive bibliography on this subject in any encyclopedia with which I am acquainted; "Africa" occupies 40 columns; Dr. Warfield's article on "Apologetics," 12 columns in length, a classic when written and still such; "Babylon" is assigned 38 columns, and "Baptists," 48 columns, in a volume extending only to the word "Basil."

The titles of some articles will come as a surprise to most readers; for instance, there is the section of two and one-half columns, and 34 lines of bibliography on "Abrasax." This is a word of mystic meaning in the system of the Gnostic Basilides upon which enormous labor has been expended in a search for its meaning and the origin of the name. (The introductory essay, "Concerning Bibliography," pp. XII-XXIV, is very important.)

The Catholic Encyclopedia, in ten volumes, published in 1907, is probably the most elaborately *illustrated* encyclopedia of religion and the Bible issued in our language. Here, in addition to the general religious and Biblical subjects one would expect to find in such a work, are included subjects seldom treated in any other dictionary, and if so, with extreme brevity; e.g., "Abbess," "Abbey" (10 columns), "Abbott," and a very interesting list of ecclesiastical abbreviations extending to 13 columns. We would expect to see an article on "Abraham," but here also is "Abraham in Liturgy." Forty columns are given to "Altar"; "Absolution" and "Abstinence" are treated with great care; and the "Bull Apostolicae Curae" has 15 columns of solid type. One regrets that the religious history of all the states of our nation, and most of the principal cities, is included here, with a Catholic interpretation, of course, e.g., "Alabama," a state in which even at the beginning of this century Catholicism had hardly any roots at all, is assigned 8 columns.

Let me here say only a brief word concerning Hastings' *Dictionary of the Bible,* in four volumes, plus a supplementary volume, published between 1898 and 1904, the most comprehensive work of its kind to appear in the English language to that time. My own reaction may not be entirely fair but I have generally felt that the articles in the dictionary proper are so technical that often they do not adequately repay a busy minister for the hours needed for reading them. The supplementary volume, however, has great value of its own, especially in the magnificent article by Sir William Ramsay on the "Religion of Asia Minor," where one finds amazing testimony to the accuracy of the second half of the first chapter of Paul's letter to the Roman Church. There is also here an exhaustive article by the late Professor Votaw on the "Sermon on the Mount," and an equally comprehensive study of "War" by the late Professor James Moffatt.

We now turn to what has been for me, apart from the *Encyclopedia of Religion and Ethics,* the most valuable of all the dictionaries edited by Dr. Hastings, *The Dictionary of Christ and the Gospels,* published in two volumes, 1906-1907, uniform with the above-mentioned work. This is a set that ought to be indexed page by page, for the reader will come upon one surprise after another in the titles of articles, written by some of the best scholars of the western world at the beginning of our century. Here is a section of 16 columns on "Christ in Art," one of 10 columns on "Consciousness," 11 pages on "Gospel Criticism" by R. J. Knowling, and 17 columns on "Dates," and who would expect to find 4 columns in a Hastings dictionary on the "Day of Judgment"; or 7 columns on "Desire"—a masterly study in human psychology? The "Divinity of Christ"—today generally referred to as the deity of Christ—is given 30 columns.

The late Professor C. W. Hodge of Princeton Theological Seminary makes an important contribution to the work with his article, "Fact and Theory," a more forceful challenge to the liberal attitude toward the Gospels than will appear in any Bible dictionary for many years to come. Here likewise are 15 columns on the "Foresight of Christ"; 30 columns on the "Aprocryphal Gospels"; 10 pages by Professor James Denney on the "Holy Spirit"; and, though the words of the title are not from the New Testament, the article "Leading Ideas" in 10 columns is a classic. Acknowledged everywhere as one of the superb contributions of modern times to the study of the "Character of Christ" is the article by Professor T. B. Kilpatrick (34 columns).

To those who know him only as the greatest Calvinistic theologian of America of his time, the precious article by Dr. B. B. Warfield, "Children" (8 columns), will come as a surprise. In my opinion, this is the best treatment of Mark 10:14, 15 to be found anywhere. The matter of the "Christian Calendar" is a difficult one, and the 28 columns devoted to the subject will be found very helpful. Professor Denney has a good study of the "Authority of Christ," and A. T. Robertson an unusually significant article on the "Announcements of Christ's Death." Even the titles of Christ not in the Gospels are here fully considered, such as "Alpha and Omega," "Amen," etc.

One group of articles I have left for the last, and that is those arising from the Gospel narratives of Christ's birth. Every minister, annually faced with the necessity, and great privilege, of preaching on various aspects of our Lord's nativity will find superb material here. Without indicating the author or length of the article—with few exceptions—let me enumerate some of the seventy titles pertaining to this one subject: "Annunciation," "Archelaus," "Augustus," "Ava Maria," "Babe," "Benedictus," "Bethlehem," "Betrothal," "Birth of Christ" (13 columns by R. J. Knowling), "Boyhood of Jesus," "Cave," "Census," "Children," "Circumcision," "Egypt," "Flight," "Fullness of Time" (on Gal. 4:4), "Genealogies of Christ," "Handmaid," "Herod" (12 columns), "Immanuel," "Incarnation" (over 30 columns), "Infancy," "Inn."

In this survey I shall not take up the last of the series of dictionaries by our renowned editor, *The Dictionary of the Apostolic Church,* in two volumes, uniformly bound with the other works. It is generally understood among New Testament scholars, I believe, that the articles are not nearly as important as those in the work mentioned just previously.

Dr. Hastings crowned his life with the greatest of all religious dictionaries published in the English language, though not specifically a Bible dictionary, the famous *Encyclopedia of Religion and Ethics,* which began to appear in 1908, when Dr. Hastings was fifty-six years of age, the twelfth, and final, volume being completed in 1921, one year before he died. The editor was able to command the scholarship of the western world for these articles, and one wonders if there will ever be another work to supersede this one on such a comprehensive scale.

The first volume of 880 double-column pages extends only to the word "Art." Not only is the Christian religion discussed here in all of its varied and complicated aspects, but all the principal religions of the world, including the cults, and fundamental themes of prophecy. Those of us who know very little about Oriental religions, especially those of India and China, are surprised at the vast amount of space given to such subjects as "Abhiseka" (8 columns); "Adibuddha" (5,000 words), which is the theistic system of Nepal. Alfred E. Garvie gives us an interesting, seven-page study of "Agnosticism." There are seven pages on "Alchemy," 11 on "Alexandrian Theology," 21 on "Altar," and 11 on "Arianism."

What surprised me most was the section on "Animals," embracing over 60,000 words—a volume in itself. This particular article has an enormous bibliography in five languages, 560 lines of fine print—enough material on one subject alone to engage a person for twenty years of research. Philosophical subjects, such as the "Absolute," "A priori," etc., are thoroughly investigated. "Anglo-Israelism" is here, along with the "Amana Society" (27 columns), an extensive article on "Ancestor Worship," and the "Cult of the Dead."

For many, the most interesting of all articles in this first volume is that on "Ages of the World" (54 columns). The subjects considered in this encyclopedia are divided into major areas, each assigned to an authority in that particular field. For example, "Ages of the World" is divided into twelve parts, each done by a different scholar—Primitive, Australian, Babylonian, Buddhist, Christian, Egyptian, Greek and Roman (25,000 words, superior to anything I know on ancient Greek and Roman thought), Indian, Jewish, Mohammedan, Teutonic, Zorastrian. Though it is a subject in which I have never had more than a casual interest, some will find the greatest treasure in this entire first volume to be the two articles, "Architecture" (pp. 667-772) and "Art" (pp. 817-888), enough material to fill two books.

How much there is to know in this world that we shall never know! But how much richer life can become by a steady application, if only thirty minutes a day, to the study of some noble subject relating to the Christian faith.

The *International Standard Bible Encyclopedia* was first published in 1915, but the third edition, thoroughly revised, is the one now generally seen and most frequently consulted —a five-volume work brought out in 1930. This is without any question at all, the most comprehensive Bible dictionary in the English language of a conservative nature, and I know of no publishing house that is planning to bring out anything comparable to it in this generation, greatly as we need it. Some of the articles here have become classics; e.g., "Apocalyptic Literature," by J. E. H. Thomson (34 columns); "Apocrypha," by T. W. Davis (10 columns); "Apocryphal Acts," by A. F. Findlay (20 columns) and "Apocryphal Gospels," by J. Hutchison (11 columns).

Dr. W. H. Griffith Thomas is the author of the article on the "Ascension"; Dr. George L. Robinson, of the "Canon of the Old Testament" (20 columns); Dr. Robert W. Rogers, in his day the outstanding Christian Assyriologist in America, contributed the pages on the Babylonian and Assyrian religions; Professor Pinches, the authoritative article on the "Tower of Babel"; and Professor Albert T. Clay, the article on "Babylonia."

The finest treatment on "Biblical Astronomy" I know of is to be found here in the 33 columns by the Astronomer Royal Professor E. W. Maunder. The late Professor Richardson, librarian of Princeton, is responsible for the article "Alphabet," and also the superb section on "Books," extending to 18 columns. Here is the famous article "Christianity," by one of the outstanding theologians of the world at the beginning of our century, Professor James Orr. But beyond all these, probably the two most valuable contributions are those on the "Chronology of the Old Testament" by the late Professor Edward Mack (20 columns) and the classic one by the late Professor William P. Armstrong of Princeton on the "Chronology of the New Testament" (pp. 644-650).

I shall never forget the day that the great New Testament scholar and defender of the faith, Dr. J. Gresham Machen, sitting with me in my study in Coatesville, Pa., pulled this first volume from the shelf, and turning to this article by Armstrong, affectionately caressed the pages, and said to me "Have you mastered this article?" I had to tell him the truth, that I had not—though I have since done so. I know of no dictionary article that so satisfactorily deals with the difficult problems in chronology, the year of our Lord's birth and the year of His crucifixion, as does this one.

Writing in 367, St. Augustine, in developing his marvelous Rules for the interpretation of Scripture, tells of his own longing for someone to produce a worthy Biblical encyclopaedia: "What then some men have done in regard to all words and names found in Scripture in the Hebrew and Syriac and Egyptian and other tongues, taking up and interpreting separately such as were left in Scripture without interpretation; and what Eusebius has done in regard to the history of the past, with a view to the questions arising in Scripture that require a knowledge of history for their solution;—what, I say, these men have done in regard to matters of this kind, making it unnecessary for the Christian to spend his strength on many subjects for the sake of a few items of knowledge, the same I think might be done in regard to other matters, if any competent man were willing in a spirit of benevolence to undertake the labor for the advantage of his brother. In this way he might arrange in their several classes and give an account of the unknown places and animals and plants and trees and stones and metals and other species of things that are mentioned in Scripture, taking up these only and committing his account to writing. . . . It may happen that some or all of these things have been done already (as I have found that many things I had no notion of have been worked out and committed to writing by good and learned Christians) but are either lost amid the crowds of the careless, or are kept out of sight by the envious" (*On Christian Doctrine,* Book II, Ch. XXXIX).

In these and other Bible dictionaries, if "search is made" we will surely find that here "treasures are laid up."

In the *Fuller Library Bulletin,* Oct. 1953, Sept. 1954, I have compiled the most extensive bibliography of Bible dictionaries thus far drawn up, should any reader be interested in pursuing this subject further.

What Augustine longed for, you and I have abundantly.

9

BIBLICAL REFERENCES TO THE TEMPLES
IN JERUSALEM, PAST AND FUTURE

With the passing of each year in which it has been my great privilege to teach an English Bible Survey course, I have become more and more aware of the tremendous significance of the City of Jerusalem in the Biblical narratives, from its first appearance in redemptive history, in that mysterious meeting of Abraham with Melchizedek (Gen. 14), down to the end of the Bible, where our heavenly home appears as the New Jerusalem. Not only was it the center of the then known world, as Ezekiel pointed out (5:5; cf. Deut. 32:8), but it was here that the major events of our redemptive history occurred.

Jerusalem is the one place where God continually says He will there set His name. It is the one *holy* city of the Bible. It is the only place where God directed that a permanent temple be erected and sacrifices be offered. It was the only divinely ordained capital for Israel, and here all the kings of the Messianic line reigned, until the city's destruction under Nebuchadnezzar. It is around this city that so many of the Psalms are gathered. It was here that the second temple was erected. Here our Lord was brought for dedication.

It was at Jerusalem that Christ was tried, condemned, and crucified, by which death our redemption has been purchased forever. Here the Holy Spirit fell upon the assembled believers, and the Church was born; in fact, here was the mother Church, and the center of Christian activity for a number of years. It is in this city that the two witnesses will appear at the end of the age (Rev. 11). This city of Jerusalem will be the center of a world-wide revival at the conclusion of this age. While Jerusalem is thus the most important geographical location on this earth, in the Word of God, and though there is an enormous literature devoted to the city, its buildings and history, I do not know any volume that adequately surveys all that the Bible has to say about it. Here is a needed work.

In the Holy City, of course the most significant building was the Temple. During the last few years I have become increasingly convinced that this subject of the Temple is, comparatively speaking, quite ignored in Biblical textbooks, and in the teaching of the English Bible. I myself must plead guilty here. While one cannot teach the Books of Kings or Chronicles, without giving some attention to the preparation for, and the erection of the Temple, or make a careful study of the Gospels without giving consideration to the Temple of Herod, as far as I have been able to discover, there is not an adequate outline of the Biblical material. This I would like to attempt here. In some places full references cannot be given, since they are too numerous; moreover, the study is not intended to be exhaustive. I trust that the outline presentation here will encourage many ministers to undertake a series of messages on this subject, realizing anew, the great significance of this holy place in the Biblical narrative.

I. The Temple of Solomon
  1. Earlier Events Occurring on This Site
     a. The offering up of Isaac by Abraham (Gen. 22:1-19; Heb. 11:17-19)
     b. David's purchase of the threshing-floor of Araunah (II Sam. 24:15-25; I Chron. 21:18-30; 22:1)

2. Anticipatory Regulations (Deut. 12:1-32)

Note the constantly recurring phrase, "the place which Jehovah your God shall choose . . . to put his name there" (vv. 5, 11, 14, 18, 21, 26). For regulations regarding the day that the temple would be erected, see 16:21, 22; 26:2-4.

3. David's Desire to Build the Temple (II Sam. 7:1-29; I Chron. 17:1-27)

The event is referred to later in I Kings 5:3; 8:17-19; I Chron. 22:7-10; 28:2-7.

4. The Erection and Dedication of the Temple

Until a few weeks ago, had I been asked to draw up a sketch of the history of the Temple of Solomon, I am afraid that immediately after the subject of David's longing to build a temple and his being forbidden to do so by God, through Nathan the prophet, I would have placed the subject of Solomon's gathering material for the temple. But there is in I Chronicles (and only there) a very extended passage on *David's preparations* for the erection of the Temple, and his three charges concerning it.

On this passage one will get almost no help from the commentaries. In the *New Bible Commentary,* published by the Inter-Varsity Fellowship, more space e.g. is given to an interpretation of the twenty-five verses of the Epistle of Jude than is allotted to the interpretation of the sixty-five chapters of I and II Chronicles! And so it is with other commentaries. Now we are ready for a full outline:

a. David's preparation of materials (I Chron. 22:2-5)

b. David's charge to Solomon (I Chron. 22:6-16)

c. David's arrangements for the temple service (I

Chron. 23:1—26:28). Here are 121 verses without a parallel reference in the Scriptures, but where can we find an adequate commentary upon the passage?

d. David's address to the people concerning the temple (I Chron. 28:1-10a)

e. David gives Solomon the pattern for the temple (I Chron 28:10b-21)

f. The offerings presented for the temple (I Chron. 29:1-9)

g. David's prayer concerning the temple (I Chron. 29:10-25)

h. Solomon's preparation for building the temple (I Kings 5:1—6:1; II Chron. 2:1—3:2)

i. The temple described (I Kings 6:2-7:49; II Chron. 3:2-5:1)

j. The ark is brought into the temple (I Kings 8:1-11; II Chron. 5:2-14)

k. Solomon's sermon at the dedication of the temple (I Kings 8:12-21; II Chron. 6:1-11)

l. The great dedicatory prayer (I Kings 8:22-53; II Chron. 6:12-42)

m. The temple is filled with the glory of God (II Chron. 7:1-3)

n. The dedication of the temple (I Kings 8:54-66; II Chron. 7:4-11)

The record of the preparations of David and Solomon, and the erection of the temple, embrace 479 verses. If to this is added the account of David's purchase of the threshing-floor, it totals 560 verses.

5. Desecrations and Restorations

The treatment of the temple by the Israelites, when

under attack from foreign powers, and its pollution in the days when idolatrous practices were rampant, forms a heart-breaking record indeed.

a. The law of a central sanctuary is violated by the unlawful altar of Jeroboam (I Kings 12:31-33; 13:1-5; 14:9; II Kings 10:29)

b. Shishak takes away the treasures of the temple (I Kings 14:26-28; II Chron. 12:9-11)

c. Two contrary actions on the part of Asa: first in enriching the temple (I Kings 15:15; II Chron. 15:18), and then in robbing it (I Kings 15:18, 19; II Chron. 16:2, 3)

d. In the reign of Joash. (He himself was hidden for a time in the temple, II Kings 11:1-3; II Chron. 22:12, 23:4-12). Cleansing and rededication of the temple (II Kings 11:18b; 12:4-16; II Chron. 23:18-20; 24:4-14)

e. Joash, the twelfth king of Israel, strips the temple of many of its treasures (II Chron. 25:24)

f. In the reign of Uzziah, the intrusion of the sanctity of the priest's office (II Chron. 26:18-21)

g. In the reign of Jotham who "entered not into the temple of Jehovah" II Chron. 27:2, 3a)

h. Desecration of the temple by Ahaz (II Chron. 28:24)

i. In the reign of Hezekiah.

There are two events, opposite in nature, recorded here in connection with the temple: his stripping of the temple of many of its treasures, with which to bribe the king of Assyria (II Kings 18:15, 16) and then the glorious revival under Hezekiah (II Chron. 29:1-36; 30:13—31:21), a total of 84 verses. Also, we must not forget the occasion on which

Hezekiah took a message and "went up into the house of Jehovah and spread it before Jehovah" (II Kings 19:14-19).

j. In the reign of Manasseh: the pollution of the temple (II Chron. 33:4-9), and then its restoration (vv. 15, 16)

k. The last great revival under Josiah (II Kings 22:3-7; 23:4-14; II Chron. 34:8-21; 29:31; 35:1-19) (For general statements regarding pollution of the temple, see Jer. 7:30; 11:15; 23:11; 32:34; also Ezek. 8:1-18; 11:1; 23:38, 39)

A number of interesting facts concerning the temple toward the end of Judah's existence are found in the Book of Jeremiah. The prophet's own ministry in the temple area is referred to in 7:2; 19:14; 20:1, 2; 26:1-10; 36:5-10; 38:14. In 27:16-21 is the pitiful phrase, "the vessels that are left in the house of Jehovah"; and in 28:1-17 is an account of Hananiah's false prophecy regarding the temple. Forewarnings of the destruction of the temple are recorded in Isaiah 43:28; Jeremiah 7:4; 12:7; Ezekial 24:21; Hosea 8:1, 15; and Amos 8:3.

6. The Destruction of the Temple by Nebuchadnezzar
In II Kings 24:13 we have an account of the stripping of the temple of many of its treasures at the time of the first deportation to Babylon. The actual destruction of the temple is recorded in II Kings 25:8, 13-17; II Chron. 36:17-19; Jeremiah 52:13; Daniel 1:2; Psalm 74:1-8.

7. The Blasphemous Use of the Utensils of the Temple by Belshazzar (Daniel 5:1-4)

8. Later Lamentations as the Ruined Temple is Beheld, (Lam. 1:10; 2:6, 7, 20b; 4:1; Jer. 7:14; 14:15; 23:11,

12; 51:51; 52:13, 14; Isa. 63:18; 64:11; Matt. 24:2). Concerning Psalm 74, we shall have more to say later. On praying toward the temple, see Jonah 2:4, 7. For those who desire to carefully study this fascinating subject, all Bible dictionaries, and many works on the Old Testament, will contain separate discussions of the following aspects of our theme: Brazen altar, altar of incense, ark of the covenant, bases, brazen sea, chambers, cherubim, courts of the temple, doors, foundation, lamp stands, pillars—Boaz and Jachin, pomegranates, porch, precious stones, table of shewbread, veil, walls, word, etc.

II. The Second Temple of Zerubbabel
  1. The Erection of the Second Temple
     a. The permission of Cyrus (Ezra 1:1-4; Isa. 44:28)
     b. The preparation for returning and a list of those who returned (Ezra 1:5—2:65)
     c. The gifts (Ezra 2:66-70)
     d. The altar erected (Ezra 3:1-7)
     e. The foundations laid (Ezra 3:8-13)
     f. Interruptions by antagonists (Ezra 4:1-24; 5:1-17; 6:1-14)
     g. The encouragement of the prophet Haggai (Hag. 1:1-15; 2:15-18)
     h. The temple is finished (Ezra 6:15-22; Zech. 1:16; 4:8-10; 8:9)
     i. The letter of Artaxerxes pertaining to Ezra's visit to Jerusalem (Ezra 7:11-28)
     j. Ezra's visit and bestowal of treasures (Ezra 8:1-36)
     k. A comparison of the temples (Hag. 2:1-9)
     l. Officers of the new temple (I Chron. 9:11-13, 26, 27; Neh. 11:16-22)
  2. Desecration and Restoration (Neh. 13:4-6, 10-14)

III. The Temple of Ezekiel (Ezek. 40:1—47:12)

It is not my purpose here to enter into this difficult problem; for I am only setting forth data, without interpretation.

IV. Additional Subjects relating to the Temple in the Old Testament

1. The Temple in the Psalter

For the most part, the references to the temple in the Psalter pertain to worship, and involve rejoicing, the glory of God, etc. Perhaps the three best-known passages are 27:4; 73:17; and 122:1. Other references to the temple in the Psalter are 5:7; 20:2; 23:6; 26:8; 29:9b; 55:14; 42:4b; 48:9; 55:14; 63:2; 66:13; 68:29; 84:4; 92:13; 93:5; 116:19; 34:1, 2; 135:2; 138:2. Some of these verses, as Psalm 23:6, must refer to more than a local temple in Jerusalem. In the first part of Psalm 74 there is a description of the desolation of the temple which has raised a great many problems, especially because of the word *synagogues* in verse 8. On three occasions at least the word *temple* indicates God's dwelling place in heaven—11:4; 102:19; 150:1. Some of the passages in the Psalter are of a general nature, and can hardly be identified with the specific Solomonic temple; for instance 36:8; 52:8; 68:17, 24; 77:13; 78:54, 69; 96:6; 114:2; 118:26; 122:9; 132:3.

2. The Temple in Old Testament Prophetic Writings

For the most part, the prophets, apart from their warnings concerning the ultimate destruction of the temple, because of Israel's sins, point to a future, final temple in Jerusalem, to which all the nations of the earth will resort to know the Word of the Lord. It seems practically impossible to spiritualize away the literal meaning of these many passages.

The classic introduction to this theme is Isaiah 2:2, 3, but other specific references are Isaiah 60:7; 66:1, 6, 20; Jeremiah 33:11; Ezekiel 20:40; 37:26-28; Joel 3:18; Micah 4:1; Zechariah 6:12-14; 9:8; 14:20, 21. No doubt some of these passages refer to the temple described in the last chapters of Ezekiel, mentioned above.

3. Two Aspects of the Temple in the Future
   a. The Messianic visitation ("Behold, I will send my messenger, and he shall prepare the way before me: and the Lord, whom ye seek, shall suddenly come to his temple"—Mal. 3:1)
   b. The abomination of desolation
      This very important theme is referred to four times in the book of Daniel: 8:11-14; 9:27; 11:31; 12:11. The only reference our Lord makes to the book of Daniel is in connection with this subject. (Matt. 24:15).

4. Other Temples in the Old Testament
   a. The temple of Nebuchadnezzar in Babylon (II Chron. 36:7)
   b. The temples of Tyre, Sidon and Philistia (Joel 3:5; see also marginal reading for Hosea 8:14)
      (For other miscellaneous references see Eccles: 5:1; Jer. 29:26; 34:15; 35:2-7; 41:5; and the strange phrase, "the vengeance of his temple," in 50:28 and 51:11; Joel 1:9, 13, 14; Zeph. 3:8; Amos 2:8; Zech. 3:7; 7:3; 11:13; and Mal. 3:10)

V. The Temple of Herod in the New Testament
   1. The Temple in Luke's Nativity Narrative
      It is interesting to note how prominent a part the temple plays in this narrative, inasmuch as Jesus was

not born in Jerusalem but in Bethlehem. The Gospel opens with Zacharias ministering in the temple (1:9-22); there follows the presentation of Jesus in the temple (2:22-24); Simeon "came in the Spirit into the temple" (2:27); Anna "departed not from the temple, worshiping with fastings and supplications night and day" (2:37). It is advantageous to place here also the second visit of Christ to the temple, when He was twelve years of age (Luke 2:41-50).

2. The Visits of Christ to the Temple during His Public Ministry

   a. At the time of the temptation (Matt. 4:5-7; Luke 2:4:9-12)

   b. The first cleansing of the temple (John 2:13-25)

   c. Another visit to Jerusalem (John 5)

   d. His teaching at the feast of the tabernacles (John 7:1—10:21—see esp. 7:14)

   e. At the feast of the dedication, in Solomon's porch (John 10:22-39)

   f. The second cleansing of the temple (Luke 19:45-47) (The remaining events in this section took place during Holy Week.)

   g. Questioned in the temple by the chief priests and elders (Matt. 21:23 ff., and parallels)

   h. "Jesus departed from the temple" (Matt. 24:1; Mark 13:1)

   i. The widow's mite (Luke 21:1-4)

   j. His daily teaching in the temple during Holy Week (Matt. 26:55; Mark 12:35; 14:49; Luke 19:47; 20:1; 21:37-38; 22:53; John 18:20)

3. Jesus' Teaching about the Temple

   a. "Destroy this temple and in three days I will raise it up . . . he spake of his body" (John 2:19, 21)

This utterance, early in His ministry, made a profound impression upon His enemies (see Matt. 26:61; 27:40; Mark 14:58; 15:29)

b. "One greater than the temple is here" (Matt. 12:6)
c. "Two men went up to the temple to pray," etc. (Luke 18:9-14)
d. Concerning oaths involving the temple (Matt. 23:16-21)
e. "From the blood of Abel unto the blood of Zachariah, who perished between the altar and the sanctuary" (Matt. 23:35; Luke 11:51)

4. Christ's Prophecy of the Destruction of the Temple (Matt. 24:1-2; Mark 13:1-2; Luke 21:5-6)
5. General References to the Temple of Herod in the Gospels (John 2:20; 12:56; Luke 21:5)
   Rending of the temple veil (Matt. 27:51; Mark 15:35; Luke 23:45)
6. References to the Temple in the Book of Acts
   a. The early Christians were daily in the temple (2:46)
   b. The visit of Peter and John (3:1-26)
   c. The angel commands Peter to speak in the temple (5:20, 25, 42)
   d. Stephen before the council (6:8—7:57)
   e. Paul in the temple (21:18-22; 24:18-21; 25:8; 26:21)
   f. Paul before the Sanhedrin (ch. 23)
7. Later Miscellaneous References to the Temple (I Cor. 9:13 and II Cor. 6:16 probably speak of this temple)

VI. Other References to "Temple" in the New Testament
1. Figurative Uses of the Idea of a Temple

    a. The bodies of Christians are temples of the Holy Ghost (I Cor. 3:16, 17; 6:19)

    b. The Church is a temple (Eph. 2:21, 22)

    c. Overcomers are called pillars in the temple of God (Rev. 3:12)

2. The Future Temple of Antichrist (II Thess. 2:4)

3. The Temple Measured in Jerusalem at the Time of the Two Witnesses (Rev. 11:1, 2)

4. The Temple of God in Heaven (Rev. 7:15; 11:19; 14:17, 18; 15:5-8; 16:1, 17)

5. References to Pagan Temples (Acts 19:27; I Cor. 8:10)

6. Miscellaneous (Acts 17:24; 19:37; Rom. 2:22)

7. References to an Altar in the Book of Revelation should be included here: 6:9, 8:3, 5; 9:13; 14:18; 16:7.

8. No Temple in Eternity ("And I saw no temple therein: for the Lord God Almighty and the Lamb are the temple of it"—Rev. 21:22)

This arrangement of material embraces 1580 different verses of the Old Testament, and 332 verses of the New Testament, making a total of 1912 verses. I have not included in the tabulation for the New Testament the passages containing the long discourses of Jesus given at the time of His visit to the temple, such as John 5, 7, 8 etc., because we are not quite sure where all these words were uttered.

Recently in examining again the books of Kings and Chronicles, I was surprised to note how often the temple was stripped of its treasures either by invading hosts or by a king of Judah for the purpose of bribing some threatening kingdom. The treasures of the temple were taken away on eight different occasions.

The occasions were as follow: (1) by Shishak, king of Egypt (I Kings 14:25, 26, II Chron. 12:9); (2) by Asa, king of Judah, as a bribe for the king of Syria in Damascus (I Kings 15:18, II Chron. 16:3); (3) by Jehoash, king of Judah, sent to Hazael, king of Syria (II Kings 12:18); (4) by Jehoash, king of Israel, when Amaziah was king of Judah (II Kings 14:14, II Chron. 25:24, 25); (5) by Ahaz, king of Judah, and sent to Tiglath-pileser, king of Assyria (II Kings 16:8; II Chron. 29:24); (6) by Hezekiah, with the hope of keeping Sennacherib from invading Jerusalem (II Kings 18:15, 16); (7) by Nebuchadnezzar, on his first invasion (II Kings 24:13 —these are no doubt the treasures mentioned in Daniel 1:2); (8) by Nebuchadnezzar, at the time of the destruction of Jerusalem (II Kings 25:13; II Chron. 36:18—these were the temple utensils blasphemously used by Nebuchadnezzar at his banquet, Daniel 5:1-4) These treasures taken by Nebuchadnezzar from the temple must have been removed to Persia by Cyrus, for he was able to put them back into the hands of Sheshbazzar when he led that first band of Jews back to desolated Palestine (Ezra 1:7-11).

One cannot help but wonder at the great wealth of the temple, to allow for its treasures to be depleted eight different times. No doubt there were periods in Israel's history, as in the revival under Hezekiah, when the lavish gifts of the people permitted at least the partial restoration of these treasures.

A SUGGESTED BIBLIOGRAPHY FOR THE STUDY
OF THE TEMPLES OF THE BIBLE

Material on the temples of the Bible can be found in the following classifications of Biblical literature: (1) books devoted exclusively to the temples of the Bible; (2) dictionary articles; (3) commentaries, especially those on Kings and

Chronicles; (4) Biblical histories; (5) biographies of Solomon and Herod; (6) books on the life of Christ; (7) most works on New Testament introduction; (8) sermonic literature. In addition to this, any volume dealing with the Arch of Titus will contain valuable information. In the following bibliography I have attempted to list only those works which discuss the Temple of Solomon, though some of these undertake consideration of the other temples of the Bible as well. The arrangement is chronological.

Samuel Lee: *Orbis Miraculum; or, the Temple of Solomon Pourtrayed by Scripture Light.* London, 1659. pp. (10) 371 (7).

By far the most important work on this subject to be published for two hundred years. A very scholarly work, with beautiful copper plate engravings, and, rare at that time, an exhaustive index of thirteen columns.

John Bunyan: *Solomon's Temple Spiritualized.* 1688.

To be found in many editions of his collected works.

Sir Isaac Newton: *A Description of the Temple of Solomon.* A rare work, appearing in Vol. V of an edition of his writings published many years ago. (I have not seen it.)

J. T. Bannister: *The Temples of the Hebrews.* London, 1861. p. 420.

James Fergusson: *The Temples of the Jews.* London, 1875. p. xviii, 304.

T. H. Lewis: *The Holy Places of Jerusalem.* London, 1880.

T. O. Paine: *Solomon's Temple; including The Tabernacle; First Temple; House of the King, or House of the Forest of Lebanon; Idolatrous High Places; the City on the Mountain (Rev. XXI); the Oblation of the Holy Portion; and the Last Temple.* Boston, 1861. 99 pages of text and 21 plates, some in color. This and the three preceding titles are exceedingly important.

E. C. Robbins: *The Temple of Solomon; a Review of the Various Theories Respecting Its Form and Architecture.* London, 1887. p. 61.

Thomas Newberry: *The Tabernacle and Temple.* London, 1891. p. 114.

Emanuel Schmidt: *Solomon's Temple in the Light of Other Oriental Temples.* Chicago, 1902. p. 65; diagrams, etc.

W. Shaw Caldecott: *Solomon's Temple, Its History and Its Structure.* London, 1907. pp. xv, 358.

Probably the most satisfactory of all recent works on this subject. Caldecott also wrote the very worth-while article on the temple in the *International Standard Bible Encyclopedia,* Vol. IV, pp. 2930-2942.

F. J. Hollis: *The Archaeology of Herod's Temple.* 1934. pp. xiv, 336 with thirty plans.

Some articles have appeared in the *Biblical Archaeologist* on this subject, especially Vol. IV, May-September 1941, and Vol. XIV, February 1951. Some of the views are critical, and are not to be accepted as final.

A very interesting brochure of more than fifty pages, with drawings and photographs, has been published recently, entitled *Jerusalem and the Temples in Bible History and Prophecy,* by an English student of the Scriptures. This may be purchased for $1.00 from the Biblical Museum, Limmer Lane, Felpham, Bognor Regis, Sussex, England. (Available in the U.S.A. from Philadelphia Bible Institute, 1800 Arch St., Philadelphia, Pa.) It is the best brief account of the temples, including the plans of Jerusalem, that I have seen, and is well worth the price. The many fine articles on the temple in our principal Biblical dictionaries need not be listed here. The literature on the temple of Ezekiel and the temple of Herod is too extensive for inclusion in these pages.

IO

THE LIFE AND WRITINGS
OF DR. G. CAMPBELL MORGAN

"The greatest living expositor of the Scriptures"—this is
the sweeping designation of Dr. G. Campbell Morgan in the
remarkable biography of him that has just appeared, *A Man
of the Word*, by Jill Morgan, the wife of the oldest living
son of Dr. Morgan, the Rev. Frank Crossley Morgan, of Taft,
Texas.

The statement is not in the slightest an exaggeration.
Twenty years ago one who was very careful in his praise of
others, and a distinguished expositor himself, who did not
in everything agree with Dr. Morgan, Dr. James M. Gray,
president for years of the Moody Bible Institute, wrote, in
a review of an earlier biography of this subject, that Dr.
Morgan was "the most outstanding preacher that this country has heard—we are not now speaking of him either as an
evangelist or a Bible teacher, though both gifts are his in a
marked degree—but the most outstanding preacher that this
country has heard during the past thirty years." (If any of
my readers wish to check this statement, they will find it in
the book review columns of *Moody Monthly*, November,
1930.)

During the active ministry of Campbell Morgan (which
covered something over sixty years, though we shall confine
ourselves to the first forty years of this century), there were
certainly well over one hundred thousand ministers in Great
Britain and America, standing in pulpits fifty-two Sundays
out of the year, preaching from the Bible, and we cannot

129

help but ask ourselves the question: how can you account for the fact that this one man would be recognized on both sides of the Atlantic as the peer of all Bible expositors over that period of time?

For one thing, it was not due to scholastic training. While Dr. Morgan had remarkable mental abilities, he never went to college, or entered a theological seminary. Strange that this should also be true of such men as Joseph Parker, Charles H. Spurgeon, F. B. Meyer, and H. A. Ironside. But Dr. Morgan believed in a thorough ministerial training, and was, for some years, the president of Chesnut College, at Cambridge University.

Nor can one say that he attained this pre-eminent position by great gifts of oratory. He was not a Charles Spurgeon nor a Gladstone, though he had marvelous ability in speaking. One could hardly say that he ever soared. Nor could one say that he had great flashes of inspiration, which almost blinded his audiences with brilliance. He never could do, or at least he never did do, with some passage of Scripture what Joseph Parker, for instance, did with the statement that man was made in the image of God, or the sending for Daniel during the night of Belshazzar's feast, or what Whyte did with the drunkenness of Noah.

If these are not the secrets of his success, let us see if we can discover what these secrets were. First of all, he had a native gift for teaching. He was a teacher in a school for Hebrew boys before he was twenty, and there he revealed a capacity for making subjects transparently clear that remained with him throughout all the long years of his ministry. In addition to this, he had a divine call to preach (though he was perhaps too young to recognize it when he first started to preach). He was only thirteen years old when, as the author says, he knew that "he must preach to people

—not one, but many, a congregation of adult men and women." Some folk in the Monmouth Methodist Chapel took him seriously, and on August 27, 1876, "a little group of men and women with boys and girls of his own age took their seats on the hard wooden benches in the schoolroom of the chapel and gave their attention to the small figure behind the desk."

Apart from these two divine bestowals, there is one word that can be written over every day of his life, and over almost every page of this book—*work*. How he toiled! He rose early; he retired late; he worked all day, except for the hours he took off for social fellowship among close friends. How little the audiences that crowded to hear his expositions saw him "in a circle of light at five o'clock in the morning with Bible and notebook spread before him. The potent message, the attentive listeners, the intangible atmosphere of union between teacher and taught was the result of arduous, concentrated toil and unremitting devotion to 'this one thing I do,' this preaching the Word—this above all."

Dr. F. A. Robinson, who was with Dr. Morgan for many days as they journeyed across Canada, in commenting on the fact that so few middle-aged clergymen seem to study, says: "One of the most famous could enjoy sight-seeing and dining out and social converse until thirty minutes before his evening address, but never once did I see Dr. Morgan neglect his sacred periods of Bible reading and preparation for even the most enticing and attractive social function." I have been told by those who lived near him during the great Northfield Conferences, that when he would be speaking at the ten o'clock hour, on a subject which he had brilliantly unfolded twenty years before, and his message had even been in print for years, he could be seen at six o'clock in the morning, bending over a table in the garden near his cottage, giving two more solid hours to meditation upon that text! Dr. Morgan himself said to a close friend that whenever he was asked by young ministers what might be the secret of his success, he replied, "I always say to them the same thing— work; hard work; and again work."

Of course, such a life of labor must have behind it enormous resources of energy. This he had, it would seem inexhaustibly, until he was at least fifty, and abundantly even after that. Before he had hardly passed his thirtieth year it was not unusual for him to preach in his pulpit at New Court on Sunday, or deliver a Bible lecture on Wednesday evening, and go immediately from the church to the station to take a train for the west of England or the south of Scotland, the Isle of Man, or the Welsh coast, where he would speak three or four times, and be back in London for his next pulpit engagement. In fact, by 1899, before he was forty years of age, he had already preached to great audiences in thirteen of the largest cities in the United States.

In 1907 he was lecturing in five other centers besides Deptford, fortnightly at the West London Central Baptist Church and the Mildmay Conference Hall, and monthly in Bristol and Cardiff and Manchester, in addition to other preaching and lecturing engagements, that carried him all over the British Isles, and even to Italy. Mr. Moody brought him to the Moody Bible Institute as early as 1896.

When he went to Westminister Chapel in 1904, forty-one years of age, for a thirteen-year ministry, he not only filled that auditorium for the first time in its history, I believe (it had a capacity of 2,500), but there he began his great Friday night Bible class, undoubtedly the most famous Bible class ever held in the city of London. This was attended regularly, year after year, by between fifteen hundred to seventeen hundred people, all with notebooks and Bibles, with the attendance sometimes rising to over two thousand.

In addition to this, he was for some years the president of Chesnut College, Cambridge; he made many trips to America; he established a Bible Teachers Association; he edited *The Westminster Record* for four years, *The Westminster Pulpit* for eleven years, *The Westminster Bible Record* for eight years, and *The Mundesley Conference Report* for eight years. (These statistics are not in this biography.)

We have not yet even mentioned the second greatest area of labor, his books. He began to publish volumes as early as 1897, at the age of thirty-four, when the little book, *Discipleship,* was issued. In 1901 he wrote one of the most remarkable books on the Decalogue that I know of, simply called *The Ten Commandments.* In 1903, at the age of forty, appeared what is probably his greatest work, *The Crises of the Christ.* This had an enormous influence over me personally, in my younger ministry, and I would commend it to every minister of the Word as a volume to read, study, absorb, and repreach. This was followed by a companion work, *The Teaching of Christ,* ten years later. In 1915 he issued four superlative volumes, *The Living Messages of the Books of the Bible.* After years of further study there appeared his three monumental volumes, the one on Acts, in 1924; on Matthew, in 1929; and on Luke, in 1931. (His volumes on Mark and John are not to be compared to these three volumes.)

I remember when I was asked to review the work on Matthew for a famous ultra-conservative religious weekly in our country, and went off to Hot Springs, Va., thirty miles from my church, to lock myself up in a quiet inn for twenty-four hours to do the review, I rose up from reading that book with a new conception of the glory of Christ, and a new appreciation of the inexhaustibleness of His teachings. Because I was compelled to place the volume high in Christian literature this periodical never published the review.

Morgan's *Parables of the Kingdom* of 1907 is a gem. His later work, *The Great Physician,* has forty chapters on the various characters with whose souls Christ dealt during His ministry. The most remarkable work in our language on the meaning of apostle, teacher, preacher, evangelist, pastor, and prophet is his now seldom seen volume, *The Ministry of the Word.* By 1930, a previous biographer tells us, he had published seventy-two volumes! No single expositor in the last seventy-five years has given us such a shelf of volumes of abiding worth as Dr. G. Campbell Morgan.

Now what kind of a being was this who could turn out work, oral and written, and command the attention of vast audiences everywhere he went? Well, he was a human being, with shortcomings, like you and me. He was the ideal husband and father, as some famous ministers have not been. He loved his home; he played with his children. He was the center of any social gathering. He could tell stories as could few Bible teachers of his generation. He faithfully practiced what he preached in the holding of family prayers. He was generous, in fact lavish, to those in need. He was exceedingly hospitable, and when his home was large enough for it, he would not hear of people who had come long distances to hear him speak, staying at a hotel.

He was immaculate in his dress. "From the shine on his beautiful hair, freshly shampooed every morning, to the perfection of his well-fitting shoes, he was always immaculate. His hands were exquisite, sensitive, long fingered, and beautifully kept."

He was extravagant, though he did not like to be called

that. He said he was *expensive*. It is even noted here that once in a two-month tour of Canada he had brought nine suits with him. Says a very close friend, "I never knew him to hesitate over the purchase of anything on account of the price. Yet everyone will admit this is true that offerings were received at all meetings without high pressure methods."

Many have testified to the fact that he was generally unapproachable, and I have seen this again and again in his meetings; but he had great love for ministers, and when he took time he could be infinitely patient and compassionate. With his friends he could be hilarious. He could be angry when there was cause for it. I will never forget hearing him once in Baltimore, at the time of the terrible Hickman murder case in California, when, his face like a thunderstorm, speaking of the hanging of this man, he cried out, "I could have helped in the hanging."

No breath of scandal ever crossed his life. "He behaved toward all women with gentleness and courtesy, and possessed a gift for making a woman feel distinctive and important to which it was impossible not to respond." He had a marvelous capacity for friendship, and what a list of friends he had: Alexander Maclaren, W. L. Watkinson, R. W. Dale, D. L. Moody, Joseph Parker, F. B. Meyer, J. Stuart Holden, John Henry Jowett, Samuel Chadwick, and his own successors at Westminster, John Hutton, and the present gifted incumbent, Dr. Martyn Lloyd-Jones.

There is one aspect of Dr. Campbell Morgan's ministry that just cannot adequately be communicated to paper. The author speaks of "the intangible atmosphere of union between teacher and taught." It has been my privilege ever since I was a boy to hear practically all the great biblical expositors of the last fifty years, and I must say that Dr. Morgan had something beyond what all others had.

I remember his lectures in Baltimore, about 1923 or 1925, when, whether it was raining or the sun was shining, fifteen hundred people would crowd into a suburban church in the *afternoon,* day after day, and hear this man expound the Gospel of Luke. There was a tenseness there, a magnetic pull, a lift, an atmosphere saturated with terrific intensity, as our souls were souls confronted with these eternal and transforming truths that sent us out of that sanctuary cleansed, ennobled, determined to go back to the Book. I have been moved by others in one way or another, but no Bible teacher in the world, in the twentieth century, could cast over his audience, without effort, without flash, without show, that mystic spell that Campbell Morgan cast when he was at his best.

Let not my readers think, however, that with all these gifts, these tremendous successes, and such invitations as probably no other man of our day received (he was called to the Fifth Avenue Presbyterian Church when he was thirty-five, received invitations to become a pastor of six prominent churches in one month, was offered positions on the faculties of three theological colleges, etc.) that there were no sorrows or tragedies, failures or disappointments. He probably had more of these than most ministers. Possibly this had something to do with his greatness.

Before he was twenty he felt his confidence in the Word of God, which he received from his Bible-believing father, crumbling. His soul came under the blackness of doubt. He knew he could not go into the pulpit unless he believed that Word to be authoritative. He cancelled all his preaching engagements. "Then taking all his books, both those attacking and those confirming the Bible, he put them all in a corner cupboard. 'I can hear the click of that lock now,' he used to say. He went out of that house and down the street to a bookshop. He bought a new Bible and returning to his room with it he said to himself, 'I am no longer sure that this is what my father claims it to be—the Word of God. But of this I am *sure:* if it be the Word of God and if I come to it with an unprejudiced and open mind it will bring assurance to my soul of itself.' " At the end of two years he emerged from that eclipse of faith with a confidence in the Bible that never left him. "I began to read and study the Bible in 1883, and I have been a student ever since, and I still am," he said fifty-four years later.

Young Morgan went up for ordination in May, 1888, before a Wesleyan Conference in Birmingham. Of 150 young men who applied at that time, 105 were rejected, and among them was Campbell Morgan. He was later ordained in the Congregational Church. His first ministry was at Rugeley. He had not been there long before he received a letter from the deacons complaining that he was absent too often *without their consent,* and of course this made him angry, though he did not let them know it. Often he had to write in his diary that he did not have liberty in preaching. Trouble with his throat pursued him year after year, once requiring a major operation.

He had a complete breakdown near the end of his first ministry at Westminster. He believed that his deacons had not fully supported him even there. Often he was restless and dissatisfied. He was exceedingly sensitive to crowds, and when he did not have them he was not at his best. At the height of his fame, after being released from his engagements in America, he became pastor of a Presbyterian Church in Cincinnati, but the audiences were never large, for some strange reason, and he resigned after a few months.

His sermon at Westminster December 26, 1913, at the age of fifty, seems pessimistic for a man at that time of life:

"These are the things I seem to have lost: the power of re-
covery; the old self-confidence that enabled me to do things
that I dare not face today; the power of resistance; and much
of the wonder of life." There were wonderful things that he
had gained and he talks about them: obedience to God,
refuge in God, the power of worship, etc. (I am quoting from
my own volume of the *Westminster Pulpit,* not from the
biography.)

He read his resignation to Westminster, but was then per-
suaded that it was a mistake and stayed on for another year
and a half, and when he offered the resignation at the end
of ten years, he said to his congregation, "I have no plans. I
see many things that might be done. I have to be content to
know that they will not be done by me. I have serious problems. One thing is now quite certain and established, and
that is that the whole of my life must be reconstructed." (I
again am quoting here from the *Westminster Pulpit.*)

Mrs. Morgan has done a magnificent piece of work. She
has made Dr. Morgan alive, as his earlier biographers did
not. She has had the assistance of all the members of the
family, but she herself has great ability in writing. There
are some things that are missing here, however, and I wish
they were not. There is no reference to Dr. James M. Gray,
who often brought him to the Moody Bible Institute—he
should be here, even though in the latter days the Institute
felt it could not invite Dr. Morgan to its platform, for reasons that need not be mentioned here. There is not a single
reference here to Grand Rapids, or to Mel Trotter, one of his
very closest friends through the years. I do not know why.
Martin Anstey did his great work on Biblical chronology for
Campbell Morgan's Bible classes in London, but he is not
mentioned here.

At times Dr. Morgan made rash statements that brought

sharp and deserved criticism, as, for example, his affirmation that all soldiers of England in the First World War, sacrificing their lives for the country in Flanders, could be sure of entrance into heaven, and some strange statements in his commentary on Jeremiah. The fact of the criticisms is mentioned in the book, but the reasons are omitted. Dr. Morgan changed his views on matters relating to the second advent of Christ in his latter days, but these are passed over.

I wish a chapter had been written dealing with Dr. Morgan's habits of study, his reading, and something about his library. Two hard days of work on the part of the Morgan family would have given us a complete bibliography of his writings, which would have been invaluable for that host of Bible students that place highest value on his expositions. There are a few errors, e.g., D. L. Moody did not draw Campbell Morgan to Northfield in 1900, for Moody passed away in 1899. I wish that the picture of the father with his four sons in the ministry, found in the biography by Mr. Harries, had been included in this book. But these are small matters. My own opinion is that this is the most important biography of an evangelical minister and laborer in the Word of God that has appeared since G. F. Barbour gave us, in 1924, his monumental life of Alexander Whyte. I wish that I could persuade every Bible-loving minister in the Western world to read this book through, behind a locked door, alone with God, as Campbell Morgan stayed behind a locked door with the Lord, and the Word of God, every weekday morning, from eight to one, year after year. The fundamental reason for the shameful weakness and barrenness of much modern preaching is transparently clear when one discovers the reasons for the power of the ministry of Campbell Morgan as he labored in the Word of God, bringing forth things new and old.

THE DISAPPEARANCE OF THE MESSIANIC HOPE
IN CONTEMPORARY JUDAISM

In 1937, while having dinner one evening in the outskirts of Jerusalem with one of the most gifted young missionaries living in that land, one who had dedicated his life to evangelism among the Hebrew people, I was told that Professor Joseph Klausner, of the Hebrew University in Jerusalem, had written (in Hebrew) a very remarkable work on the Messianic prophecies of the Scriptures. My informant added that those of us who were interested in the prophetic themes of the Word of God would find great treasures in these pages, should the book ever be translated.

During the subsequent fifteen years two persons individually undertook to translate this volume into English. One died before he could finish the task, and the other gave up his original intention when he heard that Dr. W. F. Stinespring, professor of Old Testament at Duke University, was seriously working on such a translation. At last it has appeared, a notable work, whatever else one may have to say, of some 550 pages, undoubtedly the most important volume on this subject by a Hebrew that has appeared in the last eighty years.

I would like, first of all, to say a word about the author; then to give something of the history of the book itself; and then to carefully examine its fundamental theme, and the conclusion at which the author arrives.

Joseph Klausner was born in 1874, in the province of Wilna in Lithuania, moving with his parents at the age of eleven to Odessa, at that time a famous center of Hebrew literature and learning. (For this paragraph on Dr. Klausner I am depending upon the most extended discussion of his writings with which I am acquainted, appearing in *A History of Jewish Literature* by Meyer Waxman, Vol. 3, p. 377-380. I may even use some of his phrases without quoting. Incidentally, this work by Dr. Waxman is the most comprehensive survey of Jewish literature in our language well worth knowing.) Before he was twenty years of age Klausner wrote an article on the subject "Coining Words and Terms in Hebrew and Their Proper Orthography." He was tremendously interested in European culture, which he strove to impart to his Hebrew readers, though remaining an orthodox Jew.

Klausner was always interested in the reclamation of Palestine for the Jews, believing that Israel's mission could not be carried out fully outside that land. Throughout his writings he has attempted to emphasize the unity of God, the idea of pure morality, and Messianism.

I think I am safe in saying that Klausner is the most famous and revered professor of Hebrew literature in the world today. When I was last in Palestine he was spoken of with nothing less than awe.

Probably no Hebrew writer of this century has produced as many books and articles of abiding importance in Hebrew as Klausner. In 1924 he published a work that made him internationally famous, *Jesus of Nazareth,* originally written in Hebrew, translated into French and German, and then into English. In this he pays a very high tribute to the ethical idealism of Jesus, and brushes aside with total impatience many critical verdicts of "Christian" writers regarding Jesus, e.g., that the disciples stole the body of Jesus from the tomb, a theory with which he has no sympathy whatever.

The volume we are now about to consider, *The Messianic Idea in Israel, from Its Beginning to the Completion of the Mishnah,* has three main divisions. The first part is entitled "The Messianic Idea in the Period of the Prophets" (240 pages); Part Two, "The Messianic Idea in the Books of the Apocrypha and Pseudepigrapha (140 pages); and Part Three, "The Messianic Idea in the Period of the Tannaim (130 pages). The Tannaim, we might add, for those who do not recognize the word, is a comprehensive term referring to the Jewish writers, scholars, and rabbis who wrote during the first two centuries of the Christian era and whose writings appear in the *Mishnah,* etc.

The third part of this volume (in its original form) was the first which Professor Klausner produced, far back in 1902, a doctoral dissertation written in Germany while the author was a student at Heidelberg, though it has undergone many revisions. This means that Klausner has been carefully studying the Messianic hope of Israel for half a century. The second part of this book was written in Jerusalem in 1921. The entire volume first appeared in Hebrew in 1925, the second edition in 1927, and the third edition in 1949. It is from this third edition that Dr. Stinespring has made his translation.

Professor Klausner's interesting introduction, written in 1903, revised in 1926 and again in 1949, opens with a most significant autobiographical statement which must be before us as we begin the study of his volume.

"Even in my early youth, the greatness and loftiness of the Messianic idea, that *original* Hebrew idea which has influenced all humanity so much, thrilled my soul; and I vowed in my heart to dedicate to it the labor of years, in order to examine it from every side and to grasp its essence. As early as the year 1900 I approached the work of collecting the abundant material necessary for a complete book embracing *The Messianic Idea in Israel*

from Its Beginning to the Present Time. To the best of my
knowledge, no such book then existed in any language on earth
except the Italian, in which the Jewish scholar David Castelli of
Florence had written a splendid work entitled *The Messiah According to the Jews.*"

In the same introduction Klausner says that "there is not
even one book which encompasses the Messianic hope in all
its periods from its beginning to the present time," to which
he appends an interesting compliment to the work by a
Christian scholar, James Drummond, *The Jewish Messiah,*
published in London in 1877. He re-emphasizes this by add-
ing:

"A book which arranges the Messianic beliefs and opinions in
all times and periods according to historical evolution, shows
their connection with and attachment to historical events, has
not yet been written. Therefore it occurred to me almost fifty
years ago to write such a book."

I would like to say in passing that there are really only
four volumes known to me in our language written by *Jews*
during the last fifty years on the Messianic hope, and not
one of them is in print today. In 1906 the late Dr. J. H.
Greenstone published his *Messianic Idea in Jewish History.*
Some twenty years later (1927) the famous Jewish orator and
Zionist of Cleveland, Abb Hillel Silver, published his fascinating volume, *A History of Messianic Speculation in Israel
from the First through the Seventeenth Centuries.* The
word "speculation" should be underlined in this title because that is what the book discusses; and it is tragic indeed,
as Silver is frank to confess, how many different dates were
set for the coming of the Messiah in the middle ages and
how many false Messiahs won the allegiance from time to
time of multitudes of Jewish people. The third volume is
Messianic Expectations and Modern Judaism, by Solomon

Schindler, then of the Temple Adath Israel in Boston (Boston, 1886). The first two-thirds of this book is devoted to a careful study of that tragic aspect of the history of the Jewish people since the advent of Christ, namely false Messiahs. Finally there is the very scholarly work, *The Doctrine of the Messiah in Mediaeval Literature,* by Joseph Sarachek (1932). It will be seen from the very titles of these four volumes that three of them are surveys of Messianic beliefs in the past, not a statement of present hope.

It is now time to turn to the theme of the Klausner volume. A Christian cannot help but notice with greatest interest that by the time he comes to the second line of the first page the author is compelled to use that blessed word which has been known and loved by millions down through the ages—"Christ." The book opens with these words, "The Hebrew word *Mashiah* (in Aramaic *Meshiha,* in Greek *Christos,* and from the Aramaic is derived the Greek form *Messias* (whence the English Messiah)."

We do not proceed very far in the volume before we come to a definition of the Messianic expectation, which, according to Klausner, is "the prophetic hope for the end of this age, in which there will be political freedom, moral perfection and earthly bliss for the people Israel in its own land, and also for the entire human race."

In this definition one must carefully notice two things. This is not a definition of the Messiah, which Klausner also gives and which will be repeated shortly. What is more important, *there is no hint in this definition of a personal Messiah.* Klausner, however, proceeds to give a definition of a belief in the Messiah, which he says is as follows:

"The prophetic hope for the end of this age, in which a strong redeemer, by his power and his spirit, will bring complete redemption, political and spiritual to the people Israel, and along with this, earthly bliss and moral perfection to the entire human race."

Toward the end of the volume he becomes more specific and says:

"The Messiah must be both *king* and *redeemer*. He must overthrow the enemies of Israel, establish the kingdom of Israel, and rebuild the Temple; and at the same time he must reform the world through the Kingdom of God, root out idolatry from the world, proclaim the one and only God to all, put an end to sin, and be wise, pious, and just as no man had been before him or ever would be after him."

This Messianic hope, our author says, is absolutely unique to Israel. "No other nation in the world knew a belief like this. . . . Truly the Messianic idea is the most glistening jewel in the glorious crown of Judaism!"

At the beginning of his work, Klausner admits that the Messiah hoped for in Israel must be recognized to be an individual. But as the book proceeds, we discover that *he does not believe in a personal Messiah at all,* and that he attempts to prove from the Old Testament, and then from subsequent writers, that it is not necessary to insist that the Messiah must be a human (though an exalted) person.

After carefully reading Klausner's work twice over, in preparing to write this review, I tried to read rather widely in contemporary Jewish literature regarding the Messianic hope of modern Judaism, and I must say I was astonished to find that with most Jews throughout the world the hope of a personal Messiah has vanished! Thus one of the most famous Hebrew professors in our country today, Dr. S. W. Barron of Columbia University, in his *A Social and Religious History of the Jews* (Vol. 2, p. 250) says:

"There could no longer be a belief in a personal Messiah to redeem the Jewish people and lead it back to Palestine. The true

Messianic hope is in a Messianic age when ethical monotheism, bringing justice and peace also, will be fully realized. The mission of Israel is to work collectively for this prophesied end; this is the real Messiah. All references to a personal redeemer must be discarded."

Mr. Jacob Jocz, a Hebrew Christian, in his truly remarkable and scholarly volume, *The Jewish People and Jesus Christ* (London 1949), makes the following statement:

"It is well to remember that faith in a personal Messiah does not belong to the fundamental tenets of Judaism. This is the more curious when we consider that Maimonides has included it in the Creed which is still in use in our day, and that Jewish hopes were for centuries associated with the coming of Messiah. . . . The Talmud nowhere indicates a belief in a superhuman Deliverer as the Messiah (p. 284—from A. Cohen: *Every Man's Talmud,* p. 368) . . . Liberal Jewish theology has completely abandoned the idea of a personal Messiah."

But to return to Klausner. Not only does Klausner set out to show that hope in a personal Messiah is no longer possible for the modern Jew, but he must also do everything he can, of course, to show that those fundamental factors which are identified with Christ as the Messiah are not to be found in the Old Testament predictions of a Messiah. First of all, he affirms over and over again that the Messiah of the Old Testament and the Messiah of the Jewish hope "is truly human in origin, of flesh and blood like all mortals." "In no trustworthy, authentic source of the Tannaitic period is to be found any description of the person and characteristics of the Messiah that goes beyond the bounds of human nature."

It is not possible for us here to enter into a detailed discussion of Klausner's various attempts to escape the significance of some Old Testament passages which make the Messiah to be a *divine* individual. I notice, however, in his comment on Micah 5 that he simply avoids those great phrases in which the Messiah e.g., is said to be "from everlasting to everlasting." Incidentally, it is interesting to note that Klausner says regarding this very clear prediction, that the Messiah would be born in Bethlehem, that there is no need to suppose that this king himself is to be born in Bethlehem—but he has to do a lot of squirming to get around this passage.

Over and over again Klausner refers to Isaiah 53 (of course), and constantly insists that this chapter refers, not to an individual, but to the vicarious sufferings of Israel, which must suffer for the sins of the nations of the earth. Not only is the Messiah of the Scriptures not a divine person, according to Klausner, but it is not even said that he will perform miracles. Nor does the Talmud say that he is to be a wonder worker.

What is he then to be? He will be human: he will redeem Israel from her troubles and her enemies and he will bring in an age of perfection and universal peace. Most of all the Messiah of Israel, says Klausner, must not be a suffering person, which is exactly what Simon Peter said when Christ said He must go up to Jerusalem to die. Klausner insists that in the Jewish literature written after the close of the New Testament there is no trace of a suffering Messiah.

So important is this matter of the Messiah, for Jews and Christians both, that Professor Klausner for this particular work has written a concluding chapter, "The Jewish and Christian Messiah," in which he brings out the following points of contrast: first, "Christianity is wholly based on the personality of the Messiah," implying that Judaism is not; secondly, the Messiah of the Christians is a humiliated and suffering Being, but in Judaism He is not; thirdly, Christ claimed to be a divine individual but Jews are monotheistic and they insist they could never accept any idea of Christ as divine and acquainted with suffering; finally, this Christ did come into the world to redeem from sin and evil; yet, says Klausner, "sin and evil, death and Satan still prevail in the world and therefore (Christians) are to expect his second coming."

Klausner concludes that "Jewish redemption can be conceived without any individual Messiah at all." He admits that Judaism may be defective without the Messiah, but Christianity cannot exist without its Messiah. Then in his final paragraphs he makes what seems to me to be one of the most pitiful statements for an orthodox Jew that I have ever read:

"Man must redeem himself from sin *not by faith alone,* but *by repentance and good works;* then God will redeem him from death and satan. Each man is responsible for himself, and through his good deeds he must find atonement for his sins. He cannot lean upon the Messiah or upon the Messiah's suffering and death."

Indeed Klausner now seems to be overwhelmed with his humanism and dares to say that "the progress of humanity does not depend on him (the Messiah), but *on humanity itself.*" The italics are Klausner's. So he concludes:

"The Jews can and must march at the head of humanity on the road of personal and social progress, on the road to ethical perfection . . . The Jewish Messianic faith is the seed of progress which has been planted by Judaism throughout the whole world."

I do not want to be unfair in any way to Dr. Klausner, but it seems to me that at the conclusion of this book on the Messianic hope in Israel he has no hope left at all, outside of a hope in man. I do not even see any hope depending upon God, or any reference to God, here in these final lines. It is man, humanity and progress!

I remember years ago reading a sermon of Dr. MacLaren's

on "No Man Cometh unto the Father but by Me," in which
he said, as I recall, that as the Christian age went on, not
only would men not be able to come to God without Christ,
but more than that, unless they received Christ they would
lose their knowledge of God. This is happening in Judaism.
This is why so many Jews flock to the various false cults of
our day, and this is why the Jews will be so susceptible to the
deception of Antichrist at the end of this age.

Of course, this denial of a personal Messiah in contemporary Judaism is a confession to the abandonment of the
faith of orthodox Jews through most of the centuries, before
and after Christ; e.g., the greatest Jewish philosopher, at
least since Philo, Maimonides (1135-1204) constantly affirmed in his numerous writings that a true Jew is one who
believes in the coming of a personal Messiah. In Book XIV,
Chapter XI of his *Code,* entitled, *The Book of Judges,*
Maimonides says:

"King Messiah will arise and restore the kingdom of David to
its former state and original sovereignty. He will rebuild the
sanctuary and gather the dispersed of Israel. All the ancient
laws will be reinstated in his days; sacrifices will again be offered;
the Sabbatical and Jubilee years will again be observed in ac-
cordance with the commandments set forth in the Law.

"He who does not believe in a restoration or does not look
forward to the coming of the Messiah denies not only the teachings of the Prophets, but also those of the Law and Moses, our
teacher, for Scripture affirms the rehabilitation of Israel, as it
is said: "Then the Lord thy God will turn thy captivity, and
have compassion upon thee, and will return and gather thee . . .
if any of thine that are dispersed be in the uttermost parts of
heaven . . . and the Lord thy God will bring thee into the land
which thy fathers possessed" (Deut. 30:3, 4, 5) . . . If there arise
a king from the House of David who meditates on the Torah,
occupies himself with the commandments, as did his ancestor
David, observes the precepts prescribed in the Written and the

Oral Law, prevails upon Israel to walk in the way of the Torah and to repair its breaches, and fights the battles of the Lord, it may be assumed that he is the Messiah. If he does these things and succeeds, rebuilds the sanctuary on its site, and gathers the dispersed of Israel, he is beyond all doubt the Messiah." (From the recently published edition of this work, issued by the Yale University Press in 1949, Vol. III of the Yale Judaica Series.)

In preparing this review, I wrote to my friend Dr. Aaron Judah Kligerman, for many years a leading Hebrew Christian worker of the Presbyterian Church, U.S.A., and a Judaic scholar. He replied by sending me some very interesting writings from his pen, and a letter in which he emphatically confirmed the conclusion to which I had come in studying this subject: "If you go through the religious literary field among my people, past and present, you will not find a book of a positive nature on the subject of the Messianic hope." He quotes the Columbus Platform: "We regard it as our historic task to co-operate with all men in the establishment of the kingdom of God, of the universal brotherhood, justice, truth and peace on earth. This is our Messianic goal."

I trust I am not betraying Dr. Klausner in any way by recording an experience which I had in his home, south of Jerusalem, on a Saturday afternoon in the fall of 1937. In the course of the afternoon, I asked Dr. Klausner if he would sign my autograph album. He said that he would not be able to do so that day, because *it was the Sabbath*. Later, upon returning to the American School of Oriental Research, where we were staying, I made inquiry as to the reason for this refusal, and was told by a famous Jewish scholar there—who apparently had little sympathy with Dr. Klausner's remark—that the Talmud declared that the writing of a signature, two words in succession, would be considered work, and therefore a violation of the Sabbath!

However, with another professor who accompanied me, we discussed during the hour a certain Messianic passage in the Psalms, and Dr. Klausner, to check a statement of his, ascended a three-step ladder, reached for a large folio on the seventh or eighth shelf, brought it down, opened it on the desk, and began to talk about this particular question. The reason Dr. Klausner could bring down this folio, while he could not sign his name, is that the Talmud does not say anything about taking a book off a top shelf, though it involves much more labor than signing one's name!

To me it was a perfect illustration of what our Lord was talking about when He said that the Pharisees (and Dr. Klausner is no Pharisee) were laying aside the commandments of God but holding the tradition of men (Mark 7:7, 8); "Thus have ye made the commandment of God of none effect by your tradition" (Matt. 15:6). It is tragic to think of a Jew of great learning and industry, and high ethical principles, who, though a slave to the minutiae of ancient man-made traditional precepts, has lost all hope in the coming of a personal Messiah. And there are millions of others, without his fame and learning, who just as definitely need the salvation which Christ has brought.

Note—Since this article was originally published, Dr. Klausner passed way, October, 1958.

12

THE LITERATURE OF THANKSGIVING
—A BIBLIOGRAPHY

In this brief chapter I shall attempt to arrange some references to the literature of Thanksgiving under the following headings:

I. The Vocabulary of Thanksgiving
II. The Virtue of Thankfulness
III. Thanksgiving in the Bible
   1. In relation to Israel's sacrifices
   2. In the Psalter
   3. The thankfulness of Christ
   4. The thankfulness of St. Paul
   5. Sermonic literature
IV. Thanksgiving in Prayer
   1. In the experience of prayer
   2. In the Prayer Book
V. Thanksgiving Day in America

I. THE VOCABULARY OF THANKSGIVING

The word *thank* comes from the same root as the verb *think,* and the great *Oxford English Dictionary,* before entering into an extended study of the word in its various forms (seven columns of fine print), says, "The primary sense was, therefore, *thought.*" In the Greek New Testament, the principal word for giving thanks and thanksgiving is *eucharistia,* occurring in its various forms fifty-five times, and in the King James Version never translated any other way. From this word, of course, is derived our word *eucharist,* meaning, the

152

sacrament of the Lord's Supper, from the verb used for thanksgiving for the elements (Luke 22:17; I Cor. 11:24). All articles on the eucharist contain important material on the Greek word itself; e.g., those in James Hastings: *Dictionary of Religion and Ethics,* Vol. V, pp. 540-570, and John Henry Blunt: *Dictionary of Doctrinal and Historical Theology,* pp. 247-256.

Inasmuch as thanksgiving is regarded as one aspect of prayer, as in Philippians 4:6 and Ephesians 5:20, Trench reminds us that it will "subsist in heaven (Rev. 4:9; 7:12), and will indeed be richer, deeper, fuller there than here; for only there will the redeemed know how much they owe to their Lord; and this it will do while all other forms of prayer in the very nature of things will have ceased in the entire possession and present fruition of things prayed for" (R. C. Trench: *Synonyms of the New Testament,* 12th ed., London, 1894, p. 191).

The other word frequently translated *thanksgiving* in the New Testament is *charis,* as in I Corinthians 15:57; II Corinthians 2:14; 8:16; 9:15. It is the word translated *grace* 129 times in the King James Version. In the Latin text, the term generally used is *gratia,* meaning, first of all, *favor which one finds with others, love, friendship;* then, *favor which one shows to another, kindness, service;* and thus, *a mark of favor shown for a service rendered, thanks.* This word, with all of its rich meanings in Latin literature, may be studied in *Harper's Latin Dictionary* (New York, 1897), pp. 825-826.

II. THE VIRTUE OF THANKFULNESS

It is not without significance that most encyclopedias, even many Bible encyclopedias, give no consideration to this great virtue. *The Encyclopaedia Britannica* does not have a single reference to thankfulness as such, in its vast index; the *Dictionary of Religion and Ethics,* edited by Matthews and

Smith, dismisses it with five lines; the large five-volume *Dictionary of the Bible* edited by Hastings gives it no attention; the *Dictionary of Christ and the Gospels* carries a brief (though good) article, classifying the various words used for thanksgiving, with a short paragraph on "Christ's Lessons Regarding Thanksgiving," Vol. II, p. 726; and Hastings' *Dictionary of the Apostolic Church* carries a brief comment on the subject, Vol. II, p. 567.

To the shame of Protestants, the two finest encyclopedic articles on thanksgiving are in the *Catholic Encyclopedia* (New York, 1912), Vol. XIV, pp. 554-555), significantly entitled, "Thanksgiving Before and After Meals"—in which there is a reference to a volume I have never seen, *Saying Grace,* by H. L. Dickson (London, 1903)—and, in the *Universal Jewish Encyclopedia,* Vol. V, p. 84 (New York, 1941).

For essays on gratitude and thanksgiving, one might begin far back with Seneca's "Essay on Gratitude." John Milton has some excellent things to say in his *Animadversions* (in the Columbia University edition of his *Works,* III, 145 f.), and his *Apology,* III 339 f. See also L. P. Jacks: *From the Human End* (London, 1916), pp. 186-198; Hamilton Wright Mabie: *Fruits of the Spirit* (New York, 1916), pp. 153-156; and articles—to name only a few—in *The Living Age,* July 27, 1918, Vol. 298, pp. 244-246; *The Reader's Digest,* March, 1953, Vol. 62, pp. 67-70; *Harper's Weekly,* December 1, 1894, Vol. XXXVIII, pp. 1140-1143; *The Rotarian,* January, 1949, Vol. 74, p. 2; and those appearing frequently in that noble periodical of some years ago, *The Independent,* especially from 1910 to 1915.

III. THANKSGIVING IN THE BIBLE

1. In relation to Israel's sacrifices.

The peace offering, which is recorded in the first paragraph of Leviticus 3, is indicated in the margin of the Revised

Version as a *thank* offering. These thank offerings are elsewhere referred to in Psalm 56:12; 100: 4 (mg.); II Chronicles 29:31; Amos 5:22 (mg.). On the peace offering, see: William G. Moorehead: *Studies in Mosaic Institutions,* pp. 156-167; I. M. Haldeman: *The Tabernacle, Priesthood and Offerings,* pp. 355-363; E. M. S.: *The Five Great Offerings and Their Law,* pp. 64-68, 198-228; Walter S. Moule: *The Offerings Made Like Unto the Son of God,* pp. 196-227.

2. In the Psalter

While the Psalter has many passages expressing the gratitude of the psalmist, I have not been able to find an actual study of thanksgiving in this portion of Scripture. I place this note here with the hope that someone will undertake a serious study of this edifying theme.

3. The Thankfulness of Christ

John H. Hutton: *Things That Matter Most* (1913), pp. 53-60; James Denney: *Jesus and the Gospel* (4th ed., 1913), pp. 265-277; R. C. Trench: *Miracles,* pp. 357 ff.; J. B. Mozley: *University Sermons,* pp. 253 ff.

4. The Thankfulness of St. Paul

Charles E. Jefferson: *The Character of Paul* (New York, 1923), pp. 259-274; J. S. Howson: *The Character of Paul,* pp. 195-250.

5. Sermonic Literature

The following list is only suggestive, and I must add that on some verses I have been unable to find any sermon worth noting, e.g., on Philippians 1:3; I Thessalonians 1:2; 3:9; II Thessalonians 1:3; and II Timothy 1:3. A volume of sermons devoted entirely to thanksgiving is one I have not seen—*Thanksgiving Sermons,* by E. H. Hughes (New York, 1910). There are no sermons in any modern work with which I am acquainted on the verses taken from Leviticus 7. There are many older works, from the beginning of the eighteenth century, on I Chronicles 16, but there is no need for including them here as the volumes can rarely be found today. On verse 7, however, see Joseph Parker: *City Temple Pulpit,* Vol. I, pp. 105-112.

On Psalm 50:23 see John Clifford: *The Gospel of Gladness,* pp. 185-199; on Psalm 103, Alexander Whyte, in *The Contemporary Pulpit,* Vol. VII, pp. 10-28; James Iverach: *The Other Side of Greatness,* pp. 119-135; and Henry Drummond: *The Ideal Life,* pp. 149-189; on Psalm 107:30, 31, a sermon on "Thankfulness for Mercies Received," in George Whitefield: *Seventy-five Sermons on Various Important Subjects* (London, 1812), Vol. III, pp. 118-128; and on Psalm 136, Charles H. Spurgeon: *Metropolitan Tabernacle Pulpit,* Vol. XXII, No. 1285.

Moving on to the New Testament, one will find helpful homiletical material on John 11:41 in John Henry Jowett: *The Friend on the Road,* pp. 170-172; Andrew Murray: *With Christ in the School of Prayer,* pp. 129-135; on Matthew 11:25, Alexander Maclaren: *Expositions of Holy Scripture, Matthew IX-XVII,* pp. 148-152; and on Luke 10:21, a great sermon by G. Campbell Morgan, in the *Christian World Pulpit,* Vol. 69, pp. 315-319. I am making no reference to sermons on passages which record our Lord's giving thanks at the institution of the Lord's Supper, for most of the literature deals not with this aspect of the occasion, but with the meaning of the bread and the wine.

On Romans 1:21, see Thomas Goodwin: *Works,* Vol. IV, pp. 163-187; on Ephesians 5:20, H. C. G. Moule: *Ephesian Studies,* pp. 249-251; and two sermons by Isaac Barrow on "The Day of Thanksgiving," in Volume I of his *Works.* In his marvelous volume *Lord, Teach Us to Pray,* Dr. Alexander Whyte has a sermon entitled, "One of Paul's Thanksgivings," based on Colossians 1:12, 13, pp. 157-168. On Philippians 4:6, there is an interesting sermon, "How to Obey an Impossible Injunction," in Alexander Maclaren: *Expositions of Holy Scripture, Philippians—I Timothy*, pp. 31-39, and in the same work a chapter on Colossians 1:12, pp. 106-114. On I Thessalonians 5:18, see John R. Broadus: *Sermons and Addresses*, pp. 45-56. Chalmers, on I John 4:19, has a notable sermon on "Gratitude Not a Sordid Affection," in his *Sermons*, Vol. II, pp. 375-393. McCheyne, from II Chronicles 5:13, 14, develops a sermon on "Thanksgiving Obtains the Spirit," in his *Works*, II. 244-249.

IV. THANKSGIVING IN PRAYER

1. In the experience of prayer.

The outstanding prayers of thanksgiving of the Bible are printed in full in that remarkable volume, *The Prayers of the Bible*, by the late Professor John Edgar McFadyen, pp. 273-280. (This book, published perhaps thirty years ago, is now practically unobtainable.) See also W. M. Scroggie: *Method in Prayer*, pp. 131-152, and Edward M. Bounds: *The Essentials of Prayer*, pp. 37-46.

2. Thanksgiving in the Prayer Book

The subject of thanksgiving is given more consideration in the Episcopal Prayer Book than in any other similar volume with which I am acquainted. For material on this, see Dyson Hague: *Through the Prayer Book* (London, 1932), pp. 155, 156; Walker Gwynne: *Primitive Worship and the Prayer Book* (New York, 1917), pp. 359-360; Walter F. Hank: *Church Dictionary* (London, 1896), p. 732. (This list could be extended indefinitely, but that is not necessary for this particular bibliography.)

V. THANKSGIVING DAY IN AMERICA

The first national Thanksgiving Day occurred November 26, 1789. For this, and all the early thanksgiving festivals of

New England, there is nothing to compare with the exhaustive study, which will probably never need to be repeated—*The Fast and Thanksgiving Days of New England,* by W. DeLoss Love, Jr., published in 1895, a work of over 600 pages, based upon a thorough investigation of the original sources. See also the biographies of Governor Bradford, particularly the latest one, by Bradford Smith, *Bradford of Plymouth* (Philadelphia, 1951), pp. 162-163.

The first printed account of this celebration is in a rare volume, published in London in 1622, *A Relation: or Journal of the Beginnings and Proceedings of the English Plantation Settlers at Plymouth in New England,* by G. Mourt. On October 3, 1789, Washington issued a Thanksgiving Proclamation, concerning which there is an interesting article, "Our Lost Proclamation," by M. C. Schlichter, in *Scholastic* for November 18, 1940, p. 13. Many of our earlier Presidents, however, refused to issue such proclamations, among whom were Jefferson, Taylor, Jackson, Monroe, Van Buren, Polk, Pierce and Buchanan.

There is a most informing discussion on the decision of Abraham Lincoln to issue a Thanksgiving Proclamation in 1863 entitled, "Day of Remembrance," in the *Christian Science Monitor,* November 18, 1936. "What You Do Not Know About Thanksgiving" is the title of an excellent article by Roger Butterfield, in the *Saturday Evening Post* for November 27, 1948, pp. 20, 21, 136 ff.

The finest work on the entire subject of Thanksgiving was written by Robert H. Schauffler: *Thanksgiving, Its Origin, Celebration, and Significance* (1925), pp. xxii, 269. See also *"We Gather Together": the Story of Thanksgiving,* by Ralph Linton (New York, 1949), pp. 100; Helen Philbrook Patten: *The Year's Festivals* (1903), pp. 211-234; and a chapter in a work edited by M. M. Kaplan: *The Faith of America* (1951), pp. 305-328.

In this bibliography, I have not in any way attempted to be exhaustive; for there are scores of articles dealing with this subject appearing in our religious magazines. In the index of the first thirty volumes of the *Homiletical Review,* there are sixty-four references to thanksgiving alone. No mention has been made here of the poetry, or the plays built around this theme and our national holiday. There are hundreds of these, as one will discover in examining the various volumes of *The Reader's Guide to Periodical Literature. The New York Times Magazine* generally has a worthwhile article on some aspect of the subject in one of the issues appearing in November of any year.

13

A CLASSIFICATION OF NEW TESTAMENT
PASSAGES ON THE HOLY SPIRIT

As far as I know, this is the first attempt (in print) to give a complete classification of all the passages in the New Testament containing references to the Holy Spirit or to "spiritual things." In his standard work, *Through the Eternal Spirit*, Elder Cumming prints in full all such passages, but he undertakes no classification of data. Arthur Cleveland Downer, in his *Mission and Ministration of the Holy Spirit* (Edinburgh, 1909)—a book that deserves the widest circle of readers—has an elaborate (15 pages) outline of the subject, but the work sets forth some teachings not specifically found in passages on the Holy Spirit, while some relevant passages are omitted. The most elaborate outline (known to me) is in a volume now seldom seen, *Outline Bible Studies,* by Henry W. Frost (Philadelphia, 1824) pp. 59-73, which I have purposely not used in constructing the following arrangement of data. If my analysis is complete, it would seem that in the New Testament we have 166 different *facts* about the Person and Work of the Holy Spirit, in which are 75 *different truths* about the relationship of the Holy Spirit to *all* believers.

Synopsis of the Outline

   I. Names and Titles of the Holy Spirit
      A. In general
      B. In relation to God the Father
      C. In relation to Christ
      D. In relation to the believer

II. The Holy Spirit in Relation to the Father and the Son
   A. As the Third Person of the Trinity
   B. In relation to God the Father
   C. In relation to Christ the Son

III. The Holy Spirit's Inspiration of the Writers of the Scriptures
   A. Of the Old Testament
   B. Of the New Testament

IV. The Teachings of Christ Regarding the Holy Spirit
   A. In the Synoptic Gospels
   B. In the Fourth Gospel
   C. In the Book of Acts

V. The Holy Spirit in the Early Church

VI. The Holy Spirit in Relation to the Believer
   A. In various aspects of our regeneration
   B. The fact of the Spirit's indwelling
   C. The continuous work of the Holy Spirit in and for us.
   D. Exhortations bearing upon our relation to the Holy Spirit
   E. The resultant spiritual man
   F. Spiritual gifts
   G. Sins against the Holy Spirit

VII. Some unclassified References to the Holy Spirit

The Classification

I. Names and Titles of the Holy Spirit
   A. In General
      1. the Spirit, Mark 1:10; Luke 4:1, 14; John 1:32, etc.

      In entering upon a study of this subject, one

should carefully examine the word *pneuma* in one of the larger New Testament Greek lexicons, and the various meanings assigned to *spirit* in the *Oxford English Dictionary*.

2. the Holy Spirit, Matt. 1:18; Mark 1:8, etc.

3. the Comforter, John 14:16, 26; 15:26, 16:7
This is a translation of the Greek word *parakletos*, which the Latin version translates *advocat*. "He is the Protector or Supporter rather than the Comforter. His function is not to save the Apostles from being submerged by despair, but in a very real way to succour them and strengthen them in their work of bearing witness to Christ and the Gospel." *A Companion to the Bible,* New York, 1958, p. 170.

4. the Eternal Spirit, Heb. 9:14

B. In relation to the Father (see also II-B)

1. Spirit of God, Matt. 3:16; 12:28; Rom. 8:14; 15:19; I Cor. 1:12; 2:11, 14; 7:40; 12:3; I John 4:2

2. Spirit of your Father, Matt. 10:28

3. Spirit of the Lord, Luke 4:18; Acts 5:9; 8:39; II Cor. 3:17, 18
There is some difference of opinion concerning some of these passages, as to whether "the Lord" refers to God the Father or to Christ.

4. Holy Spirit of God, Eph. 4:30

5. This Holy Spirit, I Thess. 5:8

6. Spirit of the living God, II Cor. 3:3

7. Spirit of our God, I Cor. 6:13

8. His Spirit, I Thess. 4.5; Eph. 3:16; I John 4:13

9. "the seven Spirits of God" (Rev. 4:5; 1:4) should perhaps be included here.

C. In relation to Christ (see also II-C)
1. Spirit of Christ, Rom. 8:9; I Pet. 9:11
2. Spirit of His Son, Gal. 4:6
3. Spirit of Jesus Christ, Phil. 1:19
D. In relation to believers
1. Spirit of Truth, John 14:17; 15:26; 16:13; I John 4:6; 5:6
2. Spirit of Holiness, Rom. 1:4
3. Spirit of Life, Rom. 8:2; 11:11
4. Holy Spirit of Promise, Eph. 1:13
5. Spirit of Wisdom, Eph. 1:7
6. Spirit of Grace, Heb. 10:29
7. Spirit of Adoption, Rom. 8:15
8. Spirit of Faith, II Cor. 4:13
II. The Holy Spirit in Relation to the Father and the Son
A. As the Third Person of the Trinity, Matt. 28:19; II Cor. 13:14
B. In relation to God the Father (see I-B)
1. The sending of the Holy Spirit is referred to by our Lord as "the promise of the Father." Acts 1:4; Luke 24:49
2. The Holy Spirit is said to be a *gift* of God. John 14:16; Luke 11:13; cf. I Cor. 2:12 (cf. IV-B-7)
3. Jesus referred to the Holy Spirit as He "whom the Father will send in my name" (John 14:26), or "He whom I will send unto you from the Father" (15:26; cf. 16:7 [cf. IV-B-6])
4. The Holy Spirit "proceedeth from the Father." John 15:26
From these passages the early Church developed the doctrine of the dual Procession of the Holy Spirit. The Greek Orthodox Church has always denied this, insisting that the Holy Spirit proceeds

only from the Father. For a brief discussion of
this subject see the work by Downer referred to
above, pp. 30-37; and for an exhaustive treatment,
H. B. Swete: *History of Doctrine of the Procession of the Holy Spirit* (London, 1876).

C. In relation to Christ
  1. At the birth of Christ
     a. Christ was conceived by the Holy Spirit (Matt.
        1:18, 20; Luke 1:35); thus the clause in the
        Apostles' Creed, "Who was conceived by the
        Holy Ghost, born of the Virgin Mary." See
        H. B. Swete: *The Apostles' Creed* (2nd ed.,
        1894) pp. 42-55.
     b. in relation to others at the time of the Nativity
          (1) Elizabeth, Luke 1:41
          (2) Zacharias, Luke 1:67
          (3) Simeon, Luke 2:25-27
  2. John the Baptist, who himself was "filled with
     the Holy Spirit from his mother's womb" (Luke
     1:15), predicted that Christ would baptize with
     the Holy Spirit. Matt. 3:11; Mark 1:28; Luke
     3:16; cf. John 1:33
  3. The Holy Spirit descended upon Him at the
     time of His baptism. Matt. 3:16; Mark 1:10;
     Luke 3:22; John 1:32, 33
  4. He returned from the Jordan full of the Holy
     Spirit. Luke 4:1
  5. At the time of His temptation
     a. He was driven by the Spirit into the wilder-
        ness. Matt. 4:1; Mark 1:12; Luke 4:1
     b. He returned in the power of the Spirit. Luke
        4:14
  6. "God anointed Him with the Holy Spirit and

with power." Acts 10:38, and Matt. 12:18, quoted from Isa. 42:1

7. He began and continued His ministry by the power of the Holy Spirit. Luke 4:18 ff.; Matt. 12:17, 18, 28

8. He offered Himself unto God through the Eternal Spirit. Heb. 9:14

9. The Holy Spirit in relation to Christ's resurrection. Rom. 1:4; 8:11; I Pet. 3:18. "Whatever Jesus was or is, whatever He did or does, the Spirit was an active agent in His being or doing it, and what the Spirit was to our Lord's human nature, He must be to our human nature also." —William Milligan: *The Ascension and High Priesthood of Our Lord* (London, 1901) p. 183; see also H. C. G. Moule: *Veni Creator* (London, 1890), p. 33

10. The Holy Spirit was sent by Christ, Acts 2:33

III. The Holy Spirit's Inspiration of the Writers of the Scriptures

A. The Old Testament

1. the *typical* significance of the tabernacle, Heb. 9:8

2. the Psalms (1) of David, Matt. 22:43; Mark 12:36; Acts 1:16, and (2) Psalm 95, Heb. 3:7

3. all the prophets "were moved by the Holy Spirit," II Pet. 1:21

4. particularly the prophecies of Christ's sufferings "and the glories that should follow them," I Pet. 1:11

5. Isa. 6:9, 10; Acts 28:25

6. Jer. 31:33, 34; Heb. 10:15, 16

B. The New Testament

1. concerning the truth that in Christ, Jew and Gentile are now one, Eph. 3:5
2. concerning certain demon manifestations in the last days, I Tim. 4:1
3. concerning virgins, "I think that I have also the Spirit of God," I Cor. 7:40
4. the messages of the risen Lord to the seven churches of Asia, Rev. 2:7-3:22
5. concerning the future of those who have died in the Lord, Rev. 14:13
6. the last invitation to "Come," Rev. 22:17

On the work of the Holy Spirit in the inspiration of the Scriptures, the following list is only suggestive: A. J. Gordon: *The Ministry of the Spirit* (1894) pp. 164-184; David M. McIntyre: *The Spirit in the Word* (Scotland, 1908); John H. Walvoord: *The Doctrine of the Holy Spirit* (Dallas, Texas, 1943) pp. 44-74. George Smeaton: *The Doctrine of the Holy Spirit* (2nd ed., Edinburgh, 1889), pp. 146-174; and "The Relation of the Holy Spirit to the Amanuensis," in Robert Preus: *The Inspiration of Scripture* (Edinburgh, 1955) pp. 50-75. There is one passage in the New Testament which, while it does not contain the word *pneuma* (or *pneumatika*), does contain, in one solitary place, a word that is built around *pneuma*. It is found in II Tim. 3:16, in the clause, "All Scripture is inspired of God," in which the four words "is inspired of God" are a translation of a form of the Greek word *theopneustos*. The late Dr. Warfield, in an exhaustive examination of the meaning of this word, has well said, "Scripture is called *theopneustos* in order to designate it as 'God-breathed,' the product of divine inspiration, the creation of the Spirit who is in all spheres of the Divine activity and the executive of the Godhead. The Scriptures owe their origin to an activity of God the Holy Ghost." See his full discussion in his vitally important work, *Revelation and Inspiration* (1927), pp. 251-280.

IV. The Teachings of Christ Regarding the Person and Work of the Holy Spirit

    A. In the Synoptic Gospels

       (Much has been written on why there are so few references to Christ's teachings on the Spirit in the first three Gospels.)

       1. He is given to them who ask. Luke 11:13, Matt. 7:11

       2. The Spirit would speak through the Twelve on (1) their first missionary journey (Matt. 10:19, 20; Mark 13:15); and (2) on later missions (Luke 12:2).

       3. The sin of blasphemy against the Holy Spirit (Matt. 12:31, 32; Mark 3:29, 30; Luke 12:10). There is an excellent discussion of this difficult subject, with a bibliography, in L. Berkhof: *Systematic Theology* (2nd rev. ed., Grand Rapids, 1941) pp. 252-254.

       4. The disciples were to baptize in the name of the Three Persons of the Godhead. Matt. 28:19

    B. In the Fourth Gospel

       For the teaching of this Gospel on the Holy Spirit, see a chapter in J. Ritchie Smith: *The Teaching of the Gospel of John* (New York, 1903), pp. 157-182; J. G. Simpson, "The Holy Spirit in the Fourth Gospel," *The Expositor*, 9th series, IV (1925), pp. 292-299; C. K. Barrett, "The Holy Spirit in the Fourth Gospel," *Journal of Theological Studies* (n.s., 1950), pp. 1-15.

1. The necessity for an experience of regeneration by the Holy Spirit, 3:5-8 (cf. VI-A)
2. "He giveth not the Spirit by measure," 3:34
3. "It is the Spirit that quickeneth," 6:63
4. The Apostle interprets Christ's words in 7:37, 38 as follows: "This spake He of the Spirit, which they that believed on Him were to receive: for the Spirit was not yet given: because Jesus was not yet glorified."

We come now to the central teachings of Christ on this subject, uttered on Thursday of Holy Week, and recorded only in the Fourth Gospel. Here, says Bishop Moule, "the Lord Jesus Himself teaches with His own lips the secret of spiritual life. Here speaks the Christ of God, in an hour of supreme tenderness" (*Veni Creator,* pp. 6, 7).

5. The Spirit can not be received by the world, 14:17; cf. I Cor. 2:14
6. The Spirit is sent (1) by the Father, in Christ's name, 14:26; 15:26; and (2) by Christ, 16:7. (See II-B)
7. The Holy Spirit is a gift of God, 14:6 (cf. II-B-2)
8. The Holy Spirit is to abide *with* believers, 14:16, 17; and to dwell in them, 14:7.
9. The Holy Spirit's work in believers in relation to Christ
   a. to bring to remembrance the things of Christ, 14:26 (the guarantee of the inspiration of the Gospel writers). "Never certainly did any acts or words so evidently await this subsequent illumination as those which were seen and heard by the followers of Jesus during the brief period in which He was with them."—

T. D. Bernard *Central Teaching of Jesus Christ,* London, 1892, p. 180. See John 2:22; 12:16

b. to testify of Christ, 15:26; 16:14, 15
c. to receive of the things of Christ and shew them unto us, 16:14, 15
d. to glorify Christ, 16:14

10. The teaching ministry of the Holy Spirit, 14:26; 16:13 (cf. VI-C-13)

On this Schaff has well said: "It is not omniscience or any kind of speculative or scientific truth which is promised, but the full knowledge of living practical truth as it is in Christ, and as relates to our soul's salvation. The Bible is not a universal encyclopedia of knowledge, but an infallible guide of religious faith and moral practice . . .

"Yet, in a certain sense, the Spirit of God alone can lead us *into all truth,* even in temporal and human things, since the love of truth is inseparable from the love of God, and the perfect knowledge of truth from the knowledge of God, which comes from the Spirit of God, the true illuminator of the human intellect darkened and distorted by sin and its bosom companion, error."

11. "He shall declare things that are to come," 16:13 *Anaggelei* is a word "proper to the announcement of things otherwise unknown."

See Acts 20:20; I Pet. 1:12; I John 1:5

12. The work of the Holy Spirit in the conviction of the world, 16:8-11. "The word translated *convict, elenko,* involves the conception of authoritative examination of unquestionable proof, of

decisive judgment"—B. F. Westcott. For a masterly discussion of this passage, see the volume by Arch-deacon J. D. Hare: *The Mission of the Comforter* (2nd ed., London, 1850). Sir W. Robertson Nicoll, in a sermon, makes a statement on this passage that is worth inserting here: "We cannot prove from statistics, however, apparently favourable, that Jesus is Lord, that the prince of this world has been judged. We cannot live in East London and say as the result of observation and reasoning that Jesus is Lord. But whenever the Holy Spirit unites us to Christ, then we are of His mind, and know that, however distant the end may be, the sentence has gone forth already against all the powers of evil." *Sunday Evening,* p. 204

See also a notable sermon in H. P. Liddon: *Sermons on Some Words of Christ,* pp. 342 ff.

C. In the Book of Acts

Acts 1:5 and 8 set forth two very significant statements of Christ about the baptism of the Holy Spirit, and empowerment by Him. See also Acts 11:16.

V. The Holy Spirit in the Church

(All references in sections 1-6 are to the Book of Acts.)

1. The descent of the Holy Spirit on the day of Pentecost, 2:1-39

   a. they were all filled with the Holy Spirit, 2:4

   b. the Spirit gave them utterance, 2:4

   c. this was a partial fulfillment of Joel's prophecy (2:28-32) regarding the bestowal of the Spirit, 2:17, 18

   d. those who believed were promised "the gift of the Holy Spirit," 2:38

2. Groups and individuals upon whom the Spirit came
   a. the Samaritans, 8:15-19
   b. the household of Cornelius, 10:44, 45, 47; 11:15-17; 15:8
   c. the Christians at Ephesus, 19:6
3. Those who are said to be filled with the Holy Spirit
   a. all believers, on the day of Pentecost, 2:4
   b. the disciples, after the first persecution, 4:31
   c. Peter, 4:8
   d. the seven appointed men, 6:3
   e. Stephen, 6:5; 7:5, 55
   f. Paul, 9:17, 13:9
   g. Barnabas, 11:24
4. The Holy Spirits supervision in the Church
   a. The Church was walking in the comfort of the Holy Spirit, 9:31
   b. by Him the members of the first extended missionary effort were chosen, 13:2, 4
   c. at the Council of Jerusalem, 15:28
   d. by Him Paul was forbidden to evangelize certain areas, 16:6, 7
   e. by Him was designated those to be appointed officers in the Church, 20:28
   f. Paul's coming sufferings were revealed to the Church, 21:4, 11; and to Paul, 20:23
   g. in the phrase, "Paul purposed in the spirit," to go to Jerusalem (19:21) it is disputed whether the reference is to the Holy Spirit or to Paul's spirit.
   h. individuals to whom the Spirit gave special messages

(1) Philip, 8:29; 20:39

(2) Peter, 10:19; 11:12

(3) disciples, 13:52; 21:4

(4) Agabus, 11:28; 21:11

5. The witnessing of the Holy Spirit, 5:32

6. Sins against the Holy Spirit

a. lying to, 5:3

b. tempting, 5:9

c. resisting, 7:51 (For three other sins against the Holy Spirit, see VI-G)

7. The Gospel was preached by the Holy Spirit, I Pet. 1:12; and particularly, by St. Paul, I Thess. 1:5; I Cor. 2:4

8. The preaching of the Gospel was confirmed "by gifts of the Holy Spirit," Heb. 2:4

9. The Holy Spirit testified to Paul's sorrow for Israel, Rom. 9:1

10. On two occasions St. John said he was "in the Spirit," Rev. 1:10; 4:2

11. On the work of the Holy Spirit in inspiring the writings of the New Testament, see III-B

For studies of the Spirit of God in the Book of Acts, see Arthur T. Pierson: *The Acts of the Holy Spirit,* 1910, and T. Walker: *The Acts of the Apostles,* London, 1919.

VI. The Holy Spirit in Relation to the Believer

We have already considered the relation of the Holy Spirit to believers, as revealed in the teachings of our Lord: here we shall confine ourselves to the Epistles and the Book of Revelation.

"Every grant and privilege enjoyed by the disciple of Christ is connected with the Spirit's work,"— Wm. Milligan.

A. Pertaining to various aspects of our regeneration
The basic passage here is, of course, John 3:5-8 (See IV-B-1)
By the Holy Spirit we are
1. born again, II Cor. 3:6; Gal. 4:29
2. made sons of God, Gal. 4:6 (See VI-C-1)
3. adopted into the family of God, Rom. 8:15
4. sealed until the day of redemption, Eph. 1:13
5. given His earnest, II Cor. 1:22; 5:5; Eph. 1:14
"the guarantee of the total transformation which will be completed at the day of resurrection of believers."—*Companion to the Bible,* p. 94.
6. renewed by, Titus 3:5
7. received by the hearing of faith, Gal. 3:2, 3
B. The truth of the Spirit's indwelling
1. The Spirit is *given* to us, I Thess. 4:8; Rom. 5:5
2. We are indwelt by Him, Rom. 8:9, 11; I Cor. 3:16; 6:19. "The same Spirit which was in Christ, which in His deity was one with Him, was in the coming time to be in them . . . dwelling and working within, in association with their own spirit."—T. D. Bernard, *ut supra,* p. 166. (Cf. VI-C-3)
3. "The *communion* of the Holy Spirit," II Cor. 13:14; Phil. 2:1
4. We are made *partakers* of the Spirit, Heb. 6:4
5. We are given "the *supply* of the Spirit of Jesus Christ," Phil. 1:19
6. By one Spirit we have all been *baptized* into one body, I Cor. 12:13
C. The continuous work of the Holy Spirit in and for us
1. He bears witness to the fact that we are the sons

of God, Rom. 8:16; I John 5:6, 7; cf. Gal. 4:6

2. By Him we have access to the Father, Eph. 2:18

3. He assures us that we are indwelt by Christ, I John 3:24; 4:13; Eph. 2:22 (Cf. VI-B-2)

4. He makes intercession for us, Rom. 8:26, 27; cf. Eph. 6:18

5. By Him we are made free from the law of sin and death, Rom. 8:2

6. There is a conflict between our flesh and the indwelling spirit, Gal. 5:17

7. By Him we are sanctified, Rom. 15:16; II Thess. 2:13; I Pet. 1:2

8. He helps our infirmities, Rom. 8:26

9. We are led by the Spirit, Rom. 8:14; Gal. 5:18

10. We are kept by Him, II Tim. 1:14

11. Through Him we are "strengthened with power," Eph. 3:16

12. By Him our mortal bodies are quickened, Rom. 8:11

13. By Him we are taught, I Cor. 2:10-13; (Cf. IV-B-10)

14. By Him we are changed from glory to glory, II Cor. 3:18

15. By Him the love of God is shed abroad in our hearts, Rom. 5:5; 15:30; Col. 1:8

16. He imparts joy, I Thess. 1:16

17. Our lives will display the ninefold fruit of the Spirit, Gal. 5:22, 23

18. Our lives are to be as epistles written by the Spirit of the living God, II Cor. 3:3

19. By the Spirit we witness to the truth concerning the Person of Christ, I Cor. 12:3; I John 4:23

20. "We have the first-fruits of the Spirit," Rom. 8:23

21. When St. Paul says (Rom. 8:17) that "the kingdom of God is . . . righteousness and peace and joy in the Holy Spirit."

D. In his relation to the Holy Spirit the believer is exhorted to

1. walk according to the Spirit, Rom. 8:1, 4, 5; Gal. 5:16, 25

2. live in the power of the Spirit, Rom. 15:13 (as did Paul, v. 19) Gal. 5:25

3. have the mind of the Spirit, Rom. 8:6; cf. v. 27

4. obey the truth through the Spirit, I Pet. 1:22

5. pray in the Spirit, Eph. 6:18; Jude 20; cf. Rom. 8:26, 27

6. keep the unity of the Spirit, Eph. 4:3

7. take the sword of the Spirit, Eph. 6:19

8. "commend ourselves" in the Spirit, II Cor. 6:6

9. "put to death the deeds of the body" by the Spirit, Rom. 8:13

10. "wait for the hope of righteousness" through the Spirit, Gal. 5:5

11. sow unto the Spirit, and so we "shall of the Spirit reap eternal life," Gal. 6:8

12. be filled with the Spirit, Eph. 5:18

E. The resultant spiritual man

Here must be introduced all the many and important passages which speak of the *spiritual* man (the word is *pneumatikos*) and the various aspects of his life. "*Spiritual* is in the New Testament always used of what regards the person and work of the Holy Spirit, also the work of the Spirit in the believers, with the single exception of Eph. 6-12."—F. W. Grosheide

An excellent book, sanely discussing these themes, is Lewis Sperry Chafer's *He That Is Spiritual*.

1. In general—"he that is spiritual," I Cor: 2:14, 15; 3:1; 14:37; Gal. 6:1
2. Such a man may possess
   a. "every spiritual blessing," Eph. 1:3
   b. "spiritual wisdom and understanding," Col. 1:9
3. The teaching of such a person will be marked by "combining spiritual things with spiritual words," I Cor. 2:13
4. Those who sow "spiritual things" should be permitted to "reap carnal things," I Cor. 9:11; Rom. 15:27
5. Such persons will sing "spiritual songs," Eph. 5:19; Col. 3:16
6. Only twice in the New Testament do we read of "spiritual gifts," the word being *pneumatika,* the word for *gift* not occurring in the Greek text, Rom. 1:11; I Cor. 12:1
7. Believers "are built up a spiritual house" to offer up "spiritual sacrifices," I Pet. 2:5
8. Our resurrection bodies will be "spiritual bodies," I Cor. 15:44, 46

F. Spiritual gifts

The entire twelfth chapter of First Corinthians is devoted to the subject of spiritual gifts, of which nine are specified, "but all these worketh the one and same Spirit, dividing to each one severally as He will."

There is an excellent discussion of this entire passage in F. W. Grosheide: *Commentary on the First Epistle to the Corinthians* (Grand Rapids, 1953) pp. 278-301.

G. Sins against the Holy Spirit
1. grieving Him, Eph. 4:30
2. quenching Him, I Thess. 5:19
3. doing despite to Him, Heb. 10:29
   (for three other sins against the Spirit, in historical occurrences, see V-6.)

VII. Some Unclassified References to the Holy Spirit and to Spiritual Things
1. The wicked request of Simon the sorcerer, Acts 8:19
2. The natural man cannot receive the things of the Spirit, I Cor. 2:14; Jude 19:cf. John 14:17
3. The children of Israel, when passing through the Red Sea, "did all eat the same spiritual food; and did all drink the same spiritual drink, for they drank of a spiritual rock," I Cor. 19:3, 4
4. In the phrase, "the ministration of the Spirit," II. Cor. 3:8
5. Jerusalem is spiritually called Sodom, and "Egypt," Rev. 11:8; i.e., "if one follows the *spiritual* understanding of the Scripture, Jerusalem lies concealed beneath the name Sodom."—Arndt and Gingrich (*A Greek-English Lexicon of the New Testament,* 1957, p. 685)
6. I have not attempted to relate John 4:23, 24 to the doctrine of the Holy Spirit.

14

A CHRONOLOGICAL ARRANGEMENT
OF BIBLICAL PASSAGES RELATING
TO THE BIRTH OF CHRIST
WITH SOME REFERENCES
TO SERMONIC LITERATURE

Those interested in the principal literature on the birth of Christ published up to the beginning of this century will find a list of approximately 170 titles in that remarkable bibliographical work, *Jesus Christ Our Lord,* by Samuel G. Ayres, pp. 32-43.

There is not one volume in the English language today that adequately treats of all the major subjects relating to the birth of Christ; thus, in this we have a great open door of opportunity for some serious student of the Scriptures.

I. The Genealogies
   Matthew 1:1-17; Luke 3:23-28

II. Old Testament Prophecies Pointing to the Birth of Christ
   A. Referred to in the Nativity Narratives
      Matthew 1:23—Isaiah 7:14
      Matthew 2:5-6—Micah 5:2
      Matthew 2:15—Hosea 11-1
      Matthew 2:18—Jeremiah 31:15
      Luke 1:17—Malachi 4:5-6
      Luke 1:32, 33—II Samuel 7:12-16
      Luke 1:46-56—I Samuel 2:1-10
      Luke 1:73, 74—Genesis 22:15
      Luke 1:77, 78—Genesis 22:15
      Luke 1:79—Malachi 3:1

Luke 2:32—Isaiah 42:6; 49:6
  B. Not Referred to in the Nativity Narratives
     Genesis 3:15

III. Events Preceding His Birth
  1. Annunciation to Zacharias, Luke 1:5-25
  2. Annunciation to Mary, Luke 1:26-38
  3. Annunciation to Joseph, Matthew 1:18-25
  4. Visit of Mary to Elisabeth, Luke 1:39-56
  5. Magnificat of Mary, Luke 1:46-55
  6. Birth of John the Baptist, Luke 1:57-66, 80
  7. Benedictus of Zacharias, Luke 1:67-79

IV. The Birth and Early Years of Jesus
  1. The birth itself, Luke 2:1-7
  2. Visit of the shepherds, Luke 2:8-20
     (*Gloria in Excelsis*)
  3. Circumcision, Luke 2:21
  4. Presentation in the temple, Luke 2:22-39
  5. Visit of the Wise Men, Matthew 2:1-12
  6. Flight into Egypt and the return to Nazareth, Matthew 2:13-23; Luke 2:39
  7. The growth of the Child, Luke 2:40

V. Subsequent References
  A. In the Gospels
     1. The argument with the Jews about His origin, John 7:40-43
     2. A possible reference to an evil report about His birth, John 8:41
  B. In the Epistles of St. Paul
     1. "Born of the seed of David," Romans 1:3; II Timothy 2:8
     2. "Made of a woman, made under the law," Galatians 4:4

    3. The great *Kenosis* passage, Philippians 2:7, 8

    4. "God was manifested in the flesh," I Timothy 3:16

C. In the Epistle to the Hebrews

    1. The two quotations of Psalm 2:7, "This day have I begotten thee," Hebrews 1:5; 5:5—by some interpreted as not referring to His actual birth, as Acts 13:33

    2. Christ's words upon His coming into the world, Hebrews 10:5-7, quoting Psalm 40:6-8

D. In the Book of Revelation

    1. the root and offspring of David, 5:5; 22:16

    2. The symbolic picture of the woman who gave birth to Christ, 12:1-5

VI. Special Subjects for Investigation

    1. The Five Dreams of Joseph—all recorded in Matthew 1:20, 21; 2:12; 2:13; 2:19, 20; 2:22

    2. The Six Appearances of Angels

    To Zacharias, Luke 1:11-23

    To Mary, Luke 1:26-38

    To Joseph, Matthew 1:20, 21; 2:13-15; 2:19; 2:23

    3. The Joy of the Nativity (all but one in Luke)

    "Thou shalt have joy and gladness," Luke 1:14

    "Many shall rejoice at his birth," Luke 1:14

    "The babe leaped in my womb for joy," Luke 1:44

    "They rejoiced with her," Luke 1:58

    "They rejoiced with exceeding great joy," Matthew 2:10

    "My spirit hath rejoiced in God my Saviour," Luke 1:47

    "I bring you good tidings of great joy," Luke 2:10

BIBLICAL SUBJECTS ON THE BIRTH
OF CHRIST ALPHABETICALLY LISTED

Advent	Fullness of Time	Names of Christ
Angels	Gabriel	Nativity
Anna	Genealogies	Nazareth
Annunciation	*Gloria in Excelsis*	*Nunc Dimittis*
Archelaus	Gold	Old Testament
Babe	Hail	Quotations
Benedictus	Herod the Great	in New
Bethlehem	Holy Spirit	Testament
Betrothal	Immanuel	Parents
Birth of Christ	Incarnation	Presentation
Blessed	Infancy	Purification
Boyhood	Innocence	Quirinius
Caesar Augustus	Jerusalem	Salutation
Census	Jesus	Salvation
Childhood	Jesus Christ	Shepherd
Circumcision	John the Baptist	Simeon
David, Seed of	Joseph	Slaughter of the
David, Son of	King	Innocents
David, Throne of	Luke, Gospel of	Sons of Nativity
Dayspring	Magi	Star
Dreams	Magnificat	Swaddling
Egypt	Manger	Clothes
Elisabeth	Mary	Tax
Enrollment	Matthew, Gospel of	Temple
Firstborn	Messianic	Virgin Birth
Flight	Prophecy	Zacharias
Frankincense	Myrrh	

SERMONIC LITERATURE ON THE BIRTH OF OUR LORD

The sermonic material on Biblical passages relating to our
Lord's incarnation and birth is, as would be expected, quite

vast. I am here attempting to suggest only some of the more significant sermons on the nativity narratives of the Gospels of Matthew and Luke. Among the more important works devoted almost exclusively to advent sermons are the following:

Lancelot Andrewes: *Sermons on the Nativity Preached upon Christmas Day,* 2nd. ed., 1631. This series of sermons, preached upon Christmas Day, will be found in Vol. I, pp. 1-302. I think one may safely say that this is the most notable volume of Christmas sermons that has appeared in our language. The seventeen sermons were published separately, some years ago, in the Ancient and Modern Library of Theological Literature.

John Donne (1573-1631): *Works,* Vol. I. Longon, 1839. The advent sermons are contained on pages 1-213.

Richard Clerke: *Sermons of the Nativity Preached on Christmas Day,* London, 1637.

John Hacket: *A Century of Sermons.* London, 1675. Fifteen sermons on the incarnation, pp. 1-146.

William Mandell: *The Advent of Christ Considered in a Course of Six Sermons Preached before the University of Cambridge.* Cambridge, 1817.

John Keble: *Sermons for the Christian Year: Sermons for Christmas and Epiphany.* 1876.

An abundant amount of sermonic material has been brought together in two volumes of *The Speaker's Bible; The Gospel According to St. Matthew,* Vol. I (Aberdeen, 1938), pp. 10-38, with bibliographies, pp. 225-228; and *The Gospel According to St. Luke,* Vol. I, pp. 19-165, with bibliographies, pp. 449-460. Some years ago the F. W. Barton Company of Cleveland published twelve beautiful volumes entitled *The Church Year Pulpit Library,* the first two of which contain a considerable number of choice sermons on our subject: Vol. I, *Advent Sundays,* pp. 311; Vol. II, *Advent Courses, Christmastide,* pp. 266. All of the sermons in Hastings' *Great Texts of the Bible* relating to the Birth of Christ have quite elaborate bibliographies.

In the list that follows I have in some instances used only the author's name; the volumes referred to are as follows: James Hastings: *Great Texts of the Bible,* St. Luke (1913); Alexander Maclaren: *Expositions of Holy Scripture, St. Luke* I-XII; G. Campbell Morgan: *Westminster Pulpit;* Charles Simeon: *Horae Homileticae,* Vol. XII; Alexander Whyte: *The Walk, Conversation and Character of Jesus Christ Our Lord.*

SERMONS ON TEXTS FROM THE GOSPEL OF MATTHEW

1:1-16—Alexander Maclaren: *Expositions of Holy Scripture, St. Matthew* I-VIII. pp. 1-6.

1:1—A. H. Strong: *Miscellanies,* Vol. II, pp. 277-297.

1:18—William Alexander: *Verbum Crucis,* pp. 3-18.

1:21—Morgan, Vol. II, pp. 49-56.

W. M. Clow: *The Evangel of the Straight Gate,* pp. 25-35.

Maclaren, as above, pp. 12-18.

James Hastings: *Great Texts of the Bible, St. Matthew,* pp. 2-15.

1:22, 23—H. P. Liddon: *Christmastide Sermons,* pp. 89-106.

1:23—J. D. Jones: *The Hope of the Gospel,* pp. 153-165.

F. B. Meyer: *In the Beginning God,* pp. 77-88.

2:1, 2—Alexander Whyte in *The Contemporary Pulpit,* Vol. I, pp. 339-351; H. P. Liddon, as above, 348-367.

2:1-3—Whyte, as above, Vol. VI, pp. 28-41.

Hastings, as above, pp. 18-31.

2:1-12—Maclaren, as above, pp. 19-28.

2:2—S. Baring-Gould: *The Birth of Jesus,* 76-88.

2:10—T. H. Darlow: *The Upward Calling,* pp. 266 ff.
Simeon, pp. 7-11.

2:11—J. A. Hutton: *Discerning the Times,* pp. 162-168.
G. H. Morrison: *The Unlighted Lustre,* pp. 252 ff.

2:13-22—Maclaren, as above, pp. 29-37.

2:16-18—Alfred Lee: *Eventful Nights in Bible History,* pp. 225-236.
Samuel Zwemer: *The Glory of the Manger,* pp. 145-154.
Simeon, pp. 11-16.

2:16—S. Baring-Gould, as above, 89-98.

SERMONS ON TEXTS FROM THE GOSPEL OF LUKE

1:33—Morgan, Vol. IX, pp. 409-416.

1:31, 34, 37, 38—Alexander Whyte: *The Spiritual Life,* Vol. I, pp. 22 ff.

1:35—Andrew Murray: *Holy in Christ,* pp. 125-131.
Whyte, pp. 19-28 (especially fine).

1:35, 38—Simeon, pp. 215-220.

1:78, 79—Maclaren, pp. 30-40.
Simeon, pp. 228-231.
H. P. Liddon: *Advent in St. Paul's,* pp. 127-181 (four sermons).

2:6, 7—S. Baring-Gould, as above, 51-62.

2:7—Hastings, pp. 2-21.
J. S. Holden: *The Life of Fuller Purpose,* pp. 11-29.

2:8-20—Maclaren, pp. 40-47.

2:8—S. Baring-Gould, as above, 63-75.

2:10, 11—Hastings, pp. 24-39.
Hugh Macmillan: *The Garden and the City,* pp. 31 ff.
Simeon, pp. 231-235.
Morgan, Vol. VII, pp. 401-408.

2:12—H. P. Liddon: *University Sermons,* pp. 189-219 (first series).

2:13, 14—Hastings, pp. 42-61.

R. C. Trench: *Sermons Preached in Westminster Abbey,* pp. 68-77.

Morgan, Vol. VI, pp. 401-408.

2:15—J. S. Holden: *Redeeming Vision,* pp. 117-125.

Hugh Macmillan: *Gleanings in Holy Fields,* pp. 40-55.

Simeon, pp. 240-244.

2:21—Whyte, pp. 29-39.

Simeon, pp. 245-250.

2:22-24—Simeon, pp. 251-256.

2:25—Simeon, pp. 256-260.

2:29, 30—Maclaren, pp. 55-62.

2:34, 35—Hastings, pp. 64-79.

Robert M. Edgar: *The Philosophy of the Cross,* pp. 35-50.

A. Tholuck: *Light from the Cross,* pp. 9-25; 93-109.

H. P. Liddon: *Advent in St. Paul's,* pp. 245-256.

J. G. Mantle: *The Way of the Cross,* pp. 19 ff.

T. V. Tymms: *The Private Relationships of Christ,* pp. 12-35.

2:40—Hastings, pp. 82-101.

Morgan, Vol. X, pp. 129-136.

Whyte, pp. 40-49.

T. V. Tymms, as above, pp. 36-54.

The great work by T. D. Bernard, *Songs of the Holy Nativity,* contains much sermonic material on the four nativity songs in Luke's Gospel which I have not thought necessary to index separately here. A volume by Stopford Brooke, *The Early Life of Jesus,* has a great deal of relevant material, but I have never been able to secure a copy.

The passages assigned from the nativity narratives in the International Sunday School Lesson system, for the last twenty years, are as follows:

Matthew 1:18-25
December 24, 1939

December 21, 1953
December 19, 1954
Matthew 2:1-12
December 25, 1938
Matthew 2:13-23
October 1, 1939
Luke 1:46-58
January 5, 1936
December 23, 1951
December 25, 1955
Luke 2:1-20
December 23, 1945
December 19, 1948
December 24, 1950
December 27, 1957
December 21, 1958
Luke 2:8-20
December 19, 1937
December 22, 1940
December 20, 1942
December 22, 1946
Luke 2:25-40
January 12, 1936
January 11, 1942
The Virgin Mary
August 27, 1950

In the volumes of *Peloubet's Select Notes on the International Sunday School Lessons* for these years, extensive bibliographies will be found for the study of these passages.

For references to the literature of the many subjects connected with the birth of Christ, see Chapter XVII, "A Suggestive Bibliography on the Birth of Christ and Christmas."

THREE NEW BIBLE ATLASES AND SOME NOTES
REGARDING EARLIER ONES

With the publication of three remarkable Bible atlases within a ten-month period (1956-57) the English world now has more authentic, amply-illustrated works in this field than ever before in the history of Biblical interpretation.

Is it not true that the Bible is the only great world classic (of course, it is much more than a world classic) which requires an extensive series of maps for a comprehensive understanding of thousands of its references? The only books that could be considered with the Bible in this respect would be Homer's *Iliad* and *Odyssey,* and one could read both of these works without continual reference to an atlas.

The Trojan War took place in the Near East, on the shores of Asia Minor, yet no one seems to refer to that event even in these days when the Near East is constantly on the front pages of our newspapers. Indeed, while the *Cumulative Indexes* for 1933 to 1948 give a separate heading to "Bible Atlases," I could not even find a separate heading for atlases of the United States! Actually, of the scores of atlases listed in these volumes, I was not able to detect one devoted exclusively to our own country.

On the other hand, it can be safely said that during the last one hundred years more atlases of Bible lands have been published than of any other area in the world.

Exactly when men began to draw maps illustrating Bible history I do not know. The earliest of which we have any knowledge is the famous mosaic map of Madaba, dating back to the sixth century A.D., which was discovered on the floor of a church at Madaba, east of the northern end of the Dead Sea. Passing over *many* others, in 1650 Thomas Fuller (1608-1661) issued a famous folio work with some remarkable maps entitled *A Pisgah Sight of Palestine.*

Early in the next century appeared the work by Adrian Leland (just try to find some biographical data on this Biblical geographer!), and at the beginning of the next century appeared the great volumes by E. F. K. Rosenmuller, 1823-1831.

The extended visits to Palestine of the well-known American geographer, Edward Robinson, beginning in 1837, laid the foundations for the modern study of Biblical geography, presenting data for more accurate identification of hundreds of Biblical sites. His great work, *Biblical Researches in Palestine, Mt. Sinai and Arabia Petraea,* appeared in three large volumes in 1841. The next major step in this direction was the *Survey of Western Palestine,* made for the most part by British surveyors and explorers, from 1865 to 1877.

This aroused much interest in the vast subject of Biblical geography, and atlases quickly followed one another from the presses. In the *American Catalog* for 1881, I find fifteen different titles of Biblical geographies and atlases, priced from fifty cents to five dollars! Most of these are now entirely forgotten, and rarely ever seen. At the close of the century, Hurst, in his *Literature of Theology,* listed 36 different titles in this area of Biblical study.

By far the best Bible Atlas in English before the publication of the great work by George Adam Smith, in 1915, was a quarto volume that this generation seldom sees, or even hears of. I refer to Samuel Clark's *The Bible Atlas of Maps and Plans,* my copy being the 5th ed., London, 1886, published by the S. P. C. K. (The first edition appeared in 1868).

Its trustworthiness was guaranteed by the fact that it contained "A Complete Index to the Geographical Names in the English Bible" by George Grove, Hon. Secretary to the Palestine Exploration Fund. This Index, we are told, was "intended to contain an exhaustive statement of the occurrences of every geographical name in the English version of the Old and New Testaments, and the Apocrypha, with its original in Hebrew or Greek, and the modern name of its sites, whether known or conjectured." I would judge that the text itself in this volume extends to about 70,000 words. An excellent feature is the bibliographies appended to each of the major sections of the book. Before acquiring this volume, quite recently, the name of Samuel Clark was without much significance to me. To my surprise I discovered he was thought of sufficient importance to be given three columns in the *Dictionary of National Biography*. This is the Samuel Clark to whom Frederick Denison Maurice addressed a series of letters later to appear as the fame-destined volume, *The Kingdom of Christ* (1837). The historian J. R. Green pronounced the maps in Clark's work, *Maps of the British Empire* the best he knew.

The most popular of all American Bible atlases was that compiled by Jesse L. Hurlbut (first ed. 1884) with an introduction by Bishop Vincent, *Manual of Biblical Geography*, published by Rand McNally, a work of 158 pages which sold for the substantial price (at that time) of $3.75. Later editions carried the title *Bible Atlas; a Manual of Biblical Geography and History*. This was revised down to as late as 1910, and the Rand McNally firm has passed on to me the interesting information that to within two or three years ago, this volume was still selling 4,000 copies a year!

A few details of this work should be noted: the book measured 11½ x 9½ inches; there were 51 small pictures and one full-page picture, 21 full-page maps and 37 smaller maps; the index to the map of Palestine carried 984 place names, and the index to the map of the Old Testament world, 160 names.

This is the only modern atlas I know of that lists the major wars and battles of the kingdom age of Israel (pp. 89, 90), indicated on a map of Solomon's Empire by small flags. Here also is a good detailed map of the vicinity of Nineveh, an area often overlooked in similar works, and a number of elaborate maps of various aspects and historical periods of the city of Jerusalem. The text runs to about 65,000 words. Probably no handbook of Bible study was used by as many thousands of Sunday school teachers for a half-century as this Hurlbut atlas.

A few years later, in 1897, there appeared a very scholarly work in two small volumes (7 x 4½ inches), *The Holy Land in Geography and in History*, by Townsend MacCoun, well illustrated with physical maps and some photographs, with a carefully written text. This is the only American atlas to which George Adam Smith later gives any notice; he calls it "one of the most complete and compact aids to the student, small but admirably clear and vivid."

The next notable advance in Bible atlases—and it was indeed an advance—occured when Dr. George Adam Smith published his *Atlas of the Historical Geography of the Holy Land* (Hodder and Stoughton, 1915). Twenty years in preparation, the work appeared long after the first edition of his *Historical Geography of the Holy Land*. This epochal volume was originally published in 1894. By 1931 it had reached its 25th edition, and has sold over 40,000 copies. In the beautifully written life of the distinguished Old Testament scholar, by his wife (a work first appearing in 1943, and to which one never sees any reference in subsequent literature), we are told that when the author was reminded by a friend of how useful his *Historical Geography* had been, he replied, "God was good to me when I wrote that book."

Apart from introductory notes, which we shall refer to later, there is no text in this book, the text being found in the frequently-revised *Historical Geography*. The finest maps of Palestine available at that time were included.

The title should be carefully noted: this is not simply an atlas of the Bible, but is an atlas of the geography *and history* of the Holy Land from earliest times to the twentieth century. No other atlas in the English language has ever attempted to set forth accurate maps of Syria and Palestine at the time of the Crusades, of the expansion of Christianity, of the political divisions of Palestine at that time, and of Christian missions in Palestine.

While the maps covering Biblical periods have been greatly improved upon through the years—and in that respect this atlas is now out of date—the "Notes to Maps, with Explanatory Bibliography" (pp. xi-xxxii), are still invaluable for references to the principal literature of all the various periods subsequent to the publication of this work.

The chronological tables, covering four folio pages, are the most detailed to be found in any Bible atlas of the present time. Of the 52 maps included here, 9 are double-page and 28 are full-page in size.

A comparison of the indexes of this volume with those of the new atlases which we are about to consider will reveal the changes taking place in geographical nomenclature for that part of the world. For example, Smith lists 473 sites beginning with *Wady,* while the Westminster Atlas has only three, and the other two works, none. Smith lists 233 sites beginning with *Khurbet;* Westminster, 13; Gröllenberg, 1, and Kraeling, none. Smith indexes 111 sites beginning with

Tell; Westminster 33; Gröllenberg, 8; and Kraeling, non. Of course it must be recognized that the maps in this collection cover many centuries not included in the other works.

The review of this atlas of Smith's in the *Expository Times* for December, 1915, concludes, "We are glad to have this cartographical record of the history of the Holy Land just at this time, when there is every likelihood that the fortunes of Palestine, already so varied, are in process of further change. Who can tell what the additional map of the next atlas will be like?"

The reviewer could have had no idea of what the next map would be—one including the State of Israel—though it should be pointed out, with regret, that the three more modern atlases published within the last two years, carry no map of the State of Israel.

Professor Smith could not have dreamed of what vast discoveries would be made in the forty years following the publication of his work: the Lachish Tablets, the 20,000 tablets found at Nuzi, the primitive writings uncovered by Byblos, the flood of new light thrown upon Biblical history with the excavations at Megiddo (1925 ff.), and Jericho (1930 ff.), the whole mass of epochal documents generally called the Dead Sea Scrolls, and Mr. Wiseman's most welcome publication of the Babylonian tablets giving minute details of the period in Nebuchadnezzar's reign when the city of Jerusalem was captured and destroyed.

In 1945 the *Westminster Historical Atlas to the Bible* was published, under the editorship of G. Ernest Wright and Floyd V. Filson (Westminster Press, Philadelphia). It immediately became the most widely-used Bible atlas among students, and it will no doubt continue to be used in more classrooms and by more Bible students than any other similar work of our generation.

After ten years, a revised edition of the *Westminster Atlas* was issued under the same editorial supervision. The size of the original edition, 15½ x 11 inches, was reduced to 14 x 9½ inches, and thirty columns of text was added, as well as a number of new pictures.

It is interesting to compare these two editions. The preface material is the same, except for the date, and Professor Albright's excellent opening chapter, "The Rediscovery of the Biblical World," has not been altered. There are some differences: The earlier edition spoke of a Stone Age "beginning 200,000 to 500,000 years ago," whereas the new edition says it began at least 100,000 years ago—someone must have been guessing.

More significant, however, is the readjustment of dates for some of the kings of Israel. In the early edition, the reign of Rehoboam is placed at 929-910 B.C., and in the later edition at 922-915 B.C. Subsequent reigns are adjusted accordingly, with the reign of Joash terminating in both tables at 800 B.C. The original edition places Ezra's reign at 458 B.C. and adds the phrase "some scholars date it later"; the new edition reads, "Rival dates for Ezra, 458, 432, 428, and 398 B.C."

I would judge that the text of the *Westminster Atlas* contains about 56,000 words. It is very carefully written, and based upon the latest archaeological and historical research. A chapter on "The Geography of Palestine" is followed by sections on "The World of the Patriarchs," etc., down through the subject of "The Journeys of Paul," with three concluding chapters on "The Expansion of Christianity," "The History of Jerusalem" and "Excavations in Modern Palestine."

The work includes 110 illustrations and 30 maps, 12 of which are full-page in size. The detail maps of Palestine are scaled nine miles to an inch. The editors' claim is that "the indexes, including a new index of modern place names, contain the most complete tabulation of Biblical sites ever gathered into a single atlas."

Some aspects of this indispensable atlas are however regrettable. A conservative who takes the Book of Genesis at face value, and believes in a divine revelation to the patriarchs, cannot go along with the statement that El Shaddai was merely a "patriarchal family God," and certainly he cannot accept the assertion that the patriarchs *chose* Him as their deity: it was not God who was chosen by the patriarchs, but the patriarchs who were chosen by God.

The drawing of a reconstruction of Solomon's Temple (p. 48) will come as a surprise to many, for it is radically different from the reconstructions we have been accustomed to seeing. One is surprised to find no reference to the Tabernacle in this carefully documented historical survey of Israel; nor does the word appear in the index.

I note here, as in the other atlases, a strange silence on the resurrection of Christ. References to His death are frequent, but from these pages, and those of Gröllenberg, one would hardly know that Christ rose from the dead.

In spite of these and other disappointing features, this is one atlas that all serious Bible students should possess.

The most elaborate and beautifully illustrated Bible atlas of all in the English language, is *The Atlas of the Bible*, by L. H. Gröllenberg, translated from the earlier Dutch edition by J. M. H. Reid and H. H. Rowley, published in 1956 by Thomas Nelson and Sons ($15.00). One cannot speak too highly of this work. A large volume, $14\frac{1}{4}$ x $10\frac{1}{2}$ inches, it contains 408 illustrations and 36 maps.

Father Gröllenberg is a member of the Paulist Order, but his work exhibits no particular slant toward Catholic tradition; in fact, he goes so far as to refrain from publishing any pictures of the Church of the Holy Sepulchre, because, he says, the present structure is so unlike anything originally erected there.

Some will think that his chapters are not as proportionate as might be expected; e.g., he devotes eleven columns of text to the history of Palestine between the close of the Old Testament and the birth of Christ, but only five columns to the history of New Testament times.

Here and there a sentence can be misleading; e.g., "The Gospels are not verbatim reports of a series of events, nor are they intended to be a work of history in the modern sense of the word." In contrast to this, we recall, e.g., the words of the famous historian Professor Shotwell of Columbia, that the writings of Luke can be ranked with the best historical compositions of the first century.

The map of Paul's voyage to Rome is the only one I have ever seen in which the drifting of the ship to the north, then to the south and back to the north again, is indicated— others use a straight line to mark this route, and that is not the way the ship moved in that storm.

The index itself is almost a Bible dictionary, and justifies the opening statement: "The principal purpose of this index is to catalog and describe all the *geographical indications* provided by the Bible. It therefore contains the name of every town and village, every mountain and valley, and every region, river, country, and people which occurs in the Bible."

One item from the index will illustrate the dictionary nature of these entries:

"GEBA, 'height'; loc. of Benjamin, listed Jos. 18:24; Levitical city, Jos. 21:17, I Ch. 6:60 (Heb. 45); cf. I Ch. 8:6; ment. in the battle between Benjamin and Israel, Jg. 20:33; and in Saul's battles with the Philistines, I S. 13:3, 16, 14:5; ment. under David, 2 S. 5:25 (Heb. Geba: Gk. and parallel passage of I Ch. 14:16 have Gibeon, cf. Is. 28:21); after the Disruption, on the N boundary of Judah, I K. 15:22, 2 Ch. 16:6, whence the expressions 'from Geba to Beersheba,' 2 K. 23:8, 'from Geba to Rimmon,' Zec. 14:10, to indicate the whole extent of the territory of Judah; repopulated after the Exile, Ezr. 2:26, Neh. 7:30, 11:31, 12:29; mod. *Jeba,* 6 miles NNW of the Temple terrace in Jerusalem; Maps 2, 13, 14, 15, 17, 19, 22; Pls. 189, 190, 250."

Here are some excellent tributes to the Bible—

"The Bible is an eternal book, the common heritage of men through the ages. Moreover, because of its constant use by the Church, the Bible has been instrumental, together with the legacy of Greece and Rome, in building Western civilization. It has nurtured our thinkers and saints, it has inspired our poets and artists.

"For the believer, the Bible is the sacred Book, which embodies God's message to mankind, the progressive revelation of His nature and His works and the authoritative statement of the condition and destiny of saving grace which was manifested from the Creation down to the Coming of Christ, and which continues from the foundation of the Church until its consummation in the heavenly Jerusalem. The Bible contains the Alpha and the Omega, the Beginning and the End; it bears the Word of God, which endures forever."

On the final page, Grollenberg himself makes this statement:

"The Christian of today shares the views of the Early Church. He knows that he is living in the latter days, in the closing phase of world history. Whether this period be long or short, all that now matters to each man is to find God in Christ.

"Henceforward it is impossible to propose any other way of salvation in the name of God. In Jesus He has said all and given all. Even God cannot give more than Himself. For all Christians the Bible shares the definitive character of the historic revelation of God in Jesus Christ. Like that revelation, it can never be replaced or surpassed."

The outstanding map publishers of our country, Rand McNally and Company, have just issued (1956) the *Rand McNally Bible Atlas,* edited and written by Dr. Emil Kraeling. This attractively printed work, 10 x 6-7/8 inches, is priced at $8.95. In spite of the fact that Kraeling says, "This book exists for the maps," it is the text, and not the maps, which give the greatest value to the volume, in my opinion. The maps represent excellent cartography, but they cannot compare in minuteness and detail with those in the *Westminster Atlas.*

A tremendous amount of work has gone into the selection of its 265 pictures, and some features here are superior to anything of like nature in other atlases. While one will not agree with every line, the very carefully annotated outline of the table of nations found in Genesis 10 is abreast of the latest scholarship and cannot be ignored in any subsequent study of this important chapter.

The well-written studies of the location of Sodom and Gomorrah, new archaeological light on the life of Isaac, the location of the crossing of the Red Sea by Israel, geographical features of the life of Gideon, the archaeology of the period of the Judges, the life of Saul (covering nearly 20 pages), recent discoveries of Nazareth, and the full discussion of whether or not Paul went to Spain—all are most commendable. I intend to keep this volume on my desk for constant reference when writing lessons for *Peloubet's Notes* which deal with these historical epochs.

Among writers of modern atlases and Biblical geography works, Dr. Kraeling is the only one, to my knowledge, who has dared to attempt a chapter on "The Geography of the Revelation," though he has, unfortunately, omitted the city

COMPARATIVE TABLE

Bibliographical Date	G. A. Smith	Westminster 1945	Westminster 1956	Nelson	Rand McNally
Size	18 x 9½	15½ x 11	14 x 9¾	14¼ x 10½	10 x 6⅞
Pages—number	108	114	130	166	487
Text—approximate wordage	no text as such	56,000	63,000	75,000	237,000
Maps	52	33	30	36	26
Illustrations	none	76	110	408	265
Index—number of entries	4800	c. 2700	c. 3100	c. 3600	3160
Cost	(out of print)	(out of print)	$7.50	$15.00	$8.95

of Jerusalem, and does not support the idea of a final battle at Armageddon.

One regrets that in quoting Psalm 137:5, "If I forget thee, O Jerusalem . . ." he speaks of "this mental bondage to a land and a place." Of course he has no evidence for saying that when John went into the wilderness he joined a monastic group, and he is at odds with most of the contemporary world of Biblical scholarship when he says, "Luke does not always have full and accurate reports to rely on."

These regrettable statements can be multiplied. Strange to say, while Kraeling speaks of the appearances of Christ as "visions," he proceeds to discuss these appearances as though Christ literally appeared to these diciples—as He certainly did.

There are now available some excellent small editions of Bible maps, the finest being the brochure, "Westminster Historical Maps of Bible Lands" (9½ x 6¼ inches), which contains all the principal maps of the larger atlas in reduced size, together with an index.

In 1956 the Fleming H. Revell Company issued two

pamphlets of maps (each 8¾ x 5½ inches) edited by John Stirling of the British and Foreign Bible Society, "An Atlas of the Life of Christ," with 20 colored maps and a double-page chart of the events of passion week, and "An Atlas Illustrating the Acts of the Apostles and the Epistles," with 22 maps and a sketch of the city of Jerusalem locating the events occurring there in the days of the apostles. These sell for 75¢ each, and are well worth having.

With all of these modern aids now available to Bible students, I wonder if it is not high time that many Sunday school teachers try to do what the great Bishop J. H. Vincent (1832-1920) did during his early pastoral days—but let him tell us himself what he was able to accomplish back there in the 1860's and 70's.

"During ten years of my pastoral life, wherever the itinerant system of my church placed me, I held on every Saturday afternoon, in the lecture-room of my church, a class to which old and young, and the representatives of all denominations, were admitted. It was called "The Palestine Class," and was devoted to the study of Bible history and geography.

"An outline of the facts, prepared in catechetical form, was printed, and committed to memory by every pupil. Difficult old Hebrew names of lands, cities and mountains, were arranged in a rhythmic way, and chanted after the manner of the old-time "singing geography" classes. Answers were given in concert to help the memory, and personal examinations were afterward conducted to test it. The class constituted an "ideal company of tourists to the Far East."

"The course of lessons was divided into five sections, covering the whole of Bible history. As each member, passing a personal examination, gave proof that he had thoroughly mastered "Section One," he was constituted a *Pilgrim* to the

Holy Land, and given a certificate to that effect. Having studied "Section Two" and passed a satisfactory examination, he was made a *Resident* in Palestine, and his name was associated with one town or mountain. In that way every principal place on the map was associated with the name of some member, who was held responsible to the class for information concerning its history and present condition.

"An examination in "Section Three" made our pilgrim and resident a *Dweller in Jerusalem*. Having been examined in "Section Four" he was made an *Explorer* of our Bible lands, and was located on some mountain or city of Egypt, Arabia, Chaldea, Asia Minor, etc. A final examination made him a *Templar* . . .

"The plan is practicable for every pastor. The book which I now have the honor of introducing to the public furnishes to every minister a complete preparation for directing such classes—a preparation which twenty-five years ago would have been a great benediction to me."

Actually, with all the marvelous visual aids now at the disposal of pastors and teachers, one with the same enthusiam could do even more than Vincent did in this type of work. In the study of contemporary history the whole of the Near East is infinitely more significant today than it was in Bishop Vincent's day, and the materials available for the study of Biblical history are equally richer. We should take advantage of these opportunities to the utmost.

16

A WELCOME REPRINT OF HENGSTENBERG'S MONUMENTAL WORK ON MESSIANIC PROPHECY

The greatest theme that has ever occupied the minds of men is that which concerns the person and work of the Lord Jesus Christ. Therefore, a subject of pre-eminent significance is the body of prophecy found in the Old Testament, in which the Spirit of God from age to age foreannounced the work which Christ would do on earth at His First Advent and which He shall yet accomplish when this age is brought to a close.

Without doubt, the most important work ever written on the Messianic prophecies of the Old Testament is *The Christology of the Old Testament,* by E. W. Hengstenberg (1802-1869), which first began to appear (in German) in 1829. The second edition was published in a four-volume English translation in Edinburgh, 1854-1858.

Since the last printing appeared in 1875, the work has been out of print for well over a half-century, and has become comparatively scarce, as well as expensive. All earnest students of the Scriptures will be grateful to Kregel Publications, Grand Rapids, Michigan, for reprinting, as it originally appeared, this four-volume set, totaling something over 1600 pages, and embracing approximately 680,000 words.

Before considering the volumes themselves, it might be of profit to review briefly the career of this notable German Biblical exegete. Born in a village of Westphalia, a descendant of an old patrician family, Hengstenberg was so well trained by his father that at the age of seventeen he qualified to enroll in the University of Bonn. Here he laid a thorough foundation in oriental languages and philosophy, so that at twenty-one years of age he had already issued an edition of an Arabic work in German.

Hengstenberg never enjoyed robust health, and for this reason probably was prevented from taking on active duties as a pastor. His bodily frailities (he himself said later) ultimately proved to be a benediction, for he was compelled to devote all of his energies to Study and writing.

At the age of twenty-five he, with a number of other like-minded men, including Tholuck, founded a biweekly paper defending Lutheran orthodoxy, *Evangelische Kirchenzeitung*, of which he was editor-in-chief. Soon after the launching of the paper, Hengstenberg wrote a vigorous article rebuking the government of Germany for permitting two influential German professors, one of whom was the Hebraist, Gesenius, to hold up the Word of God and the doctrine of the Church to general contempt. A biographer says of him:

"No man of our century spoke so strongly and for so long a series of years against the abuses of the day, both in high places and in low. He saw that the entire literature of religion stands or falls with the early documents which are its elements and alphabet: that if these individual books were not written by the men to whom the later Scriptures ascribed them—if they do not record facts that are historical—if the New Testament inspiration is not really an approval and guarantee of an Old Testament inspiration—if the Scriptures of the old and new covenants contradict each other—if, in short, there is not a perfect unity in the grand and complete record, then Christianity is undermined and ready to fall, bringing down with it the hopes of mankind. All this he saw, with perhaps a deeper insight than most men; and if he even exaggerated the expression of the principle, it was a venial fault. It is hard to deny that he was right in staking so much on the genuineness and integrity of the Old Testament."

We do not have space here for discussing the ecclesiastical and theological conflicts in which Hengstenberg, with vast scholarship and a profound understanding of the Scriptures, was engaged nearly all of his life. In addition to his teaching and editorial work, he wrote some of the most important commentaries on Old Testament books produced on the continent of Europe during the nineteenth century—commentaries on Ecclesiastes, Daniel, and Zechariah, two volumes entitled *The Genuineness of the Pentateuch,* a notable work on Ezekiel, and (still worth reading) *The History of the Kingdom of God under the Old Testament.*

By far his outstanding work was *The Christology of the Old Testament,* to which he brought not only a profound understanding of the Hebrew language, but a deep reverence for the Word of God, and an unusual gift for expression. Nothing has been written to compare with this in vastness of learning, and the firmness with which the writer sets forth his own convictions on the many disputed points of Messianic interpretation.

The first one hundred pages of Volume I are devoted to the Messianic prophecies of the Pentateuch, including fifteen pages on Genesis 3:15. There follows an interesting discussion of the expression, "angel of the Lord," as found in the Pentateuch and the Book of Joshua.

Hengstenberg's treatment of the prophecies is in chronological order, and consequently he begins with Hosea. To this prophecy he gives 130 pages; to Joel and Amos, 100 pages; to Micah, 110 pages—35 to the prediction of Christ's birth in Bethlehem (Mic. 5:1, 2)! It is not my purpose here to criticize various interpretations, but of this first volume I would say that the author's treatment of the Messianic Psalms is regrettably brief, probably due to the fact that he ex-

haustively considered this subject in his three-volume work
on the Psalter.

I would like simply to list the principal Messianic prophecies examined in Volumes II and III.

Isaiah 2—4, 7; 8:23—9:6, 11, 13.

Isaiah 40—66 in general, 34 pages; and on the central
prophecy, 52:13—53:12, 100 pages. In this elaborate study, he
sets forth the history of the interpretation—first with the
Jews and then with the Christians—and gives the arguments
against and for the Messianic interpretation.

Jeremiah 3:14-17 (25 pages); 23:1-8; 31:31-40; 33:14-26.

The most elaborate discussion of any prophecy in Ezekiel
is of 47:1-12.

Perhaps the best exegesis of all the prophecies is his treatment of Daniel 9:24-27, to which four verses he devotes 152
pages, or 75,000 words! No one can even pretend that he
has read the literature on this difficult and significant passage
without spending days with these pages of Hengstenberg.

To the prophecies of Zechariah he devotes 130 pages, and
to those of Malachi, 65 pages, including 20 pages on "quotations from Malachi found in the New Testament."

Do you know the location of Hadrach? It occurs only once
in the Biblical text, Zechariah 9:1, and its exact location has
been a problem with scholars for generations. To the question of the geographical data on this one place, Hengstenberg
devotes 47 pages! Here and there in these rich volumes one
comes upon treatments of passages which are generally overlooked; e.g., in Volume II, the author gives nearly 12,000
words to a discussion of Matthew 2:23.

The six appendices at the conclusion of the fourth volume
will whet the appetites of many. They are entitled:

The Importance of the Messianic Prophecies

Messianic Expectations among the Heathen

The Divinity of the Messiah in the Old Testament (45 pages)

The Saving and Atoning Christ in the Old Testament

History of the Interpretation of the Messianic Prophecies

The Nature of Prophecy

In the last essay are some of the most profound paragraphs on the basic factors of Old Testament prophecy that I have ever seen. Hengstenberg brilliantly discusses the differences between the Biblical prophet and the pagan mantic or diviner, the relationship of the playing of musical instruments to prophetic utterances, and the reasons why some prophecies are divinely intended to be obscure.

Fundamentally, I would make two basic criticisms of Hengstenberg's interpretation of Messianic prophecy in general. First of all, he affirms that the promises referring to Israel are to be fulfilled in the history of the Church, and that in the Church "there resides a strong and irresistible force urging it towards continual extension to the ends of the earth." How he can say, in supporting this view (Vol. IV, p. 332), that "the destruction of Jerusalem was not the overthrow but the triumph of Israel," I do not know.

Closely connected with this hermeneutical principle is the other, that Israel is not to be restored to her land as a nation, that there is to be no rebuilding of the temple, etc. He himself says (p. 388):

"Those passages which speak of the return of Israel to Zion in the Messianic times must be regarded as figurative because Zion always means the seat of the kingdom of God."

I often wonder if Hengstenberg would have changed his views were he living today, when so many things are happening which contradict the ideas set forth here. These volumes were not specifically meant to discuss prophecies concerning Israel, though the author cannot avoid these, but to all prophecies relating to the *Messiah;* and in most of these he brings forth truths which neither Jew nor Christian will be able to escape.

Learned as this work is—vast, linguistically slanted, profound—it can still be used by serious students in feeding the minds and souls of men and women even of this very superficial generation. And how we need solid Biblical exposition these days when there is so much froth in our pulpits! My slightly dimmed recollection of what I am about to relate has been restored by a very gracious letter, in reply to my inquiry, from the person about whom the story revolves.

Years ago—forty years, if one must confess to it—while I was a student at the Moody Bible Institute, one of my fellow-students and friends was John W. Bradbury, whose home formerly had been in England. John was a student from sunrise until midnight, and a hard worker. While in school, he was the assistant pastor of the First Baptist Church of Chicago, with a special assignment to its branch church located in the stockyards area, called Raymond Chapel.

This young man, having heard from Dr. James M. Gray, as had others of us, that Hengstenberg's *Christology of the Old Testament* was an unusually fine work, took all the money he had on hand and purchased these four volumes at Blessings Bookstore. And (so he writes), "found it so fascinating that I burned much midnight electricity—alert to the watchman, of course, because it was against the school law to do this."

Now, my friend John was in that predicament which many modern ministers seem to have escaped—he had nothing else to preach from or to teach his people but the Word of God (not even a movie to show his congregation!). Beginning with but sixteen boys and girls in the Sunday school, the young pastor, by prayer and earnest effort, saw 175 conversions in his church during the first year. His people had to be taught; so, spending these hours with Hegstenberg, he prepared weekly papers on the truths he was discovering, and read them at the mid-week services!

"The people were modest and humble, and of all ages. They filled the prayer meeting room. Attendance and interest increased while I did this, falling off when I stopped. They told me I was showing them an eternal, glorious and gracious Saviour and Lord. They knew where I was getting it all, for I told them, though I did not quote much of Hengstenberg because his style is heavy and his thought profound. I reduced his majestic thoughts to my humble prose. . . . I meet today some of my former Chapel members, and although advanced in years, they adore the greatness of the Christ of whom they learned so much in their youth. That experience did wonders for me. Those humble people revealed to me the reality of the Holy Spirit in helping God's people to comprehend Christian truth, profound though it is."

My friend was greatly blessed of God in the days following, and became pastor of one of the most influential Baptist churches in New York City. Twenty years ago he was honored in being made the editor of *The Watchman-Examiner,* succeeding that stalwart defender of the faith, Curtis Lee Laws. And so, Dr. John W. Bradbury closes his letter with a word with which I would like to conclude this review:

"I have found that, profound as the truth of God is, as infinite in scope as we find it to be, it is in God's grace and providence that we shall be illumined by the Holy Spirit to *understand* it, intuitively at least, if not always able to reduce it to the nuances of logic."

17

A SUGGESTIVE BIBLIOGRAPHY ON THE BIRTH
OF CHRIST AND CHRISTMAS

In any given period of ten years, more books are published concerning the Lord Jesus Christ than about the ten other greatest characters of history together. In the life and ministry of Christ, there are three subjects each of which has produced an enormous literature—His birth, His death, and His resurrection.

As an indication of the wealth of material available on the birth of Christ, we might just turn the pages of the great two-volume work published in 1906, *A Dictionary of Christ and the Gospels*, edited by James Hastings, and list some of the subjects to which separate articles are assigned having to do exclusively with our Lord's birth (with page numbers for articles of extended length):

Vol. I: Advent, 32-34; Anna; Annunciation, 74-78; Benedictus; Bethlehem, 194-197; Birth of Christ, 202-208; Boyhood of Christ, 224-230; Census, 274-276; Childhood of Jesus, 298-301; Circumcision; Dayspring; Egypt; Firstborn; Flight; Frankincense; Fullness of Time, 630-631; Gabriel; Genealogies of Jesus Christ, 636-639; Herod, 717-721; Immanuel, 782-784; Incarnation, 796-813; Infancy, 822-824; Inn; Innocence; Joseph.

Vol. II: Magi, 97-101; Magnificat, 101-103; Manger; Mary the Virgin, 140-142; Myrrh; Nazarene, 234-236; Nazareth; Nunc Dimittis; Parents; Presentation; Quirinius, 462-464; Simeon; Son of David, 653-654; Star, 674-676; Tax; Virgin

Birth, 804-809. For a complete list of these articles see Chapter 14.

Articles on most of these subjects can be found in other Biblical encyclopedias, and it is not necessary to construct a list for each. Apart from this work by Hastings, the best articles, overshadowed with Roman tradition but nevertheless valuable, will be found in the *Catholic Encyclopedia*.

This list, however, does not exhaust the nativity material, for if we were to make a complete study of the New Testament account of our Lord's birth, we would of necessity include all quotations from the Old Testament in the nativity narratives, works on angels, all treatises on the Holy Spirit, volumes discussing the names and titles of Christ, and even books that consider the city of Jerusalem, especially the temple in Jerusalem.

To learn the actual extent of this literature pertaining to the birth of Christ, and to Christmas, one needs only to open the pages of the two volumes of the *Cumulative Book Index* for the eleven-year period 1938 to 1948, and note that there were published during this time (I have not eliminated possible duplicates) 615 titles under the word *Christmas* alone, divided as follows: Christmas Entertainments, 54; Christmas Pageants, 53; Christmas Plays, 257; Christmas Plays, Religious, 115; Christmas Poetry, 32; Christmas Sermons, 9; Christmas Songs, 10; Christmas Stories, 73. (In the bibliography that follows, I am omitting plays, stories, etc., which multiply by the hundreds and are for the most part ephemeral.)

With this information before us, let me make one further statement, which may surprise my readers, and that is, *there is not one volume in the English language that covers all the subjects of the birth of our Lord arising from the study of the Biblical text itself.* There are many volumes that attempt to survey the New Testament teaching on the death of Christ, and some very exhaustive volumes on the resurrection of Christ, but there is not one that surveys all the available Biblical material on the birth of our Lord. Here is an open field for some earnest student, with a gift for writing. Such a book is long overdue.

Before outlining the material, we should note that many words used of our Lord's birth are never used of any other *historical* person, e.g., *incarnation* and *virgin birth*. In fact, I do not recall any book written about any great *historical* character, other than our Lord, devoted exclusively to his *birth*.

OUTLINE OF SUBJECTS CONSIDERED

I. Biblical Material
   1. Preparation of the World for Christ
   2. Birth of Christ
      a. Books
      b. Commentaries
      c. Lives of Christ
   3. Virgin Birth of Christ
   4. Virgin Mary
   5. The Advent in the Christian Calendar
   6. Genealogies
   7. Bethlehem
   8. Nazareth
   9. Magi and the Star
   10. Census of Quirinius
   11. Songs of the Nativity
   12. Characters of the Nativity
   13. Paul's Witness of the Birth of Christ
   14. The Incarnation
   15. Birth of Christ in the Christian Creeds

II. Sermonic Literature

III. Secular Literature
1. Apocryphal Gospels of the Infancy
2. Poetry
3. Drama
4. Hymns
5. Carols
6. The Nativity in Art

IV. Christmas

THE PREPARATION OF THE WORLD FOR CHRIST

All volumes dealing with New Testament history will have some material on the religious, economic, historical and intellectual background of the Gospels, though this is not exactly equivalent to a discussion of the preparation of the world for Christ. Holding, for the most part, to the topic as stated above, I would suggest the following, a list by no means complete:

Gerhard Uhlhorn: *The Conflict of Christianity with Heathenism*, Eng. trans., rev. ed., New York, 1894. pp. 13-149.

David Breed: *Preparation of the World for Christ*, third ed., New York, 1893. p. 483.

Alfred Edersheim: *Life and Times of Jesus the Messiah*. Vol. I, pp. 3-112.

George P. Fisher: *The Beginnings of Christianity*, New York, 1877. pp. 1-257. (Still of value)

F. W. Farrar: *The Early Days of Christianity*, second ed., London, 1882. Vol. I.

Philip Schaff: *The History of the Christian Church*, third ed., New York, 1882. Vol. I, pp. 56-89.

Edward Stapfer: *Palestine in the Time of Christ*, Eng. trans.

Philip Vollmer: *The Modern Student's Life of Christ,* New York. pp. 1-53.

G. W. Wade: *New Testament History,* second ed., London, 1931. pp. 1-105.

H. K. Booth: *The World of Jesus: A Survey of the Background of the Gospels,* New York, 1933.

THE BIRTH OF CHRIST

As stated above, there is no volume in the English language adequately considering all the subjects that relate directly to the advent of our Lord; in fact, there are fewer books on the general subject of Christ's advent than there are on the specific theme of His virgin birth.

Isaac Williams: *The Gospel Narratives of Our Lord's Nativity Harmonized with Reflections,* London, 1952. pp. 526.

Louis Matthews Sweet: *The Birth and Infancy of Jesus Christ According to the Gospel Narratives,* Philadelphia, 1907. pp. xiii, 365. This is the only really scholarly treatment of subjects pertaining to the advent of our Lord, and while for the most part it deals with the virgin birth itself, there are good chapters on "Influence of the Old Testament Prophecies in the Formation of the Infancy Story," and excellent appendices on, "Christ's Birth and the Messianic Hope," and, "The Apostles' Creed."

A. Morris Stewart: *The Infancy and Youth of Jesus,* London 1905. pp. xi, 290. This is a volume by a liberal, but books attempting to include the major themes of the nativity are so rare that I have included it here.

Arthur C. Knowles: *A Devotional Study of the Incarnation of the Son of God,* New York, 1905. pp. vii, 154. The concluding chapter is entitled "The Drawing Power of the Manger."

G. H. Trench: *The Birth and Boyhood of Jesus Christ,* London, 1911. pp. xi, 248. A Roman Catholic volume, with good material.

James H. Snowden: *A Wonderful Night,* New York, 1919. pp. 95.

Alfred E. P. Raymund Dowling: *The Flora of the Sacred Nativity,* London, 1900. pp. viii, 226.

Edward M. Goulburn: *The Gospel of the Childhood,* New York, 1873. pp. 245.

COMMENTARIES

All of the larger commentaries on the Gospels of Matthew and Luke will have more or less important material on the nativity narratives. Here I would give only the authors of the principal works on these two Gospels, without titles and dates, for they are well-known to all Bible students and can be found quickly in any library.

Matthew: John A. Broadus, A. C. Gaebelein, J. M. Gibson (*Expositor's Bible*), John Peter Lange, R. C. H. Lenski, G. Campbell Morgan, Alfred Plummer, E. H. Plumptre (in Ellicott's *Bible Commentary*).

Luke: F. W. Farrar (*Cambridge Bible for Schools and Colleges*), F. Godet, R. C. H. Lenski, G. Campbell Morgan, A. B. Bruce (*Expositor's Bible*), Arthur Carr, and A. T. Robertson: *Luke the Historian in the Light of Modern Research* (1920). *Notes on the Gospels* by J. C. Ryle will also be found helpful.

THE NATIVITY IN MAJOR LIVES OF CHRIST

It is most amazing that no outstanding life of Christ has been published by an American Protestant scholar for the last seventy years, and with the single exception of the work of David Smith, no exhaustive life of Christ has been published in England by a Protestant scholar of our century.

The Roman Catholics have put us to shame here. Since the beginning of the century they have issued in French and in English five different lives of Christ, each of which extends to two or three volumes. I am omitting titles for the following because they are well known and it will save space:

Samuel J. Andrews, pp. 1-111
Alfred Edersheim, Vol. I, pp. 111-254
C. J. Ellicott, pp. 37-83
Andrew M. Fairbairn, pp. 30-45
Adam Fahling, pp. 92-133
F. W. Farrar, Vol. I, pp. 1-103
Cunningham Geikie, Vol. I, pp. 14-230
J. P. Lange, Vol. I, pp. 257-341; Vol. III, pp. 491-512; Vol. IV, pp. 198-206. (Probably the profoundest discussion of the relevant themes in any language.)
Augustus Neander, pp. 13-34
David Smith, pp. 1-13

See also a magnificent discussion of the birth of Christ in
G. Campbell Morgan: *The Crises of the Christ*, pp. 67-101.
Among Roman Catholic writers I would mention:
Constant Fouard: *Christ the Son of God*, fifth ed., New York, 1891. Vol. I, pp. 17-92.
Ferdinand Prat: *Jesus Christ, His Life, His Teaching and His Work*, trans. from the tenth French edition, Milwaukee, 1950. Vol. I. In this volume we have the most scholarly, exhaustive, thorough treatment of all the principal themes of the birth of Christ to be found in any volume on the person of Christ, extending from page 41 through 144, and 478 to 493, including rich appendices on the magi, Quirinius, and the genealogies. The work is, of course, colored with Roman Catholic pre-suppositions, but we have nothing in the Protestant world to compare with it for thoroughness in this half century.

L. C. Fillion: *The Life of Christ, a Historical, Critical, and Apologetic Exposition,* Eng. trans., Vol. I, St. Louis, 1946, pp. 227-424.

John Pope: *Observations on the Miraculous Conception and the Testimonies of Ignatius and Justin Martyr on That Subject in a Series of Letters to the Rev. Mr. Nisbet,* London, 1792.

A. Hoben: *The Virgin Birth,* Chicago, 1903. p. 87

B. W. Randolph: *The Virgin Birth of Our Lord,* London, 1903

R. J. Knowling: *Our Lord's Virgin Birth and the Criticism of Today,* third ed., London, 1907. pp. 100

Richard H. Grützmacher: *The Virgin Birth,* 1907. p. 80

James Orr: *The Virgin Birth of Christ,* New York, 1907. pp. xiv, 301. A very valuable appendix in this volume contains a number of papers on the subject from Biblical scholars, gathered by the late Dr. W. W. White, including articles by William Sanday, Sir William Ramsay, R. J. Knowling, H. Bavinck, Bishop Moule, etc.

T. J. Thorburn: *A Critical Examination of the Evidences for the Doctrine of the Virgin Birth,* London, 1908. pp. iv, 179

Vincent Taylor: *The Historical Evidence for the Virgin Birth,* London, 1920. pp. 136.

Elwood Worcester: *Studies in the Birth of the Lord,* New York, 1932. pp. xvi, 300

John B. Champion: *The Virgin's Son,* Chicago, 1924. p. 160

J. Gresham Machen: *The Virgin Birth of Christ,* New York, 1930; second ed., 1932. pp. x, 415. This is the most remarkable volume on the virgin birth available in any language. Dr. Machen began writing on this subject in 1912 for the *Princeton Theological Review,* so that the volume represents twenty years of uninterrupted consideration of all the problems connected with this doctrine. The book has never been answered by New Testament liberal scholars. It should be in the library of every serious student of the life of Christ.

Douglas A. Edwards: *The Virgin Birth in History and Faith,* London, 1943. pp. 240

William Evans: *Why I believe in the Virgin Birth,* Los Angeles, 1924. pp. 104

Franklin P. Ramsay: *The Virgin Birth,* New York, 1926. pp. 111

See also articles by Dr. Adeney, "The Virgin and the Divinity of Christ," in the series, *Essays for the Times,* No. XI, and by C. A. Beckwith in the New Schaff-Herzog *Religious Encyclopedia,* Vol. CII, pp. 201-214.

THE HOLY SPIRIT AND THE VIRGIN BIRTH

While there are incidental references to this subject in the various major works on the Holy Spirit, there are only two treatments of any length in this literature that I know of. One is by the great Puritan divine, John Owen: *Pneumatologia, or, A Discourse Concerning the Holy Spirit,* Part I, Book I, Chapter 3, which appears in the edition of the works of John Owen edited by William H. Goold, Vol. III, pp. 159-167; and the other, a scholarly work by J. Ritchie Smith: *The Holy Spirit in the Gospels,* New York, 1926, pp. 53-180.

THE VIRGIN MARY

That the Virgin Mary is given an important place in the Gospels, and that upon her God conferred a great honor in making her the mother of our Lord, Protestants all acknowledge. The Roman Church, however, has developed four dogmas concerning the Virgin Mary, of which at least three cannot in any way be supported by the Scriptures, nor by ancient tradition, and one of which is blasphemous.

These dogmas are, first, the dogma of the immaculate conception; second, the dogma of the perpetual virginity of the Virgin Mary (concerning which there is nothing that can be called in any way evil or wrong, and many orthodox Protestants believe in it, but it certainly cannot be supported by the Scriptures); third, the dogma of the assumption of the Virgin Mary, that is, that she was taken to heaven in her own body; and fourth, that of prayers to God through the Virgin Mary.

On the entire question of Mariolatry, which needs re-examination today, the following may be considered:

H. Harbaugh: *The True Glory of Woman as Portrayed in the Beautiful Life of the Virgin Mary,* Philadelphia, 1858.

Thomas Hartwell Horne: *Mariolatry; or Facts and Evidences Demonstrating the Worship of the Blessed Virgin Mary by the Church of Rome,* enlarged ed., Hartford, 1844.

J. Endel: *The Worship of the Blessed Virgin Mary in the Church of Rome Proved to be Contrary to Holy Scripture and to the Faith and Practice of the Church of Christ through the First Five Centuries,* London: The Society for the Promotion of Christian Knowledge, 1851. (Part Two includes the following two chapters: "Evidence of Holy Scripture," pp. 82-101; and "Assumption of the Virgin Mary," pp. 102-132.) As far as I know, this is the most exhaustive work on the entire subject of the Virgin Mary in English Protestant literature. (According to its printed catalog, the Library of Congress does not have one of these three volumes.)

In the five years, 1938-1942, 57 volumes appeared on the Virgin Mary, all written by Roman Catholics. Of Protestant works we have very few. The best that I know of is A. T. Robertson: *The Mother of Jesus*, New York, 1925; see also an older work by A. Moody Stuart: *The Three Marys*, London, 1862.

The doctrine of the immaculate conception was first declared by the Vatican under Pope Pius IX, December 8, 1854, in the encyclical *Ineffabilis Deus*. The entire document with full discussion may be found in Philip Schaff: *The Creeds of Christendom*, sixth ed., New York, 1931, pp. 108-129. There are very important articles on Mary in J. H. Blunt: *Dictionary of Doctrinal and Historical Theology*, new ed., 1903, under the following headings: Mary, pp. 449-454; Immaculate Conception, pp. 328-331; Perpetual Virginity, pp. 562-563; Theotokos, 753-755. For an extended collection of poems, pictures, etc., relating to the Virgin Mary, see Cynthia Pearl Maus: *The World's Great Madonnas, An Anthology of Pictures, Poetry, Music and Stories Centering in the Life of the Madonna and Her Son*, New York: Harper and Bros., 1947, pp. xiii, 789. For additional material, see the Chapter "A Protestant Bibliography of the Virgin Mary."

The Advent in the Christian Calendar

L. Duchesne: *Christian Worship, Its Origin and Evolution*, third ed., Eng. trans., London, 1910. pp. 228-291.

George N. Gibson: *The Story of the Christian Year*, New York, 1945. pp. 68-106.

John Dowden: *The Church Year and Kalendar*, Cambridge, 1910. pp. 76-79.

Vernon Staley: *The Seasons, Fasts and Festivals of the Christian Year*, London, 1910.

Charles Williams: *The New Christian Year,* New York, 1941. pp. 1-21.

John Wordsworth: *The Ministry of Grace,* London, 1910. pp. 304-402.

Dom Gregory Dix: *The Shape of the Liturgy,* London, 1945. pp. 333-360.

One may also consult with great profit the various articles on the calendar, and chronology, in Bible dictionaries, especially the one by Armstrong in the *International Standard Bible Encyclopedia,* Vol. I, pp. 644-650.

Of the older encyclopedias the best articles are those in William Smith and Samuel Cheetham: *Dictionary of Christian Antiquities,* Vol. I, Hartford, 1880; "Advent," pp. 30-32; "The Festival of Christmas," pp. 356-364; and "The Festival of Epiphany," pp. 617-621. The most exhaustive encyclopedic article, however, is a very learned one by Kirsopp Lake in James Hastings: *Dictionary of Religion and Ethics,* Vol. II, pp. 601-608.

GENEALOGIES

On the complicated subject of the genealogies of Matthew and Luke, the greatest work is an older one by Lord Arthur C. Hervey: *The Genealogies of Our Lord and Saviour Jesus Christ,* Cambridge, 1853. Lord Hervey also wrote the article on this subject in William Smith's *Dictionary of the Bible,* Vol. II, pp. 665-668. See also an article by L. M. Sweet in the *International Standard Bible Encyclopedia,* Vol. II, pp. 1196-1199; and two articles in *Bibliotheca Sacra,* by H. M. Bagoum in January, 1915, and by William H. Bares, in April, 1917.

Many pamphlets have been written on this subject, of which one of the best is by the late Dr. W. M. Christie, published by the B. J. S. Mount Carmel Bible School Press, Haifa, Palestine.

BETHLEHEM

J. R. MacDuff: *The City of Bethlehem,* New York, 1870. pp. 202.

F. W. Faber: *Bethlehem,* London, 1860. pp. xiii, 536.

Gustav Dalman: *Sacred Sites and Ways,* London, 1935. pp. 17-56.

Wilbur M. Smith: "Why Was Bethlehem the Birthplace of Our Lord?" *Revelation,* December, 1936.

Wilbur M. Smith: "The Miraculous Choice of Bethlehem," *Sunday School Times,* December 5, 1936.

S. D. Gordon: *A Quiet Talk about the Babe of Bethlehem and the Crowded Inn,* New York, 1915. pp. 58.

S. W. Drake: *The Glory of Bethlehem,* London, 1915. pp. 162.

William Allen Knight: *On the Way to Bethlehem,* New York, 1912. pp. xii, 222.

Gaston Leary: *The Christmas City,* New York, 1911, pp. 191.

David James Burrell: *In David's Town.*

J. M. P. Otts: *The Fifth Gospel,* pp. 35-68.

William Sanday: *Sacred Sites of the Gospels,* Oxford, 1903. pp. 24-30.

Paxton Hood: *The Villages of the Bible.* pp. 285-297.

NAZARETH

On Nazareth, in addition to the chapters in the volumes mentioned above by Dalman, Sanday, and Hood, one should consult the following:

G. D. Drew: *Nazareth, Its Life and Lessons,* third ed., London, 1876. pp. xiv, 147.

Frederick John Scringeour: *Nazareth of Today,* Edinburgh and London, 1913. Written by a native of Nazareth, this book contains 103 pages of text, with 75 photographs of present-day Nazareth. There is nothing here of particular significance on the birth of our Lord, but it is the best work on modern Nazareth that we have.

THE MAGI AND THE STAR

I thoroughly agree with the verdict of G. H. Box, that "various attempts have been made to identify the star of this narrative with some heavenly phenomenon, and to fix its occurrence by means of astronomical calculations, but the data are too indefinite to allow for any certain conclusion in this matter." The best-known effort to solve this problem was the work by the famous astronomer Kepler, *De Jesus Christi Vero Natalito,* published in 1605.

Two significant works on these subjects were written many years ago by an author of considerable influence in his day, Dr. Francis W. Upham: *The Wise Men,* New York, 1878, pp. v, 253, with a later edition, 1901, a book that won wide acclaim from some of our best Biblical scholars, and, his later volume, *Star of Our Lord,* New York, 1873, p. 370, a very scholarly work that has never been surpassed.

I have in my possession a very rare work (only fifty copies were printed), *What Was the Star of Bethlehem?* by Elias Colbert, for several years professor of Astronomy in the Old University of Chicago, and from 1890 to 1900, president of the Chicago Astronomical Society. In this work of thirty-six pages he has much to say about the constellation Virgo in the Zodiac and the fixed star in the constellation called Spica, or the Virgin Spike.

See also the classic work by R. C. Trench: *The Star of the Wise Men,* and some very important pages by the distinguished historian William M. Ramsay in *The Bearing of Recent Discovery on the Trustworthiness of the New Testament,* second ed., London, 1915, pp. 140-149.

THE CENSUS OF QUIRINIUS

This has been a much disputed subject in the New Testament criticism. For the most recent discussion, see the great work by Sir William Ramsay, *Was Christ Born in Bethlehem?* and his later volume, *The Bearing of Recent Discovery on the Trustworthiness of the New Testament,* pp. 238-300; also relevant material in A. T. Robertson: *Luke the Historian in the Light of Modern Research* (1934) pp. 118-129.

THE SONGS OF THE NATIVITY

All of the four songs sung at the advent of our Lord are found exclusively in Luke's Gospel. The most important book on this subject is *The Songs of the Holy Nativity,* by Canon Thomas D. Bernard, London, 1895, pp. viii, 164. The Biblical text of each song is first discussed, and then the use of the song in the subsequent history of the Church.

The *Nunc Dimittis* is very fully treated in a work bearing that title by Thomas N. Gurney, London, 1906, pp. viii, 151. The *Magnificat* is treated exhaustively in a series of four sermons entitled *Magnificat,* by Canon H. P. Liddon, originally published in 1889, the fifth edition appearing in 1898, pp. x, 111. The *Gloria in Excelsis* is beautifully unfolded by Thomas Guthrie in his little volume, *The Angels' Song,* London, 1866, pp. 141. A smaller book, *The Magnificat,* was published in 1889 by R. M. Benson, pp. 99.

CHARACTERS OF THE NATIVITY

Practically all volumes devoted to the study of characters in the New Testament, except those exclusively confined to the twelve apostles or the companions of Paul, will have one or more chapters on persons appearing in the nativity story. Among these works are:

Alexander Whyte: *The Walk, Conversation and Character of Jesus Christ Our Lord.*

G. Campbell Morgan: *The Great Physican.*

James Hastings: *The Greater Men and Women of the Bible,* Vol. V, *Mary—Simon.*

T. Vincent Tymms: *The Private Relationships of Christ,* London, 1907.

Dinsdale T. Young: *Neglected People of the Bible.*

George Matheson: *Representative Men of the New Testament.*

A. T. Robertson: *Some Minor Characters of the New Testament.*

Walter F. Adeney: *Women of the New Testament,* New York, 1899. pp. 1-84. (Six excellent chapters, with a particularly good one on Anna.)

PAUL'S WITNESS TO THE BIRTH OF CHRIST

Of the many works on Paul's theology, few have any discussion of his concepts of the birth of Christ. The following list is not exhaustive, but it is all I have discovered after examining some sixty volumes on Paul and Pauline theology:

R. J. Knowling: *Witness of the Epistles,* London, 1892. Chapter 4, pp. 244-290.

R. J. Knowling: *The Testimony of St. Paul to Christ,* New York, 1905. pp. 261-265.

Charles A. Briggs: *The Incarnation of the Lord,* New York, 1902. pp. 63-80.

There is one volume devoted entirely to this subject which I believe is not today too well known, *Did Paul Know of the*

Virgin Birth? A Historical Study, by Bishop **Richard J.** Cooke, New York, 1926. p. 152.

The Incarnation

All volumes devoted to a consideration of this vast subject will have some material, necessarily, on the virgin birth, beginning with the well-known work of Athanasius, often translated and edited, *The Incarnation of the Word of God,* the latest edition being one published in New York in 1946. Another famous work on this subject is Charles Gore: *Dissertations on Subjects Connected with the Incarnation,* New York, 1895, pp. 3-70. The largest work of recent times is Robert L. Ottley: *The Doctrine of the Incarnation,* eighth ed., 1946.

The Birth of Christ in the Christian Creeds

Because of the early phrase in the Apostles' Creed, "who was conceived by the Holy Ghost, born of the Virgin Mary," there are good chapters in many books on this great expression of Christian faith. One of the most notable is in a work which every student of doctrine must possess, first published in 1655, John Pearson: *An Exposition of the Creed.* One of the best editions is that by Chevallier (Cambridge, 1882) in which the subject of the virgin birth is discussed in pp. 298-345. See also the following:

B. F. Westcott: *The Historic Faith,* 1890. pp. 59-72.

H. B. Swete: *The Virgin Birth in Relation to Primitive Christianity,* Cambridge, 1908. pp. 42-55.

A. C. Baird: *Christianity Fundamentals,* Edinburgh, 1926. pp. 70-89.

Karl Barth: *Credo,* New York, 1936. pp. 62-72.

Foundations of the Faith, edited by David J. Fant, New York, 1951. pp. 41-51.

SERMONIC LITERATURE

One of the first great sermons in the Christian Church on the nativity of our Lord was the Homily by Chrysostom, which can be found in all of his works, and in some anthologies of great sermons.

The first volume of outstanding significance devoted entirely to sermons on the birth of Christ is that by Lancelot Andrewes, the great saint and scholar, author of the inimitable *Private Devotions.* These sermons will be found most conveniently in the first volume of the edition of his sermons published at Oxford in 1841 in six volumes entitled *Ninety-Six Sermons by the Right Honorable and Reverened Father in God,* Lancelot Andrewes, pp. xxx, 454. (The nativity sermons, seventeen in number, preached at intervals over a period of about twenty years before King James I at Whitehall from 1605-1624, occupy the first 300 pages of this volume.)

An editorial in the Literary Supplement of the *London Times,* September 23, 1926, said, "His sermons are too well built to be readily quotable; they stick too closely to the point to be entertaining. Yet they rank with the finest English prose of their time, for any time. . . . Andrewes is the first great preacher of the English Catholic Church . . . His prose is not inferior to that of any sermons in the language, unless it be some of Newman's."

In 1817, William Mandell published six sermons preached before the University of Cambridge in a volume entitled *The Advent of Christ.*

There are extensive lists of Christmas sermons, containing hundreds of references, which cannot be repeated here. For the earlier ones see James Darling: *Cyclopedia Bibliographia, the Holy Scriptures, Subjects,* 1859, columns 771-778, 949-

963, 1854-1857. More recent lists may be found in the *Speaker's Bible,* St. Matthew, Vol. I, 1938, pp. 225-228—160 references to Matthew 1:21—2:16, and the same series, *St. Luke,* Vol. I, pp. 449-462—approximately eight hundred sermon references based on the verses of Luke 1:5—2:52.

Probably the greatest sermons of the nineteenth century on subjects pertaining to the advent of our Lord are those by Canon H. P. Liddon, especially *Christmastide in St. Paul's,* 1889, third ed., London, 1891, pp. xv, 426; and *Advent in St. Paul's,* 1888, new ed., 1896 pp. xx, 613. (This volume has sermons on both advents of our Lord, and contains Liddon's famous sermon, "The First Five Minutes After Death.")

In the *Church Year Pulpit Library,* published some years ago by the F. M. Barton Company of Cleveland, Ohio, there are three volumes having considerable material on the advent season: Vol. I, *Advent Sundays,* pp. 311; Vol. II, *Advent Courses—Christmastide,* pp. 266; Vol. III, *Epiphany and First, Second and Third Sundays After,* pp. 302.

Spurgeon also has a series, *Twelve Christmas Sermons,* New York, 1899, pp. 144. See also Goulburn's *Gospel of the Childhood;* John Keble: *Sermons for the Christian Year, Christmas and Epiphany;* and J. G. Greenhough: *Christmas Festivals and Anniversaries.* Most of the volumes of Christmas sermons of our generation are of infinitely less significance. I mention a few: Wil R. Johnson: *Magnetism of the Manger,* Grand Rapids, 1938. p. 131; J. Harold Gwynne: *Gospel of Christmas,* 1938, p. 150, and *Christmas Treasures,* Grand Rapids, 1940, pp. 160. There is a brilliant series of studies in Samuel M. Zwemer: *The Glory of the Manger.* N. Y., 1940, pp. 232. (For additional titles see the chapter in this volume, "A Chronological Arrangement of Biblical Passages Relating to the Birth of Christ," etc.)

Apocryphal Gospels of the Infancy, Etc.

James DeQuincy Donehoo: *Apocryphal and Legendary Life of Christ*, New York, 1903. pp. 1-188.

Montague Rhodes James: *The Apocryphal New Testament*, Oxford, 1924.

R. Travers Herford: *Christianity in Talmud and Midrash*, London, 1903. pp. 35-49.

The Birth of Christ in Poetry

The first poetic treatment of the nativity in the history of English literature was that done by Cynwulf in the eighth century. The principal work on this is Albert S. Cook: *The Christ of Cynwulf*, Boston, 1899. The advent text is found on pp. 1-17, and the exhaustive glossary for this text, pp. 227-294. See also Charles W. Kennedy: *The Poems of Cynwulf Translated into English Prose*, London, 1910.

Many others have written books on this subject. The greatest poem ever written on the birth of our Lord is, of course, Milton's glorious ode "On the Morning of Christ's Nativity," which he wrote at the age of twenty-one. For an extended consideration of this work see especially Albert S. Cooke: *Notes on Milton's Ode, "On the Morning of Christ's Nativity,"* in the *Transactions of the Connecticut Academy*, New Haven, 1909, Vol. XV, pp. 307-368. All works on Milton will have some comment on this classic.

For extensive collections of poems relating to our Lord's birth, see W. Garrett Horder: *The Poets' Bible*, New Testament Section, new ed., London, 1883, pp. 6-76. Other volumes that might be consulted are *Christmas with the Poets*, London, 1855, second ed., p. 202; Philip Schaff and Arthur Gilman: *The Library of Religious Poetry*, New York, 1881, pp. 709-737; and James Dalton Morrison (ed.): *Masterpieces of Religious Verse*, New York, 1948, pp. 135-172 (114 poems).

THE NATIVITY IN DRAMA

The birth of our Lord, of course, provided wonderfully vivid material for the English miracle plays and drama in the early life of the Church. For a consideration of this subject in general, see A. W. Pollard: *English Miracle Plays*, Oxford, 1890; Katherine Lee Bates: *English Religious Drama*, New York, 1893; and Karl Young: *The Drama of the Medieval Church*, two volumes, Oxford, 1933. There is an exhaustive list of all important dramas relating to the birth of Christ in Edward D. Coleman: *The Bible in English Drama*, New York, 1931.

CHRISTMAS HYMNS

Though I have gathered a great deal of material on about twenty-five of the most important Christmas hymns from medieval times, the length of this bibliography already prevents my including the material in this article.

CHRISTMAS CAROLS

Davies Gilbert: *Some Ancient Christmas Carols,* second ed., enlarged, London, 1823.

William Sandys: *Christmas Carols, Ancient and Modern,* London, 1833. *Ancient Christmas Carols,* London, 1860; additions in 1863.

Joshua Sylvester: *A Garland of Christmas Carols, Ancient and Modern,* London, 1861; New York, 1902, 1905.

William H. Husk: *Songs of the Nativity,* London, 1868.

H. R. Bramley and John Stainer: *Christmas Carols Old and New,* 1871.

Edith Rickert: *Ancient English Christmas Carols*, MCCCC —MDCC, New York, 1910.

A. S. W. Anson: *The Christmas Book of Carols and Songs*, London, New York, n.d.

Percy Dearmer, R. Vaughan Williams and Martin Shaw: *The Oxford Book of Carols*, Oxford, 1928.

Catherine Bailey and David Pottinger: *Old English Carols for Christmas*, Cambridge, Mass., 1929.

Edward Bliss Reed: *Christmas Carols Printed in the Sixteenth Century*, Cambridge, Mass., 1932.

In Grove's *Dictionary of Music and Musicians* (third ed., 1949) there is a very scholarly article, "Carol," Vol. I, pp. 564-468.

The Nativity in Art

Henry Van Dyke: *The Christ-Child in Art, A Study of Interpretation*, New York, 1894. pp. 15-36.

Mrs. Anna B. Jameson: *Sacred and Legendary Art*, Boston and New York, 1896.

A. Bartle: *The Madonna of the Poets*, 1906.

Julia M. Cartwright: *Christ and His Mother in Italian Art*, London, 1917. pp. xiv, 228.

John Gough: *The Virgin Mary and the Traditions of the Painters*, London, 1873. pp. xi, 263.

F. W. Farrar: *The Life of Christ as Represented in Art*, New York and London, 1900.

Estelle M. Hurel: *The Madonna in Art*, Boston, 1897. pp. 217.

Adolfo Venturi: *The Madonna, A Pictorial Representation of the Life and Death of the Mother of Our Lord, Jesus Christ*, Eng. trans., London, 1902. pp. xiii, 446. Discusses over 500 paintings and sculptures.

Cynthia Pearl Maus: *Christ and the Fine Arts,* New York, 1931. The nativity and childhood are discussed on pp. 25-94.

CHRISTMAS

Thomas K. Hervey: *The Book of Christmas, Descriptive of the Customs, Ceremonies, Traditions, Superstitions, Fun, Feeling and Festivities of the Christmas Season,* London, 1841, pp. ix, 220; new ed., London and Boston, 1888, pp. iv, 356. (This is one of the first of the larger books in our language covering the general subject of Christmas; many were to follow.)

William Sandys: *Christmastide, Its History, Festivities and Carols,* London, 1852, 1860. pp. 327.

J. P. McCaskey (Ed.): *Christmas in Song, Sketch and Story,* nearly nine hundred Christmas songs, hymns, carols, etc., New York, 1890. pp. 320.

A. Tille: *Yule and Christmas,* London, 1899. p. 218.

William Francis Dawson: *Christmas: Its Origin and Associations,* London, 1902. pp. xvi, 306.

Robert Haven Schauffler: *Christmas, Its Origin, Celebration and Significance as Related in Prose and Verse,* New York, 1907. pp. xiii, 325 (in the series, *Our American Holidays*).

The Book of Christmas, New York, 1909. (Introduction by H. W. Mabie) pp. xix, 369.

D. L. Kelleher: *An Anthology of Christmas Prose and Verse with New Stories and Poems,* London, 1908. (Much emphasis on scriptural themes.)

Clement A. Miles: *Christmas in Ritual and Tradition, Christian and Pagan,* London, 1912.

T. G. Crippen: *Christmas and Christmas Lore,* London, 1923. pp. viii, 221.

Elizabeth H. Sechrist: *Christmas Everywhere,* Philadelphia, 1931. pp. 176.

William Muir Auld: *Christmas Tidings,* New York, 1933. pp. xii, 156. The first of these two volumes has extensive material on the date, December 25, "as effected by coincident pagan festivals," chapters on Christmas trees, Christmas Bells, etc. The second volume is devoted to the Biblical material.

R. J. Campbell: *The Story of Christmas,* New York, 1935. pp. xi, 288. This includes chapters on "Tributary Festivals and Quaint Survivals," "Non-Christian Christmas Customs," and "Nativity Plays."

M. R. Heath (compiler): *Margaret Tarrant's Christmas Garland,* Bradford, 1942.

A. C. Hottes: *Christmas Facts and Fancies,* second ed., 1944.

Vivian Campbell (Ed.): *Christmas Anthology of Poetry and Painting,* 1947.

Edward Wegneknecht (Ed.): *The Fireside Book of Christmas Stories,* 1945. (This volume has sold 500,000 copies.)

Edward Wagneknecht: *A Fireside Book of Yuletide Tales,* Indianapolis, 1948. pp. xv, 553.

Walter W. Schmauch: *Christmas Literature Through the Centuries.* Chicago, 1938. pp. 418. This was privately published by Walter M. Hill, the famous book dealer of Chicago of a former generation. The work has become quite scarce. Apart from the first chapter, "Christmas History," of less than thirty pages, the author deals with the literature of Christmas, not the Biblical material. He is unique in having chapters on John Milton, Sir Walter Scott, Washington Irving, Charles Dickens, W. M. Thackeray, Phillips Brooks, Henry Van Dyke, etc. The book is valuable also because of its fifteen pages of bibliography, though not embracing literature on the Biblical material as such.

Francis X. Weiser: *The Christmas Book*. New York: Harcourt, Brace and Co., 1952. pp. 188. The author is professor of Philosophy and German at Immanuel College in Boston. Though written by a Roman Catholic, the book is really an excellent, reverent presentation of many subjects relating to Christmas. Here is the best chapter I have seen on St. Nicholas, and two chapters on Christmas trees and plants. The work shows a careful investigation of origins. The only adequate discussion of Luther's hymn, "Away in a Manger," that I have seen is in this volume.

Jane T. Stoddard: *The Christian Year in Human History,* London, New York, n.d. pp. 3-48.

Selma Lagerlof: *Christ Legends,* 1908. pp. 272.

Philip Gates: *Christmas in Song and Story,* London, 1875. pp. 385. A magnificent quarto volume.

Cynthia Pearl Maus: *Christ and the Fine Arts,* New York, 1931. Part I is devoted to "The Nativity and Childhood of Jesus," pp. 25-94, and contains eighteen pictures, fourteen poems, seven stories, and eleven hymns. A beautiful work.

Edward Wagneknecht (Ed.): *The Story of Jesus in the World's Literature,* New York, 1946. pp. 3-164. This includes T. S. Eliot's "The Journey of the Magi," and Maxwell Anderson's "The Journey to Jerusalem."

W. H. Jewitt: *The Nativity in Art and Song,* 1898.

Mary Lamberton: *The Home Book of Christmas,* 1941. pp. xx, 746.

Among the best volumes published by the Roman Catholic Church is the one edited by the Librarian of Fordham University. William J. Roehrenbeck: *Christmastide, A Catholic Treasury for Young and Old,* New York, 1948. p. 381.

Eric Posselt: *The World's Greatest Christmas Stories,* Chicago, 1949. pp. xvi, 451.

William F. Daus: *Christmas, Its Origin and Associations,* London, 1902, p. 394.

John Hadfield: *Christmas Companion,* London, 1939. pp. xvi, 560.

Katherine Lambert Richards: *How Christmas Came to the Sunday School,* New York, 1934. pp. ix, 292. A remarkable volume, but hardly known today. It is the result of research for a doctorate degree, bringing the subject of Christmas in America down to the year 1927. Such a survey will never have to be repeated. The footnotes are elaborate and the material is exhaustive. There is a good deal of material here, incidentally, regarding the *Sunday School Times.* I was interested to discover the approval of Dr. Henry Clay Trumbull in 1874 of the play, "The Christmas Chimes."

K. A. Kellner: *Heortology: A History of the Christian Festivals from Their Origin to the Present Day,* London, 1908.

Charles Wendte: *At Christmas Time,* Boston, 1917.

The earliest defense of Christmas among our colonial forefathers that has been preserved in print was one written by George Pigot in 1730. *A Vindication of the Practice of the Ancient Christian as Well as the Church of England and Other Reformed Churches in the Observance of the Christmas Day.*

NOTES

In this bibliography I have given no attention and purposely so, to such subjects as Uletide, St. Nicholas, Noel, the legends of trees, etc. These subjects may appear in some of the volumes here mentioned, but they have no place in the Biblical unfolding of our Lord's nativity.

For those who are interested in more extensive lists on the

influence of the Bible in English literature, art and music, including the subject of Christ in art, may I refer to my "Bibliography of the Influence of the Bible on English Literature, and in Part on the Fine Arts," published in the *Fuller Seminary Library Bulletin,* January—June, 1951.

If any readers of this volume are interested in books relating to the Birth of Christ published before 1820, they will find a great number in the amazingly large bibliography, under "Jesus Christ," in Robert Watt's *Bibliotheca Britannica.* Vol. IV. Edinburgh, 1824.

18

THE OLIVET DISCOURSE

Its relationship to Old Testament prophecy and the Book of the Revelation

Christ's great prophecy delivered on the Mount of Olives, on Tuesday of Holy Week, is the most neglected major discourse of our Lord in the literature that has gathered around the Gospel records of His life and teachings. One will come upon a hundred books on the Sermon on the Mount, and sections of this sermon, before he finds an adequate discussion of the Olivet Discourse. An illustration of this fact is in Hastings' famous five-volume *Dictionary of the Bible,* where in the supplementary volume an initial article on the Sermon on the Mount by Votaw extends to eighty-eight columns, but there is no article anywhere in the dictionary on the Olivet Discourse!

In spite of the fact that 160 verses are devoted to this prophecy in the Synoptic Gospels, no volumes attempting to expound this inexhaustible utterance were published in this country (apart from pamphlet literature) for over eighty years. And yet, there is hardly any passage in the New Testament, outside of the Book of Revelation, so demanding close study for the day in which we live.

NOTES:

1. The relation of the Olivet Discourse to the Book of Revelation has been worked out with greatest detail (in my opinion, not all of the conclusions therein are justified) by Henry W. Frost in his volume, *Matthew Twenty-Four and*

OUTLINE OF THE OLIVET DISCOURSE IN THE SYNOPTIC GOSPELS

Old Testament Prophecies of the Same (or related) Events	Similar Earlier Teachings of Christ	The Prophecies and Illustrating Parables	Matthew 24:1—25:46	Mark 13:1-37	Luke 21:5-36	Similar Teachings: Acts and Epistles	Prophecies Reappearing in the Revelation[1]
		INTRODUCTION					
Even before the Israelites had entered Canaan they were warned of a future destruction of their cities (Deut. 28:49-52). Prophecies of former destructions of Jerusalem often have a further reference to Jerusalem at the end of this age (see, e.g., Isa. 28; Jer. 4-6,9,16,25; Ezek. 16,22,33; Zech. 14:1-8).	Matthew 23:27-29; Luke 13:34,35; 19:41-44	1. The preliminary prediction Jerusalem will be destroyed	24:1,2	1,2	5,6		(The final attack upon Jerusalem 20:7-9)
		2. The threefold question of the disciples,	24:3	3,4	7	(cf. Acts 1:6)	
		a. "When shall these things be"					
		b. "What shall be the sign of thy coming?"[2]					
	"The end of the age" Matthew 13:39, 40,49	c. "And of the end of the age?"[3]					
		I. THE COURSE OF THIS AGE, AND "THE BEGINNING OF TRAVAIL."	24:4-14	5-13	8-24	See footnote 5	See footnote 5
		1. False Christs will deceive many[4]	4,5, also 11,24	5,6	8		
		2. Physical and economic disturbances	6-8	7,8	9-11		
War at the end of the age (see, e.g., Dan. 11:36-45; Lev. 26:25; Joel 3:9-17; etc.).		"wars and talk of wars"[6]	6,7a	7,8b	9,10		For wars—16:12-15; 17:14; 19:11 ff. 20:8
		"tumults"[7]			9		
Famine, as sent as a divine punishment (see Lev. 26:29; Deut. 28:38-42,53-57). Pestilence (see Lev. 26:25; Deut. 28:21,22,59-61.)[8]		"famines"	7b	8b	11		For famine—6:5; 6-8
		"pestilences"	7b	8b	11		For pestilence—6:8
		"earthquakes"			11		For earthquakes— 6:12; 8:5; 11:13; 16:18; 18:8
		"terrors"[9]			11		(Fear, 6:16,17)

Scripture References	Topic				Notes
Matthew 13:21; Mark 4:17; John 16:33	"great signs from heaven" 3. Moral and religious phenomena tribulation[10]	9-13 / 9	9-13	11 / 12-19	6:9-11; 11:7-10; 13:7,15; 16:6; 17:6; 18:24.
	delivered up to councils, etc.		9,11		Fulfilled, in part, I Thessalonians 2:14,15; Acts 3, etc.[11]
Luke 11:49,50	martyrdom		12	12-16	
On hatred of disciples of Christ, Matthew 5:12; 10:22; Luke 6:22; John 15:18-21; 17:14.	hatred	9,10	12,13	17-19	
Matthew 13:41	false prophets[14] increase of iniquity[12]	11 / 12			"The man of lawlessness"
	4. Gospel to be preached to all nations	14	10		II Thessalonians 2:8 (cf. v.7)
	5. Destruction of Jerusalem "trodden down of the Gentiles until the times of the Gentiles be fulfilled"[15]			20-24	
	II. "THE GREAT TRIBULATION" (MATT. 24:21) 1. Appearance of the Abomination of Desolation[13]	24:15-28 / 15-20	14-23 / 14-18		II Peter 2:1; I John 4:1

OUTLINE OF THE OLIVET DISCOURSE IN THE SYNOPTIC GOSPELS

Old Testament Prophecies of the Same (or related) Events	Similar Earlier Teachings of Christ	The Prophecies and Illustrating Parables	Matthew 24:1—25:46	Mark 13:1-37	Luke 21:5-36	Similar Teachings: Acts and Epistles	Prophecies Reappearing in the Revelation[1]
Daniel 11:31; 9:27; 12:11. Deuteronomy 28:53-57; Daniel 12:1; Isaiah 30:20; Hosea 5:15; Zephaniah 1:15.		2. The Great Tribulation[10]	21,22	19,20			(2:9,10); 7:14
False prophets, in general (see, e.g., Jer. 5:31; 29:9; 28:9; 37:19; Ezek. 13:16-19; Jer. 23:16-32; etc.).	Matthew 7:15; Luke 17:23,24	3. Appearance of false Christs and false prophets[14]	23-28	21-23			13:13-15; 16:14. (On "the false prophet," see 16:13; 19:20; 20:10)
	(John 4:48)	a. Shewing great signs and wonders					
		b. Deceiving many[4]					
		III. AFTER THE TRIBULATION	24:29-31	24-27	25-28		
Isaiah 13:10; 24:23; Ezekiel 32:7; Jeremiah 4:23,24; Zephaniah 1:15; Zechariah 14:6; Amos 5:20; 8:9; Isaiah 14:12; 34:4; Joel 2:10,31.		1. Celestial phenomena	29	24,25	25a,26b		6:12-14; 8:12; 9:2; 16:8; 12:4
Haggai 2:6,7; among other prophecies, certainly one should include Jeremiah 25:30-38.		2. International conditions "distress of nations"[16]			25b,26a		6:15-17
		"in perplexity"[17]					
		"men fainting for fear"[18]					For fear see above, for Luke 21:11
Zechariah 12:10; Dan. 7:13.		3. The Coming of the Son of Man[19]	30	26 (also 14:62)	27,28	II Thessalonians 1:7,9	1:7
	Matthew 13:30, 39-43	4. Gathering together of the elect	31	27			(14:14-20)
Joel 3:11-16.		IV. JUDGMENT OF THE NATIONS	25:31-46				
		V. EXHORTATIONS AND ILLUSTRATING PARABLES					
		1. Parable of the fig tree	24:32-35	28-31	29-33		
	Luke 17:26-31	2. The need for watchfulness	24:36-42	32,33			
		3. Faithful and unfaithful servants contrasted	24:43-51				
		4. Parable of the ten virgins	25:1-13				
		5. Parable of the talents	24:14-30				
		6. A final warning		34-37[20]	34-38		

the Revelation, published by Oxford University Press in 1924.

2. The word translated "sign" *(semeion)* is found also in this discourse in Matthew 24:24, 30; Mark 13:22; Luke 21:11, 25. Compare "signs of the times," (Matt. 16:1); and "we would see a sign from thee" (Matt. 12:38, 39), etc.

3. Christ Himself used this phrase "end of the age" in Matthew 13:39, 40, 49; and again at the time of His ascension, 28:20. It is found nowhere else in the New Testament except Hebrews 9:26. The full phrase, I think, is not in LXX, but the idea of the *end* is there, e.g., Daniel 7:26; 8:17, 19; 9:26; 11:6, 27, 35, 40, 41; 12:4, 6, 8, 9, 13.

4. While the actual word *pseudokristos* occurs only in the Olivet Discourse, the subject of deception in the last days is basic in the New Testament prophetic passages—II Thessalonians 2:11; I Timothy 4:1; II Timothy 3:13; II Peter 3:17; I John 2:26; II John 7; and especially in Revelation, 12:9; 13:14; 18:23; 19:20; 20:3, 8, 10.

5. In the last days there will also be false teachers, II Peter 2:1. The root of this word is the same as the word translated "liar" in John 8:44 and I John 2:22.

6. The word incorrectly translated "rumors" in almost all versions (Matt. 24:6; Mark 13:7), is *akoe,* meaning "what is heard" (as in Matt. 13:14; Acts 28:26), or "report" (John 12:38), hence, "talk about." And when does any major daily newspaper appear today without some article on war, generally on the first page? On the subject of war at the end of the age, see an exhaustive treatment in George N. H. Peters: *The Theocratic Kingdom,* Vol. II, pp. 102-116, 751-772, and a briefer study, wholly apart from Peters, in my volume, *World Crisis in the Light of Prophetic Scriptures,* pp. 96-119.

7. The word is *akatastasia* meaning disturbance, disorder, unruliness, I Corinthians 14:33; II Corinthians 6:5. A par-

ticipial form is used in James 1:8 and 3:8. In the Septuagint (LXX) it is used in reference to Cain as a wanderer, Genesis 4:8. (See also Isa. 54:11).

8. One form of judgment upon Israel for her continued disobedience is, strangely never referred to in the New Testament, namely, an invasion of wild beasts (see Deut. 32:24; Lev. 26:22; Hos. 13:8).

9. The word is *phobetron,* meaning a terrible sight or event. It is found in Isaiah 19:17. Fear (*phobos*) as a factor at the end of the age is referred to in Revelation 11:11; 18:10, 15.

10. Tribulation as a part of the experience of God's people, culminating in a time of "the great tribulation," is a theme frequently occuring in the New Testament (see e.g., Matt. 13:21; Mark 4:17; John 16:33; Acts 11:19; 14:22; Rom. 8:35; II Cor. 1:4; 6:4; 7:4; 8:2; I Thes. 1:6; 3:37; Rev. 1:9; 2:9, 10, 22; 7:14. For the use of the Greek word *thlipsis* in the LXX., see Deut. 28:53-57; Isa. 8:21; 10:3, 25; 26:16; 30:6, 20; 33:2; 37:3; 65:16; Jer. 10:18; 15:11; Dan. 12:1; Hos. 5:15; Obad. 12, 14; Hab. 3:16; Zeph. 1:15).

11. The initial fulfullments of this prophecy are found throughout the Book of Acts—4:1-22; 5:17-42; 6:8-8:3; 12:1-19; 14:19, 20; 16:19-29. From 21:27 to the end of the book, Paul appears before one Roman authority after another.

12. The word *anomia,* meaning "lawlessness," often translated "iniquity," is found with great frequency in the LXX text of the Old Testament prophetic writings (e.g., Isa. 1:5; 5:7, 18; 24:20; 59:3, 4, 6, 12; Ezek. 8:6, 9, 13-17; 16:43, 47, 51; 36:31, 33; Zech. 5:8).

13. This is taken literally from Daniel 11:31; see also Daniel 9:27; 12:11. The word rendered "abomination" is *bdelugma,* meaning "a foul thing," often used in LXX in passages referring to idolatry, (e.g., I Kings 11:5; 21:26; II

Kings 21:2; and, similarly, in Rev. 17:4, 5; 21:27). The word translated "desolation" is *eremosis,* in this form only in the Olivet Discourse, but as a verb *eremoo* in Matthew 12:25; Luke 11:17; Revelation 17:16; 18:17, 19.

14. On false prophets in the Old Testament especially in relation to the last days, see LXX text for Jeremiah 33:7, 8, 11, 16 (Chap. 26 in our text); 27:9; 29:8.

15. It is significant that Luke, a Gentile, should give more attention to Christ's predictions about Jerusalem and the post-resurrection appearances of Christ in Jerusalem, than any of the other three authors of the Gospels. Some have taken the prophecy regarding Babylon (Rev. 17, 18) to refer to Jerusalem, e.g., I. Williams, Bengel, Weidner, etc., but this seems quite impossible.

16. The Greek word here is *sunoche,* meaning "to be in distress," or "in prison," or "to be suffering anguish." It is found in the New Testament only here and in II Corinthians 2:4; it is not the same word as that translated "distress" in verse 23.

17. The word translated "perplexity" is *aporia,* only here in the New Testament from a verb meaning "to be without resources, to be embarrassed, to be in doubt, not to know how to decide." (Thayer), as in Luke 24:4; John 13:22; Acts 25:20. It is most interesting that the word is found in the LXX text of two well-known prophecies of the last times in the Pentateuch: "I will bring upon you preplexity," (Lev. 26:16); and "the Lord will smite thee with distress," (Deut. 28:22). Also, in the LXX text, Haggai 2:18 and Isaiah 5:30, in connection with the roaring of the sea. Also Isaiah 8:22; 24:19.

18. The verb translated "fainting for fear" is *apopsucho,* meaning, literally, "to stop breathing, and then, to swoon away." It occurs only here in the New Testament.

19. Two words are translated "coming" in relation to the Second Advent of Christ in the Olivet Discourse. Matthew alone uses the familiar *parousia* (24:3, 27, 37, 39), the word used for the second advent in I Corinthians 15:23; I Thessalonians 2:19; 3:13, etc. More frequently used in the verb *erkomai* (Matt. 24:30, 42, 44, 46, 48; 25:6, 10, 13, 19, 27, 31; Mark 13:26, 35, 36; and Luke 21:27). This is also used of the coming of false christs (Matt. 24:5, etc.). The other word used in the New Testament in relation to the second advent, *apokalupsis* (as in I Cor. 1:7; Gal. 1:12, and I Pet. 1:7) is not in the Greek text of the Olivet Discourse. In the Olivet Discourse four things are said to accompany our Lord in His return: power (Matt. 24:30); great glory (24:30; 26:31; Mark 13:26; Luke 21:27); angels (Matt. 24:31; 25:31); and clouds (Matt. 24:30). These factors are also present in other references to Christ's return, as in Matthew 16:27; 19:28; 24:64; 19:28; 24:64, and always accompany any epochal manifestations of deity (see Ex. 19:16; 34:5; 40:34-36; II Pet. 1:16, 17; Acts 1:8-11; Rev. 19).

20. Some identify this parable as unique in Mark, and call it the Parable of the Absent Householder.

19

A PROTESTANT BIBLIOGRAPHY
OF THE VIRGIN MARY

Certainly the most important woman character of Scripture is Mary, the mother of our Lord. Next to her Son, she is the dominating figure in the nativity narratives; she is one of the three persons to whom Christ spoke directly from the cross; and she is the only woman named in the gathering of the early church in the upper room immediately preceding Pentecost.

The Roman Catholic Church has grossly, and at times blasphemously, exalted the Virgin Mary to a place of worship, ascribing to her divine names (something the Scriptures never do), and has developed an enormous Marian literature much of which is fantastic and historically ungrounded. The Protestant Church on the other hand, has, for the most part, and to its own impoverishment, neglected the beautiful passages in the New Testament in which Mary appears.

As far as I have been able to discover, no extensive bibliography of the Virgin Mary has been constructed by any Protestant in Great Britain or in this country, so the list which follows may stand unique in this type of literature. How many volumes have been written by Roman Catholics on the mother of Jesus, I do not know. In the *United States Catalog* for 1938-1942, fifty-six titles by Roman Catholics are listed, whereas there is but one title on the Virgin Mary by a Protestant.

My estimate would be that in the last one hundred years there have been at least four hundred volumes written on the Virgin Mary in the English language. In the following list I have tried to include all of the major and some of the less important works by Protestants, and have added those volumes by Roman Catholics which attempt a scholarly, historical survey of the whole subject of the Virgin Mary, together with anthologies and books dealing with the controversies that have gathered around her position in the Christian church.

Works of mere adulation, meditation, and development of myths and traditions I have not felt called upon to include. In two sections of the bibliography, I have purposely refrained from attempting anything exhaustive, e.g., in periodical articles and sermons. There are scores, perhaps hundreds, of sermons which need not be listed here; and, of course, there are many pamphlets and brochures on the Virgin Mary, many of which will probably never be recovered. I have included a few of these which happen to be in my possession.

The distinguished New Testament authority, the late Professor A. T. Robertson, has well said (in his volume, *The Mother of Jesus*) : "I have felt for many years that Mary the Mother of Jesus has not had fair treatment from either Protestants or Catholics. If Roman Catholics have deified Mary, Protestants, as a rule, have neglected her. This is largely due to a reaction against the adoration by the Catholics. Protestants have often been afraid to praise and esteem Mary for her full worth lest they be accused of leanings in sympathy with the Catholics. Hence, it has come to pass that the noblest of mothers is still the most misunderstood of mothers and of women. Cold neglect on the one hand is hers, while adoring worship greets her memory in countless statues on the other hand. The God whom multitudes worship today is Mary. Protestants fight Mariolatry in order to stand up for the worship of Mary's Son, our Saviour." We may now proceed to list these works, in chronological order.

James Endell Tyler (1789-1851); *The Worship of the Blessed Virgin Mary in the Church of Rome Contrary to Holy Scripture and to the Faith and Practice of the Church of Christ During the First Five Centuries.* London, 1884. Tyler was a widely-respected scholar and preacher of Oriel College, Oxford. This is the first volume on the Virgin Mary, as far as I know, to appear in any United States catalogue.

Mathieu M. Orsini (1802-1875): *The Life of the Blessed Virgin Mary, Mother of God.* Roman Catholic. Translated from the French, Amer. ed., rev., New York, 1851, pp. 428. An enlarged edition, with steel engravings, was published in 1861, pp. 764. The early American catalogue says that by 1876 the twenty-fifth edition had been called for, and five different American publishers were bringing out editions of the book. I am including it here because of its wide vogue among Catholics.

Mason Gallagher: *The Regard Due the Virgin Mary, with an Examination of the New Roman Dogma.* New York, 1855. pp. 162. The author, rector of the Church of the Evangelists of Oswego, N. Y., says (in the introduction): "When I beheld multitudes of my fellow citizens going up in crowds to attend their churches, with their minds full of devotion to the Virgin Mary, my spirit was stirred within me, and I determined, as became a public teacher of the religion of Christ, to draw your minds to the only proper revealed object of worship—God the Father, Son and Holy Ghost." This is an excellent scholarly study of the entire subject from a Protestant viewpoint.

Henry Harbaugh (1817-1867): *The True Glory of Woman*

as Portrayed in the Beautiful Life of the Virgin Mary,
Philadelphia, 1858, pp. 263. Harbaugh wrote a number
of books on heaven which had wide circulation a century ago. The chapter headings of this work are interesting: Mary, the Ideal Virgin; Mary, the Model Be-
trothed; Mary, the Model Wife; Mary, the Model
Mother; Mary, the Model Disciple; Mary, the Model
Saint. The work defends the perpetual virginity of Mary.

*Mary, the Handmaiden of the Lord, by the author of the
Chronicles of the Schönberg-Cotta Family.* New York,
1865, pp. 152.

Xavier Donald Macleod (1821-1865): *History of the Devotion of the Virgin Mary in North America.* New York,
1866, pp. xxiii, 467. Roman Catholic. This was originally written as an appendix to the *Life of the Blessed
Virgin,* by Orsini (see above). It is mentioned here because its pages reveal how widespread was the devotion
to Mary in this country nearly a century ago.

J. J. Laborde: *The Impossibility of the Immaculate Conception as an Article of Faith.* 1876.

Alexander Stewart Walsh: *Mary, the Queen of the House
of David and Mother of Jesus.* New York, 1886, pp. 626.
Introduction by T. DeWitt Talmadge.

R. Montague: *The Sower and the Virgin.* London, 1887. This
volume was written against the doctrine of the Immaculate Conception.

Thomas Livius: *Mary in the Epistles; or, the Implicit Teaching of the Apostles Concerning the Blessed Virgin Contained in Their Writings.* London, 1891. pp. viii, 292.
A Roman Catholic work. It is included here because of
its strange, perverted interpretations of the New Testament epistles.

Richard F. Quigley: *Mary the Mother of Christ in Prophecy*

and Its Fulfillment. New York, 1892, 2nd ed., rev., pp.
493. The author of this, the most important work on
the Virgin Mary by a Roman Catholic of this continent
in the nineteenth century, was a member of the Bar of
New Brunswick and Quebec, and a graduate of Harvard
University.

Stephen M. Merrill (1825-1905) : *Mary of Nazareth and Her
Family, a Scripture Study.* New York, 1895. pp. 192. Dr.
Merrill was a bishop of the Methodist Episcopal Church.

A. T. Robertson: *The Mother of Jesus.* New York, 1925, pp.
71. Here is a delightful small volume by one of the outstanding authorities on the Greek New Testament of
our century. I have quoted from this work at the beginning of this bibliography.

T. A. Lacey: *The Hidden Life of the Blessed Virgin, Based
Solely on the Gospel Records.* S. P. C. K., 1926, pp. xi.,
83.

James Marchant: *The Madonna. An Anthology.* London,
1928. pp. xxxix, 207. When published, this work was
priced at $7.00, with a deluxe edition at $16.00.

Mary Bordon: *Mary of Nazareth,* New York: Doubleday,
1933, pp. 305.

Mary the Mother of Our Lord, by the Maréchale (Catherine
Booth-Clibborn). The tenth edition of this beautiful
booklet, published by Marshall, Morgan and Scott of
London, is dated 1949, and carries a foreword by Bishop
H. C. G. Moule.

Francis Joseph Sheed: *The Mary Book.* New York, 1950, pp.
xii, 411.

Paul F. Palmer (ed.): *Mary in the Documents of the Church.*
London: Burns and Oates, 1953, pp. xxii, 129. Though
a Roman Catholic work, it is an important one for this
study. It is significant that the author can present only

one page on Mary in the early church creeds, but is compelled to give six pages to the subject of heresies involving Mary in the same period. The remainder of the volume is devoted to the documents of Mariolatry in the post-Apostolic ages. A supplement "Titles of Mary," lists *174 different titles* given to the Virgin Mary, with references to discussions in this book.

Two pamphlets, not dated, are "Mary, the Mother of Jesus," by Arthur W. Pink, published at the Bible Truth Depot, Swengel, Pa., and a sermon by Dr. Harold J. Ockenga preached at Park Street Church, Boston: "The Pondering Heart of Mary, the Virgin Mother of Jesus."

Giovanni Miegge: *The Virgin Mary: The Roman Catholic Marian Doctrine.* Philadelphia: Westminster Press, 1956, pp. 196. The author of this recent publication is professor of Church History at the Waldensian Faculty of Theology in Rome. This is the most theological work on Mariolatry written by a Protestant in our century. Professor Miegge says: "Catholicism in our time feels itself to be living in an age that in devotion to Mary is second to no other, probably not even those great centuries of Mariology, the twelfth and thirteenth. The twentieth century presents, moreover, a doctrinal superiority over that golden age of veneration of Mary. On the one hand, Marian theology through a century of work on it has reached a definiteness and an awareness of itself that the great Marian theologians of the Middle Ages, St. Anselm, St. Bonaventura and St. Bernard, did not attain. On the other hand, the desire to make the laity Mary-conscious has never been served by means so potent or a desire so strong." Among other chapters are "Mary in the Gospel," "The Compassionate Mother," etc. In highly commending the volume, *The Converted Catholic Magazine* says, "The whole work reveals the hallmark of a finished scholar, whose theological thinking has been refined by the challenge of teaching in the very heart of the Roman Catholic stronghold."

The Virgin Mary in Legend, Art and Literature

Charles Beecher: *The Incarnation, or Pictures of the Virgin and Her Son.* With Introductory Essay by Harriet Beecher Stowe. New York, 1849, pp. ix, 227.

J. G. Clay: *The Virgin Mary and the Traditions of Painters,* London, 1873, pp. xi, 263.

Henry Van Dyke: *The Christ Child in Art.* New York, 1893, pp. xviii, 236.

H. A. Guerber: *Legends of the Virgin and Christ, with Special Reference to Literature and Art.* New York, 1899, pp. xx, 277. An excellent handbook.

Mrs. Anna B. Jameson: *Legends of the Madonna as Represented in the Fine Arts,* London, 1890, new ed., pp. lxxv, 344. The standard work on this subject.

Estelle M. Hurll: *The Madonna in Art.* Boston, 1897, pp. 217.

W. H. Jewitt: *The Nativity in Art and Song.* 1898.

Adolfo Venturi: *The Madonna. A Pictorial Representation of the Life and Death of the Mother of Our Lord Jesus Christ.* London, 1902, pp. xiii, 446. This volume discusses over five hundred paintings and sculptures.

A. Bartle: *The Madonna of the Poets.* London, 1906.

J. Vriend: *The Blessed Virgin Mary in the Medieval Drama of England with Additional Studies in Middle English Literature.* Purmerend, Holland, 1928, pp. xv, 160.

Edward D. Coleman: *The Bible in English Drama.* New

York, 1931, pp. 101-104. The indispensable guide to Biblical dramas.

Cynthia Pearl Maus: *The World's Great Madonnas: An Anthology of Pictures, Poetry, Music and Stories Centering in the Life of the Madonna and Her Son.* New York, Harper, 1947, pp. xiii, 789. This, the last literary effort of Miss Maus before her death, contains a vast amount of material, though it is not exhaustive.

The Magnificat

The principal study of the songs of the Nativity is T. D. Bernard's *The Songs of the Holy Nativity.* London, 1895, pp. 164. Difficult to come upon, but worth any price. By far the best volume of sermons on this song of Mary is that by the greatest of London preachers of his day, *The Magnificat,* by H. P. Liddon, London, 1898, pp. 111. R. M. Benson published a series of brief meditations entitled *The Magnificat.* London, 1889, pp. 100. A work I have not seen is H. H. Jeaffreson's: *The Magnificat.*

Chapters on the Virgin Mary in Books on Biblical Characters

James Hastings: *The Greater Men and Women of the Bible,* Vol. VI, Mary-Simon, New York, 1915, pp. 1-34.

Alexander Whyte: *Bible Characters: Joseph and Mary to James the Lord's Brothers,* 1900.

T. Vincent Tymms: *The Private Relationships of Christ.* London, 1907.

W. B. Doyle: *The Holy Family.* New York, 1916.

F. C. Spurr: *The Holy Family.*

Walter F. Adeney: *Women of the New Testament,* pp. 1-56. A great chapter.

A. Moody Stuart: *The Three Marys.* London, 1862.

Agnes S. Turnbull: *The Four Marys.*

Books on the Life of Christ

Of course all adequate lives of Christ will have something on the Virgin Mary. Among the more important volumes dealing exclusively with the childhood of Jesus are the following:

S. A. Brooke: *The Early Life of Jesus*. Sermons Preached at Belford Chapel. London, 1887. (A book I have not been able to secure.)

F. W. Drake: *The Glory of Bethlehem*. 1915, pp. 12-36.

E. M. Goulburn: *The Gospel of the Childhood*. New York, 1873, pp. xxviii, 242.

J. Gresham Machen: *The Virgin Birth*. New York, 1932. Consult index for many references to Mary.

George F. Pentecost: *The Birth and Boyhood of Jesus*. New York, American Tract Society, 1897. pp. 91-108, 153-192.

Louis M. Sweet: *The Birth and Infancy of Jesus Christ According to the Gospel Narratives*. Philadelphia, 1907, pp. 264-266, etc. The most comprehensive work on all the major subjects pertaining to the birth of our Lord that has yet appeared in the English language.

Encyclopedic Articles
(listed in approximate order of publication)

John Kitto: *Cyclopedia of Biblical Literature*, 1859, ed. Mary, Vol. III, pp. 92-99.

William Smith: *Dictionary of the Bible*. New York, 1871, rev. ed. "The Virgin Mary," Vol. III, pp. 1816-1827. This learned discussion, with references to the principal literature, contains a list of the many exalted titles used in reference to Mary. I did not know until I read this article that she was not only called "Queen of Heaven," but also "Queen of Heaven and Hell," and is actually called in *"The Glories of Mary"* "the Advocate," "the Mediator," "the Redeemer and Saviour."

John M'Clintock and James Strong: *Cyclopedia of Biblical Theological and Ecclesiastical Literature.* New York, 1871. "Immaculate Conception," Vol. IV, pp. 506-510. "Mariolatry," Vol. V, pp. 747-754, with bibliography. "Mary," Vol. V, pp. 833-841, includes discussion of Jewish tradition and "Mohammedan tradition regarding Mary." "Perpetual Virginity of Mary."

William Smith and Samuel Cheetham: *A Dictionary of Christian Antiquities,* Hartford, 1880. "Festivals of Mary the Virgin," pp. 1139-1159.

Encyclopedia Biblica, London, 1899. Mary, Vol. III, cols. 2952-2969.

James Hastings: *Dictionary of the Bible,* 1898. Mary, Vol. III, pp. 286-293; with bibliography.

John Henry Blunt: *Dictionary of Doctrinal and Ecclesiastical Theology.* London, 1903. Ave Maria, p. 72. Immaculate Conception, pp. 328-331.

Mariolatry, pp. 440-442.

Mary, pp. 449-454.

Perpetual Virginity, pp. 562-563.

Theotokos, pp. 753-755.

C. H. H. Wright and Charles Neil: *Protestant Dictionary.* London, 1904.

Assumption of the Blessed Virgin, pp. 51-53.

Ave Maria and Angelus, pp. 60-62.

Conception, Immaculate, pp. 127-130.

Mary, the Virgin, pp. 390-397.

As the title of this work would imply, all of these articles repudiate the dogmas here discussed, except, of course, the virginity of Mary.

The Catholic Encyclopedia. New York, 1907.

> Annunciation, Vol. I, pp. 541-542.
> Assumption, Vol. II, pp. 6-7.
> Hail Mary, Vol. VII, pp. 110-112.
> The Immaculate Conception, Vol. VII, pp. 674-681.
> The Magnificat, Vol. IX, pp. 534-536.
> The Virgin Birth of Christ, Vol. XV, pp. 448-451.
> Virgin, Vol. XV, pp. 464-472.

> There are over fifty columns of text devoted to various subjects relative to the Virgin Mary in this encyclopedia, necessitating three columns of index (more than 300 lines of type). It is significant that the article on the Virgin is longer than the article on Jesus Christ.

The New Schaff-Herzog Encyclopaedia of Religious Knowledge. 1908.

> The Immaculate Conception, Vol. V, pp. 455-457.
> The Magnificat, Vol. VII, pp. 128-129.
> Mary, Vol. VII, pp. 220-225.

> These articles carry bibliographies, though most of the titles are in Latin or German.

The International Standard Bible Encyclopedia. 1939.

> Mary, Vol. III, pp. 2001-2003.

> In this work more space is given to Mary of Bethany than to Mary the mother of our Lord.

James Hastings: *Dictionary of Christ and the Gospels.* 1921.

> For lists of these articles see Chapters 14 and 17.

Encyclopaedia Britannica 14th ed.

> Mary, Vol. XIV, pp. 999-1000.

It was my intention originally to include references to some of the more choice sermonic literature on the Virgin Mary, but the bibliography is already sufficiently extended.

"The Virgin Mary to the Child Jesus"

I have always felt that Elizabeth Barrett Browning's exquisite poem, "The Virgin Mary to the Child Jesus," is the most beautiful poetic tribute to that epochal event written in our language, as Milton's "On the Morning of Christ's Nativity" is the most majestic.

As all of her writings testify, Mrs. Browning was a true believer. Of the twelve stanzas of this poem, I quote here only the first, the eighth, the eleventh, and the twelfth.

> Sleep, sleep, mine Holy One!
> My flesh, my Lord!—What name. I do not know
> A name that seemeth not too high or low,
> Too far from me or heaven:
> My Jesus, *that* is best! that word being given
> By the majestic angel whose command
> Was softly as a man's beseeching, said,
> When I and all the earth appeared to stand
> In the great overflow
> Of light celestial from his wings and head.
> Sleep, sleep, my saving One!
>
> Art Thou a King, then? come, his universe,
> Come, crown me him a King!
> Pluck rays from all such stars as never fling
> Their light where fell a curse,
> And make a crowning for this kingly brow!—
> What is my word? Each empyreal star
> Sits in a sphere afar
> In shining ambuscade:
> The child-brow, crowned by none,
> Keeps its unchildlike shade,
> Sleep, sleep, my crownless One! . . .
>
> It is enough to bear
> This image still and fair
> This holier in sleep
> Than a saint at prayer;

This aspect of a child
Who never sinned or smiled;
This presence in an infant's face;
This sadness most like love;
This love than love more deep;
This weakness like omnipotence
It is so strong to move.
Awful is this watching place,
Awful that I see from hence,
A king without regalia,
A God without the thunder,
A child without the heart for play;
Ay, a Creator, rent asunder
From his first glory, and cast away
On his own world, for me alone
To hold in hands created, crying—"SON!"

That tear fell not on thee,
Beloved, yet thou stirrest in thy slumber!
THOU, stirring not for glad sounds out of number,
Which through the vibratory palm-trees run
From summer wind and bird,
So quickly hast thou heard
A tear fall silently?
Wak'st thou, O living One?

20

SOME SUGGESTIONS FOR THE STUDY
OF A GIVEN BIBLICAL PASSAGE

In this study I should like to present not a full bibliography of a given portion of Scriptures, here the first three chapters of Genesis, nor an outline of this section, but the major areas of study which might be followed in a more or less exhaustive investigation of a Biblical passage. One will readily see by such an outline that the study of just three chapters in the Word of God, with their influence in history and literature, could occupy a person for twenty years.

I. LOCATION OF THE PASSAGE

The first three chapters of Genesis would be out of place elsewhere in the Bible. Upon this passage much of the later theology of the Scriptures solidly rests. Similarly, the last three chapters of the Book of Revelation could not rightly appear in any other place but at the end of the marvelous unfolding of divine revelation. Ultimately "location" leads to the larger problem of the present canonical order of the books of the Bible.

II. LITERARY FORM

The Old and New Testaments embrace some books that are strictly historical, some which are principally made up of laws and statutes, and many which consist of series of prophecies; some, for example Job, are written in dramatic form; others, such as the Gospels, are biographical; and then, we have the great body of devotional literature, at the forefront of which stands the Book of Psalms. The literary *genus* must never be ignored in the problem of Biblical interpretation. A masterly arrangement of Biblical material according to literary form will be found in Moulton's epochal work, *The Literary Study of the Bible.*

III. TEXTUAL CRITICISM

This involves the determination of the most ancient and accurate text of a passage in the Hebrew Old Testament or in the Greek New Testament. It requires years of study in the ancient languages. Inasmuch as my field is not Biblical languages, and as these columns are written for those who study the Bible principally in the English text, I am not giving references here to relevant literature.

IV. VOCABULARY OF THE TEXT

There are over 8,600 different Hebrew words in the text of the Old Testament, and a few more than 5600 different words in the Greek New Testament. For a study of the Biblical vocabulary, one needs the finest lexicons available. In the next twenty years, the Christian church will no doubt be producing Hebrew lexicons far superior to those now in print.

For the New Testament, lexicons of the *entire* Greek language will prove of value, as the later editions of the monumental two-volume work by Liddell and Scott. Checking the occurrence of words of a text in other parts of the Bible requires a Hebrew or Greek concordance, and the indispensable *Concordance to the Septuagint* by Redpath and Hatch. The recent discoveries in the Near East, Ras Shamra, Mari, Byblos, Qumran, etc., will enrich the lexical study of the Scriptures.

A recently-published lexicon, translated from the German with some English and American additions which will stand for many years to come as the essential lexical tool for the New Testament is the truly epochal *Greek-English Lexicon of the New Testament* by Wm. F. Arndt and F. Wilbur Gingrich (Univ. of Chicago Press, 1957).

V. VERSIONS

The most important single version of the Old Testament is in Greek, the Septuagint, written before New Testament times. Next in order, for the entire Bible, is the Latin Vulgate version, of the age of Jerome. Innumerable versions follow, down to the English versions which have been changing through the years, even to the present time.

I would like to recommend here the excellent articles on "Texts and Versions" in Hastings' *Dictionary of the Bible,* Vol. IV, pp. 727-741, and Vol. V, pp. 208-271, 402-420. A reprint of the comprehensive articles by Metzger, and others, in the *Twentieth Century Encyclopedia of Religious Knowledge* has just been issued (Grand Rapids: Baker Book House). Two helpful books, fundamental for Bible study, are F. F. Bruce: *The Books and the Parchments* (London, 1950), and H. W. Robinson (ed.): *Ancient and English Versions of the Bible* (Oxford, 1940).

For any who are sincerely interested in the study of versions, I would suggest the great six-volume *Hexaglot Bible,* published in this country (by Funk and Wagnalls) in 1901, and still seen, occasionally, in second-hand bookstores. These are quarto volumes, $9\frac{1}{2}$ x 12 inches. In the first volume, e.g., six versions of the Pentateuch are given, in parallel columns: on the left-hand page, the Hebrew, the Greek (Septuagint) and the Latin (Vulgate); on the right-hand page, the Authorized English Version, the German, and the French. This six-version arrangement is carried through from Genesis to Revelation.

The best interlinear translation of the Hebrew Old Testament for Genesis and Exodus known to me is that issued by Wilcox and Follett (Chicago) in 1946, *The Interlinear Literal Translation of the Hebrew Old Testament with the King James Version and the Revised Version Conveniently Presented in the Margins for Ready Reference and with Explanatory Textual Footnotes Supplemented by Tables of the Hebrew Verb and the Hebrew Alphabet*. This was edited by Dr. George Ricker Berry, once of the Department of Semitic Languages of the University of Chicago.

VI. CIRCUMSTANCES ATTENDING COMPOSITION OF THE PASSAGE

Here must be determined as far as possible, the name, life and character of the original author, the time in which he wrote, the historical conditions prevailing in that part of the world in which he wrote, the purpose of his writing, peculiarities of style, etc. Most of these subjects are considered in works on Biblical Introduction.

VII. PRINCIPAL SUBJECTS

In the first three chapters of Genesis, all of the following great themes are touched upon:

1. Creation
2. The Creator; Attributes of God
3. Origin of the Universe; Cosmology; Cosmogony
4. Origin of Life
5. Origin of Man
6. Man in God's Image
7. Adam (and Eve)
8. Unity of the Race
9. Eden
10. Marriage

11. Sabbath Day

12. The Tree of the Knowledge of Good and Evil; The Tree of Life

13. The Serpent; Satan

14. The Fall

15. Original Sin

16. Death

17. Messianic Prophecy

There is an enormous literature on all these subjects, even in Bible dictionaries; e.g., in Hastings' *Encyclopedia of Religion and Ethics,* not strictly a Biblical reference work, there are over 175 columns of printed text on the subjects Creation, Cosmology, Man in God's Image, Adam, the Fall, and Original Sin, and in the index, over 330 lines of references to these subjects!

VIII. REFERENCES TO RELATED PASSAGES IN LATER BIBLICAL LITERATURE

This line of investigation will unfold as one studies, principally, the influence of the Old Testament upon the New Testament; there are also a number of passages in the epistles which arise from the Gospel records, e.g., the eschatology of St. Paul's Thessalonian letters derives directly from Christ's Olivet Discourse. It has been estimated that 1170 portions of the Old Testament are quoted or referred to in the New Testament, of which approximately 400 are in the Book of Revelation. These three chapters in Genesis exercised profound influence over later Old Testament literature as well. The concept of creation set forth in Genesis 1 and 2 is referred to in more than forty Old Testament passages, in addition to many more in the New Testament.

A complete list of all quotations from the Old Testament, arranged in order of Old Testament books is found in the more recent editions of Nestle's *Novum Testamentum Graece* (pp. 658-671; this standard edition of the Greek New Testament is available at any Bible house). Some years ago F. W. Grant issued an interesting volume, *Genesis in the New Testament,* which has almost been forgotten. We need a new study of this subject.

IX. PARALLELS IN NON-BIBLICAL LITERATURE

Here some attention must be given to parallels in Mesopotamian and, occasionally, Egyptian literature. The essential work for this type of study is *Ancient Near Eastern Texts Relating to the Old Testament,* edited by James B. Pritchard (Princeton, 1950, rev. ed., 1956; pp. xxi, 525).

The most comprehensive listing of parallels in the Greek and Roman classics is in *The Testimony of the Heathen to the Truths of Holy Writ,* by Thomas S. Millington (London, 1863; pp. 31, 647). This rare work, now practically unobtainable, deserves thorough revision. A bibliography of the creation in all the principal European languages is in Stith Thompson: *Motif-Index of Folk-Literature* (Helsinki, 1932).

For parallels in ancient Mesopotamian literature, one may consult the earlier well-known work by George Smith: *The Chaldean Account of Genesis* (new ed., New York, 1880), and the more recent volume by Alexander Heider: *The Babylonian Genesis: The Story of Creation* (Chicago, 1942), in which high tribute is paid to the infinite superiority of the Genesis text over any secular accounts (pp. 117-118).

X. LITERATURE TO CONSULT FOR THE INTERPRETATION OF PASSAGE

1. *The Writings of the Church Fathers.*

It is very strange that the only worth-while commentary on the Book of Genesis produced in the first five centuries of the early church, that by the mighty Augustine, has never appeared in an English translation. The full Latin text may be found in Migne's *Patrologiae cursus completus,* Latin Series, Vol. XXXIV. It would be a boon to the Church if someone would translate this for us.

2. *Commentaries*

Material on the first three chapters of Genesis will be found (1) in those commentaries that cover the entire Bible, (2) in those that embrace only the books of the Old Testament, such as the great Keil and Delitzsch series, (3) in works on the Pentateuch, (4) in commentaries devoted exclusively to the Book of Genesis, and (5) in volumes on these chapters only. I will not here attempt to list commentaries on the Book of Genesis. Extensive bibliographies are given in the volumes by Lange and others. See also the extensive list in M'Clintock and Strong: *Cyclopaedia,* III. 784.

The American Biblical Encyclopedia Society of New York has recently undertaken a project called Encyclopedia of Biblical Interpretation, and in 1953 published the first volume, covering only the first six chapters of Genesis. Here for the first time in English, is a collection of the more important comments by the leading scholars of Judaism on these opening chapters of our Bible. The Appendix contains most interesting discussions of "The Atom in Jewish Sources" and "Creation and the Theory of Evolution."

In earlier literature the six days of creation were known as the *hexaemeron.* A scholarly study of the commentaries on the Book of Genesis for the century 1527-1633 is that by Arnold Williams, *The Common Expositor* (University of North Carolina Press, 1948), with an adequate bibliography.

3. *Bible Dictionaries*

The major themes of Genesis 1-3 have been listed. The larger Bible dictionaries will prove of great help in the study of the more significant Bible passages. The article on Adam, e.g., in Kitto's *Cyclopedia of Biblical Literature* extends to over seventeen columns (Vol. I, pp. 56-65).

4. *Theological Works*

Here it will be advantageous, I think, to illustrate with specific references. All systematic theologies devote one or more sections to the doctrine of Creation. In the *Systematic Theology* of Charles Hodge, this appears late in the first volume (Chapter X, pp. 550-574), though there are many earlier pages in his chapters on Theism, and the Nature and Attributes of God which have to do with this Genesis passage.

Biblical theologies likewise must give (early) consideration to the doctrine of creation, as the *Biblical Theology* of W. L. Alexander, Vol. I, pp. 130-134. All volumes on the doctrine of God will include this subject, e.g., the still great work by Samuel Harris: *God the Creator and Lord of All* (1897) Vol. I, pp. 463-518; the later influential study by J. Oswald Dykes; *The Divine Worker in Creation and Providence* (Edinburgh, 1909); and the Roman Catholic work by Joseph Pohle, *God the Author of Nature and the Supernatural* (St. Louis, 1942).

Almost all volumes on theism, such as that by Robert Flint, will treat extensively the doctrine of creation. The large *Studies in Theology:* by Randolph S. Foster is still worth reading; and Theodore Graebner's *God and the Cosmos* (1932 and later) has hardly been surpassed.

For a history of the earlier conflict of science and religion, see Charles C. Gillespie: *Genesis and Geology, a Study in the Relations of Scientific Thought, Natural Theology and Social Opinion in Great Britain,* 1790-1850 (Harvard University Press, 1951). In that volume which every serious student of the Scriptures should possess, *Systematic Theology* by my friend Dr. L. Berkhof (Eerdmans, 1941), there is a fine treatment of Creation in the Scriptures (pp. 126-164), with a good bibliography. See especially, Bernard Ramn's widely discussed volume, *The Christian View of Science and the Scriptures.* I have only hinted at a few titles in this vast literature.

5. *Special Volumes of Biblical Studies*

Scores of works comprised of essays on various Biblical themes will contain chapters on the Creation or the opening verses of Genesis. Godet, e.g., has some worthwhile things on this.

Among innumerable related publications see Merrill Unger: *Archaeology of the Old Testament* (1954), Chapters 2 and 3, with excellent footnotes. The *Cumulative Book Index,* 1949-1952 lists forty volumes as having been issued during those four years on the origin of man, and the origin of the universe, all of which bear upon these opening pages to some extent.

6. *Apologetic Literature*

One must include here the already large, and constantly-growing literature on science and religion. In the *Cumulative Book Index,* 1949-1952, forty-five titles are listed under the single heading Science and Religion.

7. *Sermonic Literature*

This type of literature can be ignored when one is simply attempting to ascertain the *meaning* of the text; however, for the *history* of the interpretation of the text, and some of the richer spiritual values, sermonic material must be consulted. There is no hard-and-fast rule for quickly discerning what is good and what is ordinary.

In James Darling's large *Cyclopedia Bibliographica* (1859) there are eighteen columns of references (many of the earlier works being in Latin) to literature on these three chapters! The first volume of *The Sermon Bible* (1900) lists 230 references to sermons based upon texts from this single passage. *The Speaker's Bible: Genesis* gives 220 textual sermon references, very few of which duplicate those of the *Sermon Bible* or of Darling. I would estimate that these three works alone contain at least a thousand references to sermons from Genesis 1-3.

8. *Devotional Works*

Two distinguished preachers of an earlier generation, J. Stuart Holden and F. B. Meyer, each did a helpful series of devotional studies, a page on one verse from each chapter of the Bible. I would classify as more or less devotional the writings of C. H. Macintosh on the Pentateuch.

The classic on Genesis in this type of literature is James Strahan's *Hebrew Ideals,* of which Alexander Whyte once said, "Let that fine piece of evangelical scholarship be in every house."

XI. INFLUENCE OF THE PASSAGE IN HISTORY AND LITERATURE

1. *In Jewish Apocryphal Literature and the Talmud*

(This would not apply to New Testament passages.)

2. *In the Writings of the Church Fathers*

In the index to the Church Fathers of the Ante-Nicene period only, there are over 300 references to these initial chapters of Genesis.

3. *In Ecclesiastical and Doctrinal Literature*

The works on theology mentioned previously belong here. The following subdivisions are suggestive:

    a. *The Creeds*

The Apostles' Creed, e.g., begins, "I believe in God the Father Almighty, Maker of heaven and earth." All works on the creeds will have extended discussions on the Creation. Pearson devotes forty pages to the one phrase, "Maker of heaven and earth" (in the Sinker edition, pp. 89-129).

    b. The development of the liturgy

    c. Doctrinal discussions and heresies.

4. *In Art and Architecture*

The very interesting work by Cynthia Pearl Maus, *The Old Testament and the Fine Arts* (Harper, 1954) contains full-page reproduction of some famous pictures based upon the opening chapters of Genesis, with comments.

5. *In Government: Legislation*

(The influence of certain Biblical texts upon national legislation is one of the most neglected areas of Biblical research.)

6. *Upon the Lives of Men*

A good illustration is available here in the development of chloroform by Sir James Young Simpson and his study of "sleep" in Genesis 3:16-18, concerning which I have a chapter in *Chats from a Minister's Library*, pp. 21-25.

7. *In Musical Composition*

The abundance of musical compositions based upon the first chapter of Genesis is evident from the index of Julian's *Dictionary of Hymnology,* which lists fifty-five hymns beginning with the word *Creator.* For a discussion of Haydn's great oratorio, "The Creation," see, among other volumes, H. E. Jacob: *Joseph Haydn* (1950) pp. 258-291.

8. *In Language*

While it is true that for the exact meaning of any passage, one must examine the original text, still each nation reads the Bible in its own native tongue; and thus, for us, the meaning of English words is pre-eminently important in the interpretation of the English Bible. Confining ourselves to the first two chapters of Genesis, we note that the word *Eden* came into our language as early as 1225 A.D., a century before Wycliffe.

The *Oxford English Dictionary* gives a number of early references to such words as Adam, Adamic, Adamical, Adamite, and Adam's apple. Incidentally, one of the mysteries of this dictionary is that while considerable space is given to Adam, the name Eve does not even appear, though it certainly has had wide use in English literature.)

To the terms *create, creation, creator* and *creature,* the *Oxford Dictionary* gives over five columns, and to the word *day,* the meaning of which in this text is still being debated, eight columns, embracing *twenty-four primary definitions* for this three-letter word.

9. *In Literature*

The influence of these three chapters of Genesis upon literature, and especially European literature, is a subject which has never been adequately explored. Holding strictly to the English language, let me here point out some of the volumes which might be used as guides in such a study.

In W. G. Horder's *The Poet's Bible: Old Testament* (London, 1889) portions from seventy-four different poetic compositions taken from the themes of Genesis 1-3 are quoted. Cook's *Index to the Works of Ruskin* indicates that Ruskin quoted from these three chapters 120 times.

All of Milton's *Paradise Lost* centers in this passage, and there are scores of references to these verses in other writings of Milton. The small volume on Genesis in the Temple Bible series has an excellent appendix, "Biblical References in English Literature." Who compiled these lists I do not know, but they were expertly done.

There is a remarkable list of Miracle Plays of the Middle Ages relating to creation, and Adam and Eve, as well as of modern plays depicting the same themes, in Edward D. Coleman: *The Bible in English Drama* (New York, 1931) pp. 38-42.

The most complete compilation of quotations from prose and poetry bearing upon this section of scripture with which I am acquainted is in a volume by the late Solomon Goldman, *In the Beginning* (Harper, 1949), pp. 166-404.

XII. CONFIRMATION IN THE FIELD OF ARCHAEOLOGY

This is applicable, of course, only to the historical records of the Bible. An enormous literature has appeared in this field in the past two generations, with much more to come.

XIII. TRIBUTES TO THE PASSAGE

My own volume *Therefore Stand* contains some interesting tributes to the beauty and significance of these particular verses (pp. 332-341, 572-573); see also the volume by Samuel Goldman mentioned above.

XIV. BEARING UPON YOUR OWN DEVOTIONAL LIFE AND PREACHING

1. The Devotional Value of the Text.
2. The Relation of the Passage to Contemporary Problems.
3. The Sermonic Worth of the Text and Possible Treatments.
4. The Use of the Passage in Evangelism and Personal Work.

Note: No comprehensive bibliography of the Book of Genesis in the English languages has been drawn up, as far as I know. The most extensive list of commentaries is that in the *British Museum Catalog.* The bibliographies in Lange's work on Genesis are still helpful.

What a boon it would be to all students if someone would now undertake a volume on the Old Testament similar to *New Testament Literature, an Annotated Bibliography,* by Lyons and Parvis (Vol. I, Chicago, 1948). Until that is forthcoming, we must be satisfied with the book-lists of the Society for Old Testament Studies; 1956 list was edited by H. H. Rowley.

An illustration of the wealth of literature issuing from but *one* verse of this portion of Scripture is Dominic J. Unger's *The First Gospel: Genesis 3:15* (St. Bonaventure, N. Y.: The Franciscan Institute, 1954) which lists 334 different works discussing the interpretation of this single verse down through the centuries.

That these opening chapters of Scripture continue to exercise extraordinary influence on the thought patterns of modern man is obvious, e.g., from the title of a recent book which has had a wide sale, originally in Germany, then in France, and now in our own country, *In Search of Adam; the Story of Man's Quest for the Truth about His Earliest Ancestors,* by Herbert Wendt (Boston: Houghton-Mifflin, 1956).

The entire field of periodical literature bearing upon these chapters awaits a critical bibliography. Hundreds of worthwhile articles published during the last two generations in scholarly journals are lost to the ordinary student for want of bibliographical listing. The index to *The Expository Times,* for instance, for the two decades 1889-1909, has 86 references to these three chapters alone.

21

SUGGESTIONS FOR READINGS IN THE GREAT CHRISTIAN CLASSICS

There has always been available—in the classical period of Greek and Roman literature, increasingly so during the Middle Ages, and more so than ever after the invention of printing—a vast amount of literature that is *not* worth reading at all. Of literary material of a second-rate nature we must read some, for our particular work, to keep abreast of some areas of thought, or to be prepared to meet the problems of some who have skeptical tendencies.

Then there are the pre-eminently worthwhile books that have permanent value, generation after generation, writings that can inspire and quicken the mind, cleanse the soul, and stir us to greater endeavors in our Christian life. Almost all earnest Christian men and women know times in which they long to lay hold of some volume that will lift them above the humdrum monotony of life, but they too often may not know what particular books to look for.

After some years of considerable thinking, as well as some teaching along this line, I have attempted to list here approximately 180 outstanding authors whose works make some definite contribution to Christian thought (plus seven works not identified with any particular author). Of course, some of these writers represent greater influence and genius than others here listed. The last eighty years have not produced much Christian literature that will be of any particular worth one hundred years from now, should the Lord tarry. The list includes, here and there, men who cannot be called Christians strictly speaking, as Alfred Tennyson. This list of authors is definitely not to be taken as complete.

I. *The Field as a Whole*

No book in human history has exercised such an enormous influence over the literature of the world as has the Bible, and around no other book has such a vast, important, and often transcendent literature been written as that prompted by the study of the perennial pages of the Holy Scriptures, and the great themes of which they speak.

Included in this body of literature are the writings of the Church Fathers, climaxed in the works of Augustine, which represent the major contribution to literature in the Western World from the close of the New Testament canon to the end of the fourteenth century.

Then there are the great liturgies of the East and West, the thousands of volumes of commentaries and works of Biblical exegesis provoked by the ever-present longing on the part of both Jews and Christians to know more of what God has said through His ancient oracles, and that massive (and in part unexplored) library, in innumerable languages, of books about the person and work of the Lord Jesus Christ. (I would estimate, e.g., that in *modern* times, at least sixty thousand volumes concerning Christ have been written in the principal western European languages.)

To these must be added the large works in the area of systematic, Biblical and historical theology, apologetic works, hymns, poems, books on Biblical ethics, dramas based on Biblical subjects, inspirational writings, and the unnumbered volumes of homilies and sermons from the days of Chrysostom to the present.

In addition to literature written for the specific purpose of interpreting the Scriptures, one must recognize the influence

of the Bible upon what might be called non-religious literature. The four-fold outline of the empires in Daniel 2 and
7, e.g., dominated European historiography down to the end
of the seventeenth century. Until most recent times, the opening chapters of Genesis have always been considered in works
on natural science. The influence of the Bible on general
literature is beyond all estimation. Dr. Albert Cook says, "The
Bible possesses a universality which has placed it at the foundation or the head, or both, of all modern literature," and
then gives a number of reasons why this is so (*The Authorized
Version of the Bible and Its Influence,* New York, 1910, p.
17). A better-known contemporary of Professor Cook, the
late Professor William Lyon Phelps of Yale, after a lifetime
of brilliant teaching, declared, "The Bible has been a greater
influence on the course of English literature than all other
forces put together; it is impossible to read standard authors
intelligibly without knowing something about the Bible, for
they all assume familiarity with it on the part of their readers"
(W. L. Phelps: *Reading the Bible,* New York, 1919, p. 17).

As an illustration of the influence of the Bible on English
literature, it is interesting to note that in the Index of the
Columbia Edition of Milton's *Works* there are over six
hundred lines of references to quotations from the Pentateuch
alone, and over fourteen hundred lines of index to the one
word *Christ!* In the index of E. T. Cook's great edition of
Ruskin's *Works,* over three thousand different Scripture
passages are listed.

I have not explored the subject of studies on the influence
of the Bible in continental Europe, but the following books
will be of help to anyone wishing to pursue this fascinating
theme:

R. V. Raumer: *Die Einwirkung des Christentums auf die
  althochdeutsche Sprache,* 1845.

E. Stein von Nordenstein: *Uber den Einsluss der Bibel aud deut. Sprache und Litt.* 1856.

J. Trenel: *L'Ancien test et la langue francaise du moyen age,* 1904.

II. *Introduction to World Literature*

Since many books dominated by Biblical themes are found in works on world literature, it might be well here to give a brief bibliography on this subject.

Cassell's Encyclopedia of World Literature, ed. by S. H. Steinberg. 2 vols. (New York, 1954, xxiii, 2086 pp.). The outstanding work of its kind, though weak in some areas.

World Literature, in the College Outline Series. 2 vols. (New York: Barnes and Noble, 1953, 280, 383 pp.).

Anne C. Lynch Botta. *Handbook of Universal Literature.* Rev. ed. (Boston, 1902, xiii, 562 pp.). Still of real value, though fifty years old.

Laurie Magnus. *A History of European Literature.* (London, 1935, xiii, 318 pp.).

Richard G. Moulton. *World Literature and Its Place in General Culture.* (New York, 1911, 502 pp.). A famous work; still worthwhile.

Barrett Wendell. *The Traditions of European Literature from Homer to Dante.* (New York, 1920, 669 pp.). Splendid bibliographical notes.

A Summary of the Literature of Modern Europe (England, France, Germany, Italy, Spain) from the Origins to 1400. Compiled and arranged by Marian Edwardes. (London, 1907, xvi, 532 pp.).

Frederic Loliee. *A Short History of Comparative Literature from Earliest Times to the Present Day.* (Eng. trans., London, 1906, xii, 375 pp.).

III. *Some Anthologies of World Literature*

The best anthology of literature of all nations published in our country is that edited by the late Richard Garnett, of the British Museum, entitled *Universal Anthology,* issued simultaneously in London and New York in 1899 in fifty volumes. Another work—not as well edited, in my opinion —appeared in sixty volumes, *The World's Greatest Literature.* This was in part a uniform reprinting of some of the classics of English and European literature, though it did extend back as far as the Babylonian, Assyrian, Greek and Roman classics. There was also President Elliott's famous *Five-Foot Shelf of Books,* perhaps the best known of all such anthologies.

During the last half-century, anthologies of world literature in one and two volumes have become quite numerous, excellently edited and attractively printed. Two of the more important are *Western World Literature,* edited by Harry Wolcott Robbins and William Harold Coleman (New York, 1938, xix, 1422 pp.); and *Writers of the Western Word,* edited by Addison Hibbard (Boston, 1942, xxii, 1225 pp.).

In my opinion, the best of these is *The World in Literature,* edited by George K. Anderson and Robert Warnock, in two attractively printed volumes (Chicago and New York, 1951, xv, 440, 575, 15 pp; xv, 624, 492, 14 pp; i.e., 2131 double-column pages of text).

IV. *The History of Christian Literature*

No adequate systematic survey of the great writings of the Christian Church, including the influence of the Bible on the literatures of the Western World, has even been undertaken. Scores of books have been written on the literary history of early Christianity, e.g., by Crittwell, Krueger, Goodspeed, and the monumental work on the Church Fathers by Johannes Quasten, now in process of publication, *Patrology* (two volumes, coming down to the time of Lactantius, having been completed, and the third to appear soon), and on the general literature of the Reformation. We have an excellent work surveying all the early Latin Literature of the Christian Church—Pierre De Labriolle: *The History and Literature of Christianity from Tertullian to Boethius* (xxiii, 555 pp.).

There are also some good surveys of the religious literature of certain nations, e.g., the three-volume work by Henri Bremond: *The Literary History of Religious Thought in France from the Wars of Religion Down to Our Own Times* (1928). However, there is no general satisfactory survey of the entire field of Christian literature through the ages. In 1926, Macmillan published a work by George L. Hurst: *An Outline of the History of Christian Literature* (547 pp.), but the chapters are of a very sketchy nature. What we need is an exhaustive work covering the subject of the influence of the Word of God on the literatures of the Western World, on the same scale as Gilbert Highet's rich contribution to scholarship, *The Classical Tradition, Greek and Roman Influences on Western Literature* (Oxford University Press, 1949, xxxviii, 763 pp.).

Before the advent of modern scholarship, a serious attempt was made to survey the history of the versions of the Bible, and major works directly related to the Bible, by a Methodist scholar in England, James Townley, a work originally published in three volumes in 1821, and reprinted in two volumes, of some 1200 pages, in our own country in 1842. The title indicates the content: *Illustrations of Biblical Literature Exhibiting the History and Fate of the Sacred Writings from the Earliest Period to the Present Century;*

Including Biographical Sketches of Translators and Other Eminent Biblical Scholars. Apparently since that time no one has dared to undertake a survey of such scope.

V. *Anthologies of Christian Literature*

The most extensive anthology of *devotional* literature, of our century is the ten-volume set (of about 220 pages each) *Selections from the World's Devotional Classics,* edited by Robert Scott and George Gilmore, and published by Funk and Wagnalls in 1916. Perhaps the best one-volume work of this kind is *The Book of Christian Classics,* edited by Michael Williams in 1913, and republished in 1937 with the title, *Anthology of Classic Christian Literature* (xvi, 466 pp.). A later work is *The Christian Reader: Inspirational and Devotional Classics,* ed. by Stanley Irving Stuber (Association Press, N. Y., 1952, 514 pp.).

A good selection is found in J. M. Connell: *A Book of Devotional Readings from the Literature of Christendom* (London, 1913, 295 pp.)—quotations from 114 authors, chronologically arranged, including some, however, who were certainly not Christians, as Kant, Goethe, Emerson and Shelley. Arranged in the form of a devotional manual is *A Lectionary of Christian Prose from the II to XX Century,* compiled by A. C. Bouquet (London, 1939 xxvi, 390 pp.).

For an anthology of poetry, one will want to consult *Masterpieces of Religious Verse,* by James Dalton Morrison, a quarto volume of 700 double-column pages, published by *Harper and Brothers,* 1948. Still indispensable, with excellent notes, is *A Library of Religious Poetry,* edited by Philip Schaff and Arthur Gilman (New York, 1881, xxi, 1004 pp., double column).

A scholarly and quite exhaustive anthology of Anglican

literature of the seventeenth century, *Anglicanism,* compiled by Paul Elmer More and Frank Leslie Cross, appeared in 1951 (London, S.P.C.K., lxxvi, 811 pp.).

VI. *Authors of Famous Christian Books*

It is not an easy task to draw up a list of what might be called the more important authors of Christian literature, from the days of the Apostolic Fathers to the beginning of our century. No two students would construct identical lists. The list I have drawn up would be somewhat different if compiled by a Protestant, living on the continent of Europe, and would be quite emphatically altered if drawn up by a Roman Catholic.

I have included only those writers (and of course not all of them) whose books are in themselves rich in content, works that have had wide influence, not only at the time of publication, but in subsequent centuries or decades, that have made a vital contribution to the history and corporate life of the Christian Church, and that contain pages that can still speak to us and inspire us.

Writers whose books had a marked influence and large circulation in the years immediately following their original publication, but today are acknowledgedly unimportant, have been omitted. Thus, e.g., the Church of England clergyman James Hervey (1713-1758) wrote a volume, *Meditations and Contemplations,* which went through twenty-five editions in forty-five years, but his name awakens no memories today, and the volume cannot be said to have permanent value. Similarly, Charles M. Sheldon's *In His Steps* (1896) had a phenomenal circulation of approximately ten million copies, but I believe that work cannot be called a permanent contribution to the literature of the Christian Church.

One area of Christian literature I have not attempted to

cover in this list is early English religious drama, the Chester Cycle of Plays, etc. To mention one of these would require the introduction of a large number. These plays carry no particular message for today, and their study belongs rather in the history of English literature. My list does not include living authors. Of course there have been many famous Christian writers whose writings did not in themselves relate to Biblical themes; a good illustration of this would be Sir Walter Scott.

During the sixteenth, seventeenth and eighteenth centuries, the larger number of the more influential writers were not only devout Christians, but wrote extensively on Christian themes. This has not been true since at least the dawn of the nineteenth century. As Gilbert Highet has said, "Christianity has been hated and despised by many of the most ardent lovers of the classics during the nineteenth century." Early in 1951, the *New York Times* published an article on "The One Hundred Greatest Books of the Last One Hundred Years, 1851-1951." A careful study of this list will reveal that not ten of these authors were Christians, and the majority were actually enemies of the Christian faith.

Because of their basic importance in the history of Christian literature, as well as in the history of the Christian Church, my list of Church Fathers is rather extended.

REFERENCE LIST OF AUTHORS AND LITERATURE

PERIOD OF THE CHURCH FATHERS

Clement of Alexandria	2nd century	Athanasius	c297-373
Polycarp	2nd century	Gregory of Nyssa	d. 353
Justin Martyr	2nd century	Cyril of Jerusalem	313-386
Tertullian	150-240	Jerome	340-420
Irenaeus	fl. 180-190	St. Ambrose	340-397
Hippolytus	fl. 217-235	Rufinus	345-410
Origen	185-253	Chrysostom	347-407
Lactantius	250-317	Augustine	354-430
Eusebius	260-339	Theodoret	390-457

THE MIDDLE AGES

Boethius	480-524	Thomas Aquinas	1227-1274
Gregory the Great	540-604	Raymond Lull	c1232-1315
Isidore of Seville	560-636	*Dies Irae*	1250
Caedmon	d. 680	Meister Eckhart	1260-1329
Venerable Bede	673-735	Dante	1265-1321
Cynewulf	fl. 750	Duns Scotus	1265-1308
Aelfric	955-1020	Nicholas de Lyra	d. 1340
Anselm	1033-1109	William Ockham	1290-1349
Peter Abailard	1079-1142	John Ruysbroeck	1293-1381
St. Bernard of Clair-		Henry Suso	1295-1366
vaux	1091-1153	*Stabat Mater*	c1300
Hugh of St. Victor	1096-1141	John Tauler	1300-1361
Peter Lombard	1100-1160	John Wycliff	1324-1384
Robert Grosseteste	1175-1253	William Langland	c1332-c1440
Holy Grail	c1190	Geoffrey Chaucer	1340-1400
Francis of Assisi	1182-1226	Catherine of Siena	1347-1380
Albertus Magnus	1193-1280	*Cursor Mundi*	c1350
Roger Bacon	1214-1292	*Theologica Germanica*	c1350
Bonaventura	1221-1274	*Cloud of Unknowing*	14th cent.

FIFTEENTH AND SIXTEENTH CENTURIES

Thomas a' Kempis	1380-1471	John Calvin	1509-1564
Nicholas of Susa	1401-1464	John Fox	1516-1587
Savonarola	1452-1498	Diego de Estella	1524-1578
Erasmus	1466-1536	Thomas Cartwright	1535-1603
John Colet	1467-1519	Torquato Tasso	1547-1616
Martin Luther	1483-1546	*Book of Common*	
William Tyndale	1484-1536	*Prayer*	1549-1552
Thomas Cranmer	1489-1556	Edmund Spenser	1552-1599
Ignatius Loyola	1491-1556	Richard Hooker	1554-1600
Martin Bucer	1491-1551	Robert Southwell	1561-1595
Philip Melancthon	1497-1560		
John Knox	1505-1572		

SEVENTEENTH CENTURY

Lancelot Andrewes	1555-1626	Robert Herrick	1591-1674
Francois de Sales	1567-1622	George Herbert	1593-1633
James Ussher	1581-1656	Samuel Rutherford	1600-1680
John Donne	1573-1631	Thomas Goodwin	1600-1680
Joseph Hall	1574-1656	William Chillingworth	1602-1644
Jacob Boehme	1575-1624	William Laud	1573-1645
Phineas Fletcher	1582-1650	Sir Thomas Browne	1605-1682
Johann Gerhard	1582-1637	Hugh Latimer	1605-1683
Hugo Grotius	1583-1645	Thomas Fuller	1608-1661
Giles Fletcher	1588-1623	John Milton	1608-1674

Brother Lawrence	1611-1691	John Flavel	1630-1691
Robert Leighton	1611-1684	Isaac Barrow	1630-1677
John Pearson	1612-1686	John Locke	1632-1704
Richard Crashaw	1613-1649	Robert South	1634-1716
Jeremy Taylor	1613-1667	Jacob Spener	1635-1705
Richard Baxter	1615-1691	Edward Stillingfleet	1635-1699
John Owen	1616-1683	William Beveridge	1637-1708
Richard Cudworth	1617-1688	Thomas Traherne	1637-1677
Thomas Guthrie	1620-1665	Increase Mather	1639-1723
Blaise Pascal	1623-1662	Gilbert Burnet	1643-1715
Henry Vaughan	1622-1695	Madame Guyon	1648-1717
George Fox	1624-1691	Henry Scougal	1650-1678
Jacques Bousset	1627-1701	Francois Fenelon	1651-1715
Stephen Charnock	1628-1680		
John Bunyan	1628-1688		

EIGHTEENTH CENTURY

Matthew Henry	1662-1714	John Woolman	1720-1772
August Herman		Henry Venn	1724-1797
Francke	1663-1727	F. G. Klopstock	1724-1803
Isaac Watts	1674-1748	John Newton	1725-1805
William Law	1686-1761	William Cowper	1731-1800
Joseph Butler	1692-1752	William Paley	1743-1805
William Warburton	1698-1779	Johann Herder	1744-1803
Philip Doddridge	1702-1751	Thomas Erskine	1750-1824
Jonathan Edwards	1703-1758	Andrew Fuller	1754-1815
John Wesley	1703-1791	William Carey	1761-1834
William Romaine	1714-1795		

EARLY NINETEENTH CENTURY

Charles Simeon	1759-1836	John Keble	1792-1866
William Wilberforce	1759-1833	Jean Henri D'Aubigne	1794-1872
F. E. D. Schleiermacher	1768-1834	F. W. Krummacher	1796-1868
R. V. de Chateaubri-		F. A. G. Tholuck	1799-1877
and	1768-1848		
William Wordsworth	1770-1851	J. J. I. von Dollinger	1799-1890
Samuel Taylor		Cardinal N. P. S.	
Coleridge	1772-1834	Wiseman	1802-1865
Thomas Chalmers	1780-1847	A. L. F. Monod	1802-1856
Reginald Heber	1783-1826	Horace Bushnell	1802-1876
Richard Whately	1787-1863	J. P. Lange	1802-1884
Robert Haldane	1787-1864		
Johann August		John Henry Newman	1802-1890
Neander	1789-1850	Robert S. Candlish	1806-1873
Alexander Campbell	1788-1866		

LATER NINETEENTH CENTURY

Charles Hodge	1797-1878	Christina Rossetti	1830-1894
George Borrow	1803-1881	Joseph Parker	1830-1902
John Greenleaf		James Thompson	1834-1882
Whittier	1807-1892	Alexander Whyte	1836-1921
R. C. Trench	1807-1886	Robert Flint	1838-1910
Robert Murray McCheyne	1813-1843	Abraham Kuyper	1837-1920
Soren Kierkegaard	1813-1855	Andrew M. Fairbairn	1838-1912
A. P. Stanley	1815-1881	George Matheson	1842-1906
Alfred Tennyson	1809-1892	Baron von Hugel	1852-1925
Robert Browning	1812-1889	Charles Gore	1853-1932
Austin Phelps	1820-1890	Herman Bavinck	1854-1921
B. F. Westcott	1825-1900	William Temple	1881-1944
H. P. Liddon	1829-1890		

Suggested Literature for Research on Authors Studied:
The finest one-volume companion for the study of the literature and history of the Christian Church is the new scholarly, authoritative *Oxford Dictionary of the Christian Church,* edited by F. L. Cross (1957). All important histories of the Christian Church devote some space to Christian literature; the volumes by Schaff are especially rich.

Of help also are the larger Christian encyclopedias, such as Schaff-Herzog, the *Catholic Encyclopedia,* and the many articles on some of these authors in the truly great work edited by Hastings, *The Encyclopedia of Religion and Ethics.* Histories of doctrine, and the interesting post-humously-published work by Charles Briggs, *History of the Study of Theology,* 2 vols. (London, 1916), contain relevant material; also McGiffert: *History of Christian Thought,* 2 vols. (1932-1933), and H. B. Workman: *Christian Thought to the Reformation* (1911).

For the Christian literature of the Middle Ages, there are the many volumes of the Loeb Classical Library, and the long scholarly articles in the four-volume *History of Christian Biography,* edited by Smith and Wace, covering the first eight centuries. There is only one history of the Latin literature of this period in our language: *A History of Later Latin Literature (from 350-1700)*, by F. A. Wright and T. A. Sinclair (New York, 1931).

We are living in an age in which more attention is being given the Church Fathers than ever before. We have, first of all, the standard set published by Scribners some years ago, *The Ante-Nicene Fathers* (9 vols.); *The Nicene and Post-Nicene Fathers* (14 vols., covering Chrysostom and Augustine), and *The Nicene and Post-Nicene Fathers*, 2nd series (14 vols.). In addition three series are in process of publication: *The Ancient Christian Writers* (Newman Press, Westminster, Md.), works of true scholarship, with superb notes; *The Fathers of the Church*, issued by The Fathers of the Church, New York, with few notes but indexed; and the invaluable *Library of Christian Classics* (26 vols.) being published by the Westminster Press, Philadelphia.

Perhaps this is the place to introduce several titles on the great hymns of the Church. The indispensable work here is John Julian's *Dictionary of Hymnology*, 1892. The following list is only suggestive.

Armin Haeussler: *The Story of Our Hymns* (St. Louis, 1952, xi, 1088 pp).

Edwin F. Hatfield: *The Poets of the Church*, a series of biographical studies of hymn writers, with notes on their hymns (New York, 1884, 719 pp.).

Albert Edward Bailey: *The Gospel in Hymns* (New York, 1950, xx, 600 pp.). Beautifully illustrated.

Hymns Ancient and Modern, the Historical Edition, with Notes on the Origin of Both Hymns and Tunes, etc. (London, 1909, cxi, 911 pp., with many indexes).

On authors who lived in the British Isles there is an abundance of material; in the indispensable *Dictionary of*

National Biography; The Cambridge History of English Literature; and the later exhaustive *Cambridge Bibliography of English Literature.*

Inasmuch as *The Book of Common Prayer* played such a major role in the history of the Church in the British Isles, we should mention here the definitive work of John Henry Blunt; *The Annotated Book of Common Prayer* (London, 1869; quarto, lxxx, 610 pp.); Francis Proctor: *A History of the Book of Common Prayer,* 15th ed. (London, 1881), and Charles Neil and J. M. Willoughby: *The Tutorial Prayer Book* (London, 1918, xxxi, 669 pp.).

NOTE—For some anthologies of Christian literature for the first six centuries of our era, one might consult the following:

Abbe Bardy: *The Christian Latin Literature of the First Six Centuries* (London, 1930, 222 pp.). In the Catholic Library of Religious Knowledge.

H. M. Gwatkin: *Selections from Early Writers Illustrative of Church History to the Time of Constantine* (London, 1897.).

A Treasury of Early Christianity, edited by Anne Fremantle (New York, 1953, xiv, 625 pp.). Brief extracts from about 120 authors.

INDEX

This index lists the name of every author whose book or article is actually commented on in this volume; however, there are scores of authors referred to in the text, in various bibliographies, without comment whose names I have not felt it necessary to include here, e.g., those appearing on pages 154-156, 182 ff., 211 ff., etc. Only the Biblical texts on which there are extended discussions are listed. The subjects of the book, principally chapter headings, are indicated by capital letters.

**BIBLICAL PASSAGES CONSID-
ERED AT LENGTH**